WHERE CORRUPTION LIVES

Where Corruption Lives

**Gerald E. Caiden, O. P. Dwivedi,
and Joseph Jabbra**
editors

Kumarian
Press, Inc.

Dedicated to Dr. Michael C. Jabbra
and
to the memory of David Gould,
a pioneer in corruption studies

Where Corruption Lives

Published 2001 in the United States of America by Kumarian Press, Inc.,
1294 Blue Hills Avenue, Bloomfield, Connecticut 06002-1302 USA.

Design by Nicholas A. Kosar. Copyedited by Beth Richards.
Proofread by Jody El-Assadi. Indexed by Robert Swanson.
The text of this book is set in New Baskerville 10/13.5.

Printed in Canada on acid-free paper by
Transcontinental Printing and Graphics, Inc.
Text printed with vegetable oil-based ink.

∞ The paper used in this publication meets the minimum requirements
of the American National Standard for Information Sciences—Permanence of
Paper for Printed Library Materials, ANSI Z39.48–1984.

Library of Congress Cataloging-in-Publication Data
Where corruption lives / Gerald E. Caiden, O.P. Dwivedi, and Joseph Jabbra, editors.
    p.   cm.
    Includes bibliographical references and index.
    ISBN 1–56549–134–3 (cloth : acid-free paper). — ISBN 1–56549–133–5
(pbk. : acid-free paper)
    1. Political corruption. I. Caiden, Gerald E. II. Dwivedi, O.P III. Jabbra,
Joseph G.
    JF1525.C66 W54 2001
    320.9—dc21   2001038242

10 09 08 07 06 05 04 03 02 01   10 9 8 7 6 5 4 3 2 1

First Printing 2001

Contents

International Association of Schools and Institutes of Administration (IASIA)

The International Association of Schools and Institutes of Administration (IASIA) is an association of organizations and individuals whose activities and interests focus on public administration and management. Its main emphasis is on the development and use of human resources. From a concept first articulated in Vienna in 1962, the Association, which is a constituent organ of the International Institute of Administrative Sciences (IIAS), was formally incorporated in Rome during the IIAS Congress of 1971. IASIA now has a worldwide membership of over 170 institutions in 70 countries as well as several international organizations. Members are grouped in seven geographical regions. The activities of its members include education and training of administrators and managers, and related research, consulting, and publications. Its offices are at the headquarters of the IIAS in Brussels, Belgium.

The worldwide membership of IASIA provides individuals and organizations from various parts of the world, having the same concerns, with the opportunity to consider and advance their interests from a global perspective. This capacity at once makes mutual support and assistance more possible and helps serve the needs arising from the increasingly international nature of the environment in which governments and their public services are called on to operate. It also facilitates initiatives which may enhance the institutional and operational effectiveness of member organizations and of the public sector internationally.

IASIA is a not-for-profit association supported by membership fees, income from services, the voluntary services of its members and contributions from funding organizations.

IASIA Secretariat
Rue Defacqz 1, Bte 11, B-1000 BRUSSELS, BELGIUM
Tel: 32/2-536.08.89   Fax: 32/2-537.97.02
E-mail: iasia@iiasiisa.be   Web site: http://www.iiasiisa.be

The co-editors acknowledge with gratitude the International Association of Schools and Institutes of Administration's generous grant which made this publication possible.

Contributors

TOMASZ ANUSIEWICZ, graduate of the University of Warsaw, works for the Good Governance program at the UNDP Regional Support Center in Bratislava; previously he held positions at UNDP offices in Warsaw and Lusaka and in multinationals operating in Central and Eastern Europe. He specializes in human rights protection and anticorruption activities in the countries of the region.

DEMETRIOS ARGYRIADES, graduate of the London School of Economics and Political Science, is currently a consultant in human resources development and governance issues for the European Union and the United Nations and teaches at the Robert F. Wagner School of Public Service at New York University. He has held senior positions within the United Nations organization and has taught at universities in the United States and abroad.

ANTOANETA L. DIMITROVA, graduate of Leiden University, is currently working on a project on Constitutional Change and Enlargement in the European Union. She has published on the European Union and governance in Bulgaria and Slovakia and on security and conflict prevention.

GERALD E. CAIDEN, a graduate of the London School of Economics and Political Science, has served on the faculties of London University, Carleton University, Australian National University, Hebrew University, University of California, Berkeley and Haifa University, and has published extensively in public policy and administration. He has acted as consultant, researcher, and editor for international organizations and is currently professor of Public Administration at the University of Southern California.

O. P. DWIVEDI has been on the faculty of the Department of Political Science at the University of Guelph, Ontario, since 1967 and has published 30 books on public policy, management, and the environment. He has been president of professional and academic bodies in Canada and abroad and is active as a consultant and officeholder in many international organizations.

FREDRIK GALTUNG, a Norwegian national, researches on the political economy of corruption control at Cambridge University, England. He is a founding staff member and senior research associate at Transparency International where he coordinates the annual Corruption Perceptions Index and the Bribe Payer's Index and other corruption measures. He has published several studies and articles on corruption and lectured in more than 30 countries.

PETER GRABOSKY, a graduate of Northwestern University, is research director at the Australian Institute of Criminology and has published widely in public policy and criminology, particularly on electronic crime. He is President of the Australian and New Zealand Society of Criminology and Deputy Secretary General of the International Society of Criminology.

VICTOR GROVE HILLIARD, a graduate of the University of South Africa, worked mainly in semigovernmental and private sectors before he joined the University of Zululand, and then Venda University and Vista University. He is currently head of the Department of Public Management at Port Elizabeth Technikon. He has published widely in public policy and administration and is active on international academic bodies.

JOSEPH G. JABBRA is Academic Vice President at Loyola Marymount University, Los Angeles where he is Professor of Political Science and International Law. He has published extensively on the Middle East and is active in the International Association of Schools and Institutes of Administration. He is currently researching on the international environment law and comparative legal systems.

NANCY W. JABBRA is director of women's studies at Loyola Marymount University, Los Angeles where she researches gender roles, politics, ethnicity, immigration and environment issues in the Middle East and North America. Currently, her research is directed at the breakdown of the Lebanese political system, family planning in Iran and Egypt, and affirmative action in California.

PETER LARMOUR directs the postgraduate Development Administration program at the Australian National University where he teaches a course on corruption and anticorruption designed jointly with the New South Wales Independent Commission Against Corruption. He researches on South Pacific politics and good governance.

STEPHEN K. MA is Professor of Political Science at the California State University, Los Angeles and has published *Administrative Reform in Post-Mao China: Efficiency or Ethics?* (University Press of America, 1996) and *US Civil Service and Ethical Codes* (in Chinese by Tsinghua University Press, 1999). He is a member of the editorial board of the *International Journal of Public Administration.*

MAUREEN MANCUSO, a graduate of McMaster, Carleton, and Oxford Universities, is Associate Academic Vice President at the University of Guelph where she teaches political science. Her main research interests include political ethics and corruption, comparative politics, legislative behavior, and American politics. She has been a consultant to the Canadian House of Commons on legislative codes of conduct and conflict of interest legislation.

JORGE NEF, a graduate of the University of Chile, is Professor of Politics, International Development and Rural Extension Studies at the University of Guelph and has done extensive research on administrative reform. He has been Vice President of the Chilean College of Public Administration and President of the Canadian Association of Latin American and Caribbean Studies and editor of its journal.

DELE OLOWU, a graduate of the Universities of Ibadan, Ile-Ife and Indiana, teaches at the Institute of Social Studies in the Netherlands. He has held academic positions in Nigeria and served as an expert on governance and capacity building with the United Nations Economic Commission for Africa. He has published extensively on governance and democratization.

JON S. T. QUAH is Professor of Political Science at the National University of Singapore and a member of Transparency International's Governance Research Council. He led the UNDP's mission to Mongolia where he formulated its National Anti-Corruption Plan. He has published widely on Singapore politics and on anticorruption strategies, administrative reform, and public resources in Asian countries.

PAULINE F. TAMESIS, a graduate of Georgetown University, has been a career officer with the UNDP where she has worked in the Philippines analyzing best governance practices. She is global coordinator for integrity improvement initiatives within the UNDP and adviser to PACT.

TONY VERHEIJEN is Chief Technical Adviser on Governance at the UNDP Regional Support Center in Bratislava as expert on administrative reform in transition states. He previously held positions at the European Institute of Public Administration, The University of Limerick, the OECD, and Leiden University. He has published on administrative reform and is currently completing a book on Eastern Europe.

RICHARD D. WHITE, JR., a graduate of Pennsylvania State University, is Milton J. Womack Professor for Developing Scholars at Louisiana State University. His research interests include public ethics, the American Presidency, and administrative history. He has published extensively and is a contributor to *The International Encyclopedia of Public Policy and Administration.*

HENRY F. WISSINK, a graduate of the University of Stellenbosch, teaches at the Port Elizabeth Technikon where he is Dean of the Faculty of Commerce and Governmental Studies. He is the author of three texts on public management and has published on policy analysis and development policy, planning and development. He is active in the International Associations of Schools and Institutes of Administration.

DOUGLAS ANDREW YATES, a graduate of Boston University, is on the faculties of the American University of Paris and the University of Cergy-Pontoise. He has been researching the French oil industry and has published *The Rentier State in Africa: Oil-Rent Dependency and Neocolonialism in the Republic of Gabon* (Trenton/Asmara, 1996).

1

Introduction

Gerald E. Caiden, O. P. Dwivedi, and Joseph Jabbra

ON DECEMBER 29, 2000, Rachel Ehrenfeld, director of the Center for the Study of Corruption and the Rule of Law in New York, wrote a column in the 6 January 2001 *Washington Times* in which she criticized the current war on corruption kicked off by the World Bank in 1996 for failure to reduce capital flight, laundered money, and political instability arising from official kleptocracy. A week later, Jim Wesberry, director of the USAID Americas Accountability/Anti-Corruption Project agreed with her that indeed there was not a clear definition of corruption, no objective, uniform means of identifying vulnerable countries, and too few international agencies with teeth. But Ehrenfeld's academic solution of an International Integrity Standard would be costly and no more successful because of the very nature of corruption.

[O]fficial corruption . . . thrives on darkness and invisibility. It is anonymous and unmeasurable. It is rooted in the very human vices of greed and lust for power through wealth . . . [defying] . . . normal approaches to definition and measurement. . . .

The solution for corruption for many years was simply to ignore it, to pretend it did not exist or to agree that a certain amount was unavoidable, accepted cost of development. . . .

Corruption is colorless, shapeless, odorless, collusive, secret, stealthy, shameless. Even when it becomes pervasive, it still retains those qualities. It often leaves no trail but that impressed in human minds, memories and perceptions. . . .

In today's globalized, democratized, informatized world, incorruptible governments can be constructed only using incorruptible citizens as their bricks and mortar. Are our educational, familial, social and spiritual systems helping form incorruptible new citizens? Or are they doing just the opposite?

The essays in this book provide ammunition to both sides. Avoiding the temptation to highlight, as does the sensationalist mass media, the most scandalous illustrations of how the corrupt exploit their public positions to enjoy their ill-gotten benefits with impunity, academic authors probe the whys and wherefores of contemporary corruption. They raise deeper philosophical issues about the nature of this particular form of human wrongdoing, how people confront it, and what they expect others to do about it. If other forms of misbehavior, once commonplace and legitimate, have become increasing unacceptable, why does corruption persist and expand? The very notion of civilization and civilized conduct defines societies that seek to banish, or minimize, or reduce these other forms of abhorrent human acts. So why have they been so unsuccessful in combating corruption, given the overwhelming evidence of how harmful it is to good governance, sustainable development, and human justice?

Ambiguous Attitudes

This book illustrates how societies differ widely as to prevailing attitudes about corruption. At the one extreme in some countries—particularly among the poorest but by no means confined to them—anything goes in the conduct of public business and contemporary governance. Corruption is a habitualized, indeed institutionalized, part of the social fabric. People are socialized into its ways from youth. They become so accustomed to it that they no longer recognize it for what it is. Corruption is so expected, so much a part of everyday life, that they cannot conceive of any other way of conducting public affairs or see that anything could be much different. They are genuinely puzzled when outsiders try to point this out to them because they know that these outsiders do not face the situation daily. People are surprised to see efforts by the rebels within because they have seen so many such efforts end in vain. Attempts to change things are defeated or, worse still, self-defeating. Few outwardly deny or resist suggestions to change; they just will not act on them. When this is pointed out, they rationalize, justify, or explain away their inactivity and lip-service in perfectly reasonable-sounding terms and promise that when times are more propitious, things will change or be changed. This situation can continue for decades and even generations until things get so bad that the whole system of conducting personal and public affairs eventually collapses because of its very rottenness or the system becomes incapable of facing major outside challenges. Then, the price is very high in terms of uncertainty, loss of trust, and risky supersession at best—and civil unrest, revolt, and bloody revolution at worst.

At the other extreme are societies and countries, particularly in the long-established democracies, where good governance is actively sought. Having once experienced corruption on such a scale, these countries remain determined to admit to the presence of corruption in their midst and seek to rid themselves of it or at least reduce it to a more tolerable level. In time, they have changed their institutional arrangements to reduce the possibilities and opportunities for corrupt practices and to reinforce their changes with an ideology of conducting personal and public business that condemns corruption and supports moral behavior. They back their changes in law with effective law enforcement, with models of expected conduct in every walk of life, and with easy access to remedial organizations that are capable of rooting out corruption, corrupt practices and the corrupt. They welcome advice and assistance from the outside although they prefer to do things for themselves and devise their own methods for combating corruption. Doing business in these societies contrasts profoundly with doing business in the corrupt societies. The atmosphere is different, the conduct is different, and the beneficial outcomes usually speak for themselves.

There seems to be a direct correlation with the extent to which people as citizens are empowered in their societies. Where they fully participate in governance and where a lively civic culture thrives, those in authority have greater difficulty hiding corruption. Even where the governors exercise censorship over mass media and employ secret agents, people talk freely. Their moral indignation at corrupt practices they encounter soon registers in official circles and the machinery of democratic governance is set in motion to track down the source of the rumors, investigate the charges, expose the culprits, isolate the incidents, instigate action to prosecute the accused, and readjust the machinery of governance to see that repetition is made harder. A truly democratic regime seeking to improve its governance and public outcomes has great difficulties being hypercritical. Protection of corruption does not wash. Sooner or later, the truth comes tumbling out and the people react by using whatever channels of redress are available to them. They complain. They write. They vote. They organize protests. Even those who find that they inadvertently participated in or covered up corrupt activities confess error and try to atone. In these ways, the blot on society is diluted even if not totally erased.

In contrast, people in autocratic or nonliberal democratic regimes where effective power is confined to a small elite that dominates society have no voice. They do not count. Indeed, if they voice an opinion, they become targets for suppression and elimination. They have no choice other than to go along with corruption unless they stand aloof, which takes much moral courage. Their failure to go along with corruption may have grave consequences because they stand out, they are identifiable and they cannot be trusted by the corrupt. Furthermore, there are ample instruments to make them conform against their better judgment; they may face physical harm, even death. If they are not punished directly, they can be deprived of any benefits that could otherwise be theirs. They are on their own and must fend for themselves as best they can—something difficult to do in modern society where they are so dependent on others. Their situation is rather precarious. All they can hope for is to be left alone, to survive and prosper regardless, and eventually to find more and more support for their independent stand just as the successful nonconforming whistle-blowers even in democratic regimes hope for but rarely experience. Perhaps working together in tandem or underground, they may be able to exercise autonomous power of their own, sufficient to defy the corrupt and to burrow from within until the rottenness that so weakens institutional effectiveness is exposed and begins to crumble.

In the real world, these extremes are rarely found. Most societies and most regimes from the most democratic to the most autocratic are mixtures. None is totally corrupt for there are always exceptions, islands of honesty, decency, integrity, and principle that can be trusted and are reliable. Likewise, in societies relatively free of corruption, there are shady or fuzzy areas, not necessarily disguised, hidden or secret, and there is also a closed arena where the corrupt conduct their business. In them, the corrupt are not innocent. They know what they do and the consequences of what they do. So they have to be quite clever at hiding what they do. They have to win over their victims, certainly gain their silence and convince them that they provide a valuable service to them that is unattainable by other means. They have to evade possible detection and exposure. They have to offer tempting bribes and may well have to be merciless in dealing with suspected traitors and striking fear in potential informers. Consorting with the corrupt has its dangers in all societies, but so does exposing them—even when the whistle-blowers are legally supported and publicly heralded.

Human Susceptibility

So why should people be so susceptible to corruption? There seem to be three major explanations concerning scarcity, morality, and governance. First, economically, there is simply not enough to go around in most societies to satisfy people's needs; the poorer the society, the greater the scarcity and the worse the consequences of being poor. The worst situation is where the basic needs of large numbers of people are not being met. Those being left behind will soon suffer irreparable harm. In desperation, they will do their utmost to survive or ensure a better life for their loved ones. The haves can exploit their advantages and can command a price (or economic rent) for their favors. Thereafter, greed may well take over. Never really short themselves, the haves seek to increase their advantages and move even further ahead of those less fortunate. Those who resist may find themselves slipping back and eventually overtaken. Paradoxically, societies that can least afford corruption are the most mired in it as people strive to get ahead. Yet there is no guarantee that as they get richer and more able to guarantee a decent standard of living to their poorest members and provide a wider safety net for their most disadvantaged, they will tackle corruption without a marked change in moral climate, which takes possibly generations to achieve.

Second, there has to be a change in moral behavior and a higher standard of general ethics demanded. Some poor societies do encourage and require greater self-discipline and regard for others less fortunate. But others too often reward excesses and preach self-advancement to everyone else's disregard. The former frown on corruption while the latter tend to rationalize, justify, and even legitimize it. Corruption is shrugged off as being part of human behavior that has always existed and will always exist. Corruption, it is claimed, is in the blood; it cannot be helped. In contrast, more disciplined societies see human behavior as a choice, a deliberate choice on the part of individuals between doing right and doing wrong. People instinctively know right from wrong, and they know the consequences to society if they prefer to do wrong rather than right, if they remain passive when wrong is being done and if they fail to stand up for right over wrong. The remedy for corruption is in everyone's hands; they should choose not to participate in doing wrong. People are reminded constantly what society considers to be right or wrong and they always have a choice. This, they are told, should be taught to the young and enshrined in law; it should be the subject of model behavior and the standard by which to measure other's conduct, even if people slip occasionally because they are not perfect.

Third, social norms have to be universally acknowledged and then effectively enforced. The problem with corruption is not so much that there is scarcity or that people do not know what to do, but the lack of institutional enforcement. Organizations and people within them do not practice what they preach because no harm comes to them when they do go astray. Everybody gives lipservice, but the enforcement fails to ensure compliance because it is defective. The expected rules of the game are vacuous, faulty, uncertain, ambivalent, unclear, contradictory, deficient, defective, too loose, too narrow, too restricted, and so forth. Whatever the reason, few feel the need to follow them. Those who are empowered to see that others conform lack the ability, resources, competence, and efficiency to do anything effective and, worse still, may present a bad example themselves. All this denotes defective governance, not just deficient means and reprehensible morals.

So what? Who cares? Do not corrupt regimes and societies prosper regardless, despite all the dire predictions about their forthcoming collapse? Besides, there are far worse evils being perpetrated in society just as there are far worse behaviors exhibited by human beings who fight, hate, exploit, enslave, exterminate, steal, lie, cheat, deceive, rape, plunder, and pillage, individually and in groups. War and other human-made disasters continue. There are worse evils and injustices in human society than corrupt practices. These other misdeeds rightly have priority attention because they do more harm. First things first; we'll get around to corruption after we've tackled these more severe problems. At this point an issue arises that is more than merely semantic. What constitutes corruption? What human conduct is included or excluded? Where is the line between corrupt behavior and other kinds of behavior such as ignorance, incompetence, bias, indifference, carelessness, and so forth? What are the links between corruption and other social ills? Undoubtedly they are interconnected. Where should a start be made? Clearly, where a difference can be made. The studies in this book indicate that a start can indeed be made on combating corruption and in so doing other social ills can be targeted at the same time. One thing leads to another. Combating corruption involves battling other social ills, too. Successful anticorruption campaigns do indeed improve society all around, especially strengthening moral fiber. The benefits, for instance, of clean and good governance are clearly demonstrated and demonstrable.

The Challenge

One message that comes through in this book is not so much that people do not know what to do about corruption as that they tend to lack sufficient will, fortitude, stamina, resolution, and persistence to do anything about it. To some extent, there is a lack of conviction. The odds at first seem so great. People seem to be their own worst enemies. They claim to be against corruption in general but not against specific corrupt acts that benefit themselves or their communities. Sometimes their own guilt compromises them into paralysis. Even if they correct their own behavior, they are never quite sure that others will do the same; on the contrary, others may appear outwardly to change their behavior while furtively persisting in the same way. What then if reform gives a false sense of security? After all, does not corruption eventually reappear somewhere else in a different guise—more sophisticated, less obvious, less objectionable? Possibly so, but then its pervasiveness is gone. Nevertheless, is that sufficient excuse to do nothing here and now to try to stop unacceptable public conduct, obvious injustices, and unfairness arising from corruption and its continued corrosive effects on the social fabric?

Is the need to tackle corruption any greater today than it has been in the past? What is the urgency? A decade or so ago, there did not seem to be such urgency especially as corruption was not recognized by many international agencies. Several events since then have made combating corruption a higher priority. First, corruption seems to have increased or, rather, awareness of corruption and its damaging effects on world development and governance have increased. Stories about corruption appear daily in global mass media. Indeed, it is difficult to keep track of every incidence. Several international agencies, such as Transparency International and the United Nations Development Programme, now operate special Web sites for anyone interested in trying to keep abreast of revelations of corrupt practices and attempts to combat them around the globe. But does more frequent mention of corruption necessarily indicate its more frequent practice or just its greater newsworthiness?

Second, the many taboos that used to hide corruption have now been broken. Where once the World Bank, for instance, would never mention the subject, it now admits to corruption and moreover has committed itself to reducing it. Much the same can be said of other members of the United Nations family of organizations. International recognition has both preceded and followed country recognition, business concern, and nongovernmental organization action. The global society and the incidence of corruption within it touch all. No one can remain aloof or unconcerned. The cancer of corruption endangers all. A start has been made by placing it on the public agenda, by bringing it into the open, by discussing where its many manifestations do the most harm, and by debating what might be done to reduce its dysfunctions. There has definitely been a change in international attitudes toward corrupt practices, toward their ubiquity, and toward the unwillingness to confront its dysfunctions. But will this change in attitude result in any different outcomes?

Third, after a period of questioning the worth of government intervention and trying to get government out of where it should not be, international organizations have realized the impossibility of separating government from other societal institutions that govern contemporary global society; thus their substitution of the word governance for government to indicate the fusion of all societal institutions and the need for governments to use other instruments to implement public policy and deliver public services. They have also realized the greater importance of quality over quantity, that is, the primacy of effective, impartial, and good governance over the selection of which particular instrument should govern which specific human activities. Corruption undermines all instruments, public and private, governmental and nongovernmental, and its presence in one set of instruments is likely to contaminate other sets. Attention should not be confined to government alone. But what chance is there that a more universal code of conduct can govern all instruments of public business?

Fourth, there is increasing concern by leaders, adults, and teachers that ethics and morality have declined globally in recent years as evidenced by the general decline in manners and the incivility or rudeness exhibited not just by the younger generations and the spread of the cult of selfishness and inner concerns. Standards of conduct seem to be changing. What was once considered unacceptable is becoming commonplace and likewise what was once considered the norm is becoming increasingly rare or exceptional, less tolerated, and less supported. For instance, unacceptable but more commonplace behavior, such as increases in crime, violence, and disrespect have received much attention. However, less attention has been paid to the other side, such as making officeholders more directly responsible and accountable for acts and consequences of such acts taken on their watch, particularly those considered harmful to the public. Likewise, underlings and followers are no longer so easily excused for their unquestioning obedience or for carrying out harmful orders. So changes are in the air, but they can be difficult to pinpoint. There are increasing pressures to reexamine contemporary ethics, particularly as they apply to the conduct of public affairs and governance, and a reassessment of the links between good governance and the persistence of corrupt practices which by definition constitute bad governance. So what should be recommended for the global society and its future governance? What should be kept and reinforced or redefined, redrafted and even abandoned?

These are some of the questions that this book attempts to raise and to which answers are sought on four distinct but linked levels, namely international, country and regional, institutional and organizational, and individual and personal. First, international corrupt practices flow globally, replete with an international cast of bad characters and criminal organizations that deal in outlawed or immoral goods and services, operate beyond national and international conventions, and infiltrate where they can, often where people least suspect their presence. Their impact is global as they contaminate wherever they go and whomever they touch. But even without their insidious influence, world organizations are far from perfect; they also have their share of corrupt and corrupted staff and corrupt practices. Second, there are regional and national cultures in which corruption is a way of life; to do business, outsiders have little choice but to go along with the corruption. Such immorality presents a bad example to neighbors and others who are used to different ways and attitudes. To combat corruption in them requires better if not good governance and probably international incentives to change agents. Third, even in countries that pride themselves on their cleanliness, there are islands of depravity. Some institutions and organizations are systemically rotten: good people are made bad, corrupt practices persist despite efforts to eliminate them, and reforms do not last. No country can afford to be complacent; in recent years some countries have been shocked, or at least disturbed, by scandals involving some of the most respected positions in the land. Finally, there are untrustworthy people everywhere who knowingly deviate from the norms of their society and try to hide their nefarious activities from others. They operate just within the letter of the law but not in its spirit, or they act unethically in their own selfish interests and harm others. Combating this individual level is possibly the hardest task of all because there are always some people who take unfair advantage of everyone else's trust.

The Contribution

This book does not attempt to provide complete coverage of all the issues surrounding corruption and governance. It is impossible to cover every country, every aspect of every form of corruption, every anticorruption institution and agency, or every reputable expert. Given time constraints, not every promised contributor could meet the set publication deadlines. But contributors were encouraged to provide an original perspective and not stick to a standard format so that the spectrum together would throw light on the most important concerns. The result is that this book has something for everyone, from a detailed account of a specific scandal embarrassing one country to a detailed account of the many societal factors making for corruption in another, from the simple concerns of fairly clean governance in one part of the world to the worries of citizens experiencing very dirty governance in another, from long-term institutional failure to short-term success, from the pessimistic to the optimistic, from the circumspect to the ambitious, from the half-hearted to the resolute, from the idealistic to the pragmatic. All of these reflect the current state of the art.

The book opens with an overview of the world of corruption in chapter 2, Corruption and Governance, in which Gerald Caiden points out that corruption is as old as governance itself. Its causes, forms, and consequences seem to be timeless. The temptations to misuse public office have been overwhelming in all societies, political regimes, economic systems, and national cultures although there have been marked distinctions between communities where corruption has been a way of life and where it has been reduced to only an incidental and exceptional fact of life. Though corruption is timeless, this has not prevented endless disputes over what exactly constitutes corrupt practices, to what extent corruption is functional or dysfunctional, who benefits and who loses, what should be done about tackling it, and where to start first.

Following this overview of corruption comes a series of selected representative regional and country case studies of corruption around the world. The order selected is merely conventional. Although in contemporary governance it is difficult to separate political corruption from administrative corruption, private sector corruption from public sector corruption, and personal corruption from occupational corruption, Richard White in chapter 3, Corruption in the United States, confines himself to the American governmental system. He shows that whereas the public service professions are relatively free of corruption given the size and reach of its administrative state, the American political system is plagued with corruption and some corrupt practices remain institutionalized and systemic; certainly they are habitual and endemic. Nevertheless, it has proven possible to exclude deliberately sizeable areas of politics and administration from partisan considerations and to draw boundaries around crucial official activities where corrupt practices are not tolerated.

Neighboring Canada does not appear to be so beholden to political money, according to O. P. Dwivedi and Maureen Mancuso in chapter 4, Governance and Corruption in Canada. Canada is relatively corruption-free and has gone much further in establishing and enforcing institutional safeguards against ethical lapses in government and forcing offenders out of public life. If corruption persists, it is likely due to individual lapses although there may be isolated areas of systemic vulnerability. Much the same conclusion applies to many countries in Western Europe. With some exceptions in recent years, they seem to be slipping off their high moral perch as illustrated by Douglas Yates in chapter 5, France's Elf Scandals.

The countries of Central and Eastern Europe are quite a contrast. Although their Communist regimes preached the merits of the virtuous, disinterested public official, they added a superstructure that in itself was immoral and unethical. Eventually the systems collapsed because they were so hollow as Tomasz Anusiewicz, Tony Verheijen, and Antoaneta Dimitrova point out in chapter 6, Tackling Corruption in Central and Eastern Europe. Bureaucratic sterility has been replaced by administrative chaos, and systemic corruption has been compounded by economic hardship, official entrepreneurship, greater license to organized crime, privatization and deteriorating conditions of employment. The causes of corruption in the Middle East are different but the outcomes are much the same. Public business has largely remained personalized. Public office gives holders access to spoils and patronage. As described by Joseph Jabbra and Nancy Jabbra in chapter 7, Corruption and the Lack of Accountability in the Middle East, corruption is more or less systemic. Here again can be found the mixture between kleptocracy at the top and the sheer struggle to survive among street-level officials. Much is attributed to the lack of public account-ability and the absence of effective accountability mechanisms.

Countries south of the Sahara have the reputation of being among the most misgoverned and the most corrupt. Dele Olowu in chapter 8, Corruption and Governance in West Africa, examines the three former British colonies of Sierra Leone, Ghana, and Nigeria in some detail to illustrate the inhibiting effects of systemic corruption on African development in general. His compari-son gives hope that all is far from lost, especially in civilian-ruled Nigeria where beneficial results have been brought by openness, accountability, and restora-tion of the rule of law. Less optimistic is the situation in South Africa, according to Victor Hilliard and Henry Wessink in chapter 9, Understanding Corruption in the South African Public Sector, where the new regime is trying to contain the spread of corruption fed by many factors.

Perhaps things are not as bad in some parts of Asia although some coun-tries in this continent rank among the lowest in governance simply because corruption has always been a way of life. An overwhelming sense of fatalism pervades. But Jon Quah in chapter 10, Combating Corruption in the Asia Pa-cific Region examines attempts in one subregion to tackle corruption and shows that with determined political will, honest government, and public education a significant difference can be made. China is singled out in chapter 11, The Culture of Corruption in Post-Mao China, by Stephen Ma to illustrate what has gone wrong in a country once led by self-sacrificing idealists determined to radically change by example the way the country had been governed and the corrupt way public business had been conducted. They partially succeeded but were considered too harsh. Only after Mao's death could objections to this new scheme of things be voiced when it failed to produce the desired results and be loosened to allow more freedom but also greater connivance and collabora-tion. In time, opportunism spread and people took advantage to promote self-interest. Information about deviance and corrupt practices could not be sup-pressed. As something had to be done to prevent further rot, political will to take effective rather than token action has been strengthened although this still may be insufficient.

Jorge Nef points out in chapter 12, Government Corruption in Latin America, that incoming rulers in many countries of that continent also promise to root out the corruption bequeathed by their predecessors, only to continue the same practices and make matters even worse while they hold office. Political will fades once the new rulers see the advantages to themselves of perpetuating corruption for much the same reasons as poor governance and widespread corruption persist elsewhere in the world. In contrast, according to Peter Larmour and Peter Grabosky in chapter 13, Corruption in Australia: Its

Prevention and Control, Australia has virtually eliminated systemic corruption and minimized individual corruption; however, there are some black spots where corrupt practices have been cleverly and deceitfully hidden by leaders with declining political morality.

Evidence of corruption in poor countries prompted Peter Eigen to openly confront the ostrichlike attitudes that characterized the international community. So he created Transparency International (TI) in 1993; its inner story is related by Fredrik Galtung in chapter 14, Transparency International's Network to Curb Global Corruption. At the time, other international agencies that were becoming more concerned about poor governance and corrupt practices provided a receptive audience. With TI as a catalyst, international attitudes have changed as evidenced by Pauline Tamesis in chapter 15, The UNDP's Integrity Improvement Initiatives, which details the change in policy within the United Nations organization and the UNDP, which is now TI's partner. This is reinforced by Demetrios Argyriades in chapter 16, The International Anticorruption Campaigns: Whose Ethics?, which also raises the question whether the reasoning behind this sudden burst of interest is so benign. Argyriades argues that it may also be related to the antistatist rhetoric of neoliberalism to weaken the state and deprive it of other crucial functions that need to be strengthened in the global society to reduce corruption.

Gerald Caiden shows in chapter 17, Corruption and Democracy, that all countries are guilty of corruption, which pervades all regimes. Indeed, the newly emerging democracies are possibly worse off than they were before their transition phase. This perception is undermining the democratization process and the credibility of all public institutions. Even the long-established democracies are worried by scandals which reveal that wrongdoing may be too protected, sophisticated, and tolerated to yield to traditional anticorruption practices, especially where political money is involved and holding on to office so compelling. Finally, chapter 18, Official Ethics and Corruption, by Gerald Caiden and O. P. Dwivedi goes beyond governance to consider the changing nature of global morality. Official, governmental, or public service ethics cannot be isolated from these general trends or changes in public attitudes. Growing awareness of the dysfunctions of corruption has produced the impetus to propagate higher standards of official conduct, but this greatly depends on good governance supported by moral leadership and example. A key appears to be more effective public accountability not just imposed from the outside but also attributable from the moral spirit within—the inner voice of conscience, rectitude, and integrity that makes public service a righteous enterprise.

Acknowledgements

This project needed the cooperation and support of many organizations and people. We thank the editors of *The Asian Journal of Public Administration* (Hong Kong University), *Scripta* (The American University, Paris) and *The Asian Journal of Political Science* (National University of Singapore) for permission to draw upon material used in Chapters 2, 6, and 17, respectively. Gerald Caiden thanks Naomi Caiden for all her assistance on this project together with Artimese Porter for her efforts in the production of the manuscript. O. P. Dwivedi is indebted to T. N. Chaturvedi, Professors R. B. Jain (Delhi University), B. D. Dua (Lethbridge University), J. E. Hodgetts (Queen's University) and J. Meisel (Queen's University) for their guidance and help. Joseph Jabbra thanks Mrs. Nora Romero and Mr. Shayan Samii for their dedication and assistance. We gratefully acknowledge the skills of Linda Beyus and the staff at Kumarian Press.

2

Corruption and Governance

Gerald E. Caiden

EVER SINCE THE DAWN OF CIVILIZATION, it has been recognized that anyone put in a position of exercising communal, collective, or public power and commanding public obedience is tempted to use public office for personal gain and advantage. Perhaps it is asking too much of mere mortals to put aside personal ambition and prejudice and ignore all group and peer pressures to rule in a completely disinterested manner. Deviant conduct has been expected and fairly accurately recorded by historians brave enough to write about Chinese rulers, Hebrew kings, and Roman emperors. Indeed, the most wicked who wallowed in perversion and depravity even welcomed the idea that their evil deeds would be known forever and showed no shame or remorse.

Guilt about public misbehavior is a relatively recent phenomenon, at least the guilt that denies and hides such behavior. Guilt had to await the universal acceptance of the idea of free will and choice governing human conduct, optimism about the human condition, the possibility of progress, and acknowledgment of limitations on the exercise of official power. These in turn required belief in the betterment of human behavior, the discernment of right, good, fair and just, and the recognition of norms of official conduct. So much has the pendulum swung that in some puritanical societies, misuse and abuse of public office is considered shameful, spelling the end of any further public career with disgrace lasting beyond the grave.

Otherwise, offensive behavior by public officials had long been taken for granted, so much assumed that little systematic study was given to it, not even when its occurrence was particularly scandalous or its consequences especially disastrous. The world had to wait until Ibn Khaldun diagnosed that all societies, even the greatest and most brilliant, were doomed to decay, their energies dissipated, their genius suffocated, their power diminished, their rulers isolated and distant, unable to command respect and, eventually, any following. Then Machiavelli analyzed how rulers could improve their image, enrich themselves, increase their power, and postpone the fading of their light by cunning realpolitik, deception, and unsavory actions, thus rationalizing if not justifying objectionable public conduct. What was the purpose of seeking and retaining public office, if not for personal gain? Why should anyone take on the burdens and responsibilities of public leadership if there were no personal advantages, no compensating rewards? Naturally, public office was to be used in self-interest; otherwise, why bother to enter the harsh, competitive arena of public life? But this very self-interest, said Ibn Khaldun, would inevitably doom the republic.

The fullness of time proved that this was not the inevitable fate of human-kind. People sought public office and the exercise of public power for nobler causes than pure self-interest. They could successfully put aside their own personal advantage and rule disinterestedly. They could recognize conduct unbecoming public office, legislate against it, and drive it underground with harsh prosecution of offenders. A higher standard of conduct could be expected, inculcated, and practiced—one that added stature and esteem to public office, that strengthened loyalty between rulers and ruled, that made government work in the interests of all and not just a privileged few. Yet misuse and abuse of public office persisted, perhaps because the wrong people were still getting into office or because when they got into office they found the exercise of power too easy to manipulate. If every exercise of power were tainted with evil, if power degraded and demoralized those who exercised it, if officeholders came to love power for its own sake, if no one at all could be entrusted with power, then one would have to conclude with Lord Acton, "Power tends to corrupt and absolute power corrupts absolutely" (Payne 1975, 179). What else needs to be said? Why study this sleazy side of public life? Muckraking has its place but hardly within the halls of academe. So scholarly research shied away until the pervasiveness and persistence of corruption could not be ignored. Despite largely fragmentary, biased, anecdotal, misleading, impressionistic, inadequate, clandestine, sensitive, soft, unreliable, and distorted evidence, possibly more studies of corruption have been conducted in the past forty years than at any time in history.

As so often occurs in science, the more attention a subject receives, the more complicated it becomes. Corruption comes in too many forms to permit easy generalization (see Table 2.1). There is high-level and low-level corruption, and there is predominantly political and predominantly bureaucratic corruption. There are endemic, pervasive forms and isolated, infrequent forms. There are mutually reinforcing networks of complex, indirect and subtle transactions; and isolated, simple, direct, and bilateral transactions that have contradictory effects.

Table 2.1

Most Commonly Recognized Forms of Official Corruption

- Treason; subversion; illegal foreign transactions; smuggling
- Kleptocracy; privatization of public funds; larceny and stealing
- Misappropriation; forgery and embezzlement; padding of accounts; diverted funds; misuse of funds; unaudited revenues; skimming
- Abuse and misuse of power; intimidation; undeserved pardons and remissions; torture
- Deceit and fraud; misrepresentation; cheating and swindling; blackmail
- Perversion of justice; criminal behavior; false evidence; unlawful detention; frame-ups
- Nonperformance of duties; desertion; parasitism; cronyism
- Bribery and graft; extortion; illegal levies; kickbacks
- Tampering with elections; vote rigging: gerrymandering
- Misuse of inside knowledge and confidential information; falsification of records
- Unauthorized sale of public offices, loans, monopolies, contracts, licenses, and public property
- Manipulation of regulations, purchases and supplies; bias and favoritism in decision making
- Tax evasion; excessive profiteering
- Influence-peddling; favor-brokering; conflicts of interest
- Acceptance of improper gifts and entertainments; "speed" money; junkets
- Protecting maladministration; cover-ups; perjury
- Black market operations; links with organized crime
- Misuse of official seals, stationery, residences, and perquisites
- Illegal surveillance; misuse of mails and telecommunications; improper use of electronics and computers

There is large, disruptive corruption and petty, trivial corruption. Corrupt exchanges may be rare or frequent, open or closed, between equals or unequals; the stakes may be tangible or intangible, durable or nondurable, routine or extraordinary; and the channels may be legitimate or illegitimate (Johnston 1986). Nonetheless, this confusion does not invalidate certain universal generalizations:

1. Corruption has been found in all political systems, at every level of government, and in the delivery of all scarce public goods and services.

2. Corruption varies in origin, incidence, and importance among different geographic regions, sovereign states, political cultures, economies, and administrative arrangements.

3. Corruption is facilitated or impeded by the societal context (including international and transnational influences) in which public power is exercised.

4. Corruption has multitudinous causes, assumes many different patterns and guises and cannot be accurately measured because of its often indeterminate and conspiratorial nature.

5. Corruption is deeply rooted, cancerous, contaminating, and impossible to eradicate because controls tend to be formalistic, superficial, temporary, and even counterproductive.

6. Corruption is directed at real power, key decision points, and discretionary authority. It commands a price for both access to decision makers and influence in decision making.

7. Corruption is facilitated by unstable polities, uncertain economies, maldistributed wealth, unrepresentative government, entrepreneurial ambitions, privatization of public resources, factionalism, personalism, and dependency.

8. Corruption favors those who have (over those who have not), illegal enterprises, underground economies, and organized crime.

9. Corruption persists substantially as long as its perpetrators can coerce participation, public attitudes towards it vary widely, and it greatly benefits a privileged few at the expense of the disadvantaged mass or benefits all participants at the cost of nonparticipants.

10. Corruption can be contained within acceptable limits through political

will, democratic ethos, fragmented countervailing power, legal-rational administrative norms, inculcation of personal honesty and integrity, and effective enforcement of public ethics—although its complete elimination is still beyond human capability.

These findings indicate that corruption can be reduced and contained through appropriate countermeasures, but as long as the underlying causes persist, corruption is unlikely to be eliminated altogether. Indeed as long as human beings are imperfect corruption will persist. What anticorruption measures seek to do is drive it out of major areas of governance, reduce its scope, lessen its occurrence, implement fail-safe devices. These measures should improve the image of governance, increase effectiveness and efficiency, streamline operations, and make for more civic activity and greater public participation.

Definition

The word corruption means something spoiled: something sound that has been made defective, debased, and tainted; something that has been pushed off course into a worse or inferior form. Whoever corrupts sets out to make something impure and less capable, an adverse departure from an expected course. When applied to human relations, corruption is a bad influence, an injection of rottenness or decay, a decline in moral conduct and personal integrity attributable to venality or dishonesty. When applied to public office, rather than referring to departures from ideal or even generally expected standards of incumbent behavior, the practice has been to spell out specific acts of misconduct that disgrace public office and make the offenders unfit to remain there.

In virtually every society, historians and anthropologists have found that public affairs are distinguished by their exceptional privileges and trappings. Public officials so graced have been expected to exercise their special communal authority in a manner that dignifies the office, credits the officeholder, and comforts those out of office. Long before the modern state, the Code of Hammurabi, Mosaic laws, and Confucian principles shared similar notions of what was and was not acceptable official conduct. Only the best people should hold office. They should be the most righteous and wisest; persons of character and distinction, of honor and integrity; they should be dependable. These worthy people should set an example and insist on the highest standards of performance. Their task was to advance the public interest, maintain the peace, promote the general welfare, and deal kindly with their people. They were to administer public affairs with wisdom, compassion, justice, and sensitivity. They were to protect and safeguard public property as a sacred trust and to account for their actions to the public. They were to proclaim just laws and see they were carried out honestly and fairly. They were to be judged by their good deeds and remembered for their good works. They were to be condemned for wickedness, treachery, deceit, cruelty, rapaciousness, immorality, and all conduct that demeaned public office.

Even though politics has commonly been viewed as the most unprincipled of human pursuits, codes of conduct have evolved to regulate international relations, armed conflicts among states, obligations between politicians and officials, the execution of civil laws, and the conduct of public professionals. Alongside have grown legal definitions of public misconduct and dereliction of duty. The enforcement machinery has also been strengthened. Most contemporary states have outlawed specific acts of official corruption and have in place machinery to prosecute suspected officials. To this extent, corruption has been universally recognized. But beyond this area, uncertainty begins with a lack of consistency, as not all states outlaw certain acts. In other instances, the law is not enforced uniformly. Such differences thwart the acceptance of legal, moral, and public interest definitions. Similarly, even if public attitudes could be measured accurately and were not so "divided, unsuitable, ambiguous, and inconsistent" (Williams 1987, 19), definitions based on public opinion are not universal enough.

In the absence of an all-purpose definition, in recent years the public office definition coined by Nye has been the most widely accepted, namely, that corruption is *"behavior which deviates from the formal duties of a public role because of private-regarding (personal, close family, private clique) pecuniary or status gains; or violates rules against the exercise of certain types of private-regarding influence"* (1967, 419). Nye specifically included bribery, nepotism, and misappropriation. This operational definition—when extended to include unscrupulous performance, undue pressures to influence official decisions, and failure to act—should suffice as a working definition in most instances. It stresses the behavioral element of intentional deviation for personal gain. It covers most market-centered definitions that concentrate on maximizing pecuniary gains (Rose-Ackerman 1978), and it can be stretched to include public interest definitions identifying corrupt acts as those that favor private interests over public concerns. It even includes a strictly Marxist-Leninist interpretation of corruption as all official activities that protect the interests of the dominant (capitalist) class "whether they be spending, taxing, regulating or policing" (Greenberg 1974, 25) but not the public office definitions actually employed in Communist regimes. Perhaps the only area that is not covered is that of "noble" or "patriotic" corruption where public officials supposedly turn their private vices into public benefits (Werner 1983, 147), where they do not personally gain and no improper considerations induce the violation of duty. However, as a result of their noble actions, their ignoring the law and expected public ethics may, in turn, be ignored with impunity, secreted, and viewed as making up inadequate past compensation.

This public office definition does not see corruption as beneficial to the public, to the credibility of public institutions, to the status of public officials, to public trust in officialdom, to the promotion of public ethics, to open and honest government, or to common decency. Corruption prevents the public realm from pursuing the general welfare, "a just society which preserves the liberty and security of each citizen," a society in which citizens "under a wise system of laws and institutions, good customs and proper mores . . . are capable of identifying their own good and the common good" (Philp 1987, 7). Corruption leads to a breakdown in shared concerns and results in factional pursuit of special interests and a reliance on coercion over consensus. Indeed, reliance on coercion indicates a corrupt or corrupted state, perverted and rotten, where every person is on guard against everyone else in a society of amoral familism. It also indicates a state in which organizational integrity collapses amid a race for selfish advantages.

Contributory Factors

Just as there are many varieties of corrupt behavior, so there are multitudinous factors contributing to corruption. Public officials, or a significant portion of them around the globe, fail to pursue the common good and to live up to the moral standards expected of them. Perhaps these standards are set too high, given human frailty. Perhaps the personal gains for self-indulgence are too tempting. Perhaps the chances of being caught are too low and punishment too lenient to be a serious deterrent. Whatever the explanation, it is also true that their colleagues do behave themselves, that some public organizations are more trustworthy than others, and that some administrative cultures exhibit higher standards of integrity than others. What, then, accounts for such variations? So many explanations are offered that it is difficult to classify them in any systematic manner (see Table 2.2).

Psychological

Human beings are flawed, some more than others. Some are by nature sweet, self-sacrificing, public-spirited, kind, decent, obedient. They try to set a good example to others who in contrast are mean, selfish, egotistical, greedy, and devious, out only for themselves and not caring about anyone else. Usually, the latter victimize the former but even when the victims know such advantage is being taken of them, they still refuse to act that way. As a result, they tend to

Table 2.2   A Simplified Typology of Corruption

Type	Main Actors	Mode	Background
1. Foreign-sponsored	• Public officials • Politicians • Representatives of donors and recipient countries	a. Bribery and kickbacks b. Collusion to defraud the public	a. Economic dependency b. Multidimensional value systems c. Dyadic, plural, loosely structured society d. Comprador bureaucrats
2. Political scandal	• Bureaucratic elites • Politicians • Businessmen and middlemen	a. Large-scale embezzlement and misappropriation through public tender and disposal of public property b. Economic privileges accorded to special interests c. Large political donations and bribes	a. State capitalism, scarcity of capital, competition for domestic markets and public funds b. Unpatriotic, self-serving officials c. Corruption as a way of life d. Ineffectual bureaucratism
3. Institutionalized	• Politicians • Businessmen • White-collar workers	a. Large-scale disbursement of public property to special and privileged interests under the pretext of "national interest" b. Favoritism and discrimination exercised in favor of ruling parties in exchange for political contributions	a. Industrialization, concentration of capital, monopolies, statism b. Class systems c. Petty bourgeoise values d. Spoils system e. Managed economies
4. Administrative malfeasance	• Petty officials • Interested individuals	a. Small-scale embezzlement and misappropriation b. Bribes c. Favoritism and discrimination d. Parasitism	a. Domestic systems of production b. Social insecurity c. Clanism, office as perquisite d. Maladministration and incompetence e. Gossip and rumor

lose out and hope that social arrangements minimize the damage and compensate for their losses. In contrast, the victimizers exploit their opportunities to get ahead and come out winners, boastful of their success and even spiteful and sadistic, deliberately tightening the screws on their weaker victims to show their alleged superiority. As no one enjoys being a perpetual loser, the temptation is eventually to follow suit. Thus, unless strong in character and willing to forgo the benefits of corruption, the victims may find themselves sucked into corrupt conduct against their will and better judgment simply because there seems no advantage to sticking it out. In short, the root cause of corruption is found in the defects of human character inherent in the human condition; few are above temptation and corruption should be seen as the norm, not the exception.

Ideological

There are ideologies that endorse corruption or prevent remedial action, nihilistic ideologies and their tyrannical exponents who believe themselves above and beyond morality. Then there are religious doctrines that preach that all is divinely determined, including corruption, and that nothing is to be questioned or challenged lest divine retribution occur. There are also those who believe that in a righteous cause, the means justify the ends, apparently any means to justify their particular ends in an amoral pursuit of power. Life is about winning, if need be at the expense of others. And if the "good" is limited, winning at the expense of others is inevitable. The environment is seen as a world one can extract from but not shape:

In popular perception wealth and even decent well-being have no relationship to work and can only be the result of accident, luck, good connections or criminal practices. A redistributive orientation is the most rational attitude in these circumstances—connections, powerful patrons and the skillful exploitation of one's office . . . are more effective than hard work and frugality (Tarkowski 1988, 48).

Such realpolitik has obvious appeal in highly competitive and individualistic societies, in atomistic societies where few common bonds exist, and in very poor societies where death and starvation are daily companions.

External

Corruption is contagious. As no society is isolated or cut off from any other, corruption crosses boundaries. It is externally induced. Forbidden and inaccessible fruits are smuggled in across porous borders. All manner of illegal goods are traded or carried by international travelers. All foreigners bring with them foreign values whose legacy lingers as the new indigenous rulers continue their practices, exploiting the fruits of office and expecting the same deference, while their peoples engage in underground defiance. Among the fruits of office is the ability to borrow on international money markets and to siphon off a certain portion and secrete ill-gotten gains abroad. Another is the ability to negotiate the entry of multinational corporations whose voracious appetite for new business enables public officials to demand and receive personal favors in the form of monopoly dealerships, kickbacks, and influence peddling. Yet another is to indulge in spying and other covert activities both at home and abroad. Globalization has exacerbated these and other opportunities for externally induced corruption, aided and abetted by weak international bodies and ineffective country safeguards.

Economic

Scarcity is clearly a key source of corruption. Without unfulfilled demand, suppliers could not command any additional price and potential purchasers would not seek unfair access. Any temporary shortage brings out the best and worst in people. But with prolonged scarcity, as in permanently impoverished economies, there may be no second chance. Failure to gain access means certain deprivation and probable death. Suppliers can squeeze whatever can be squeezed out of the desperately needy. Wherever wealth is maldistributed to produce a permanent underclass of underprivileged and dispossessed people who, unaided, cannot improve their lot, their state of dependency becomes exploitable. Poor societies lack sufficient resources all around, but they are especially short of public resources. Governments are too poor to provide sufficient public goods and services, to maintain public facilities, or to pay their employees a decent wage. Thus a mad scramble ensures to obtain whatever is going and to make up for underpayments. Planning and regulation of economic activities to ensure greater access and fairer distribution only distort market conditions, setting into action corrective underground arrangements wherein a black market economy coexists with the official economy and the regulated come to capture the regulators. Public monopolization of scarce resources only exacerbates the situation: public officials may run their public businesses as private concerns. Privatization scarcely helps because in private business different and less demanding norms apply.

Political

Public officials are powerful because they determine in large part the personal fortunes of everyone affected by their decisions. If they had no such power, there would be no point in influencing them. Conversely, the more important their personal decisions are to any individual, the more worthwhile it is to try to influence them. Hence, corruption seeks out key decision makers and the most powerful officials. When public office is confined to a narrow, unrepresentative elite, extraordinary means have to be employed to enlarge vision and obtain concessions. Similarly, when the masses are excluded from public life and beholden to autocratic, omnipotent, discretionary rule—as in the case of military dictatorships, theocracies, and single party regimes—extralegal ways have to be found to influence public decisions and to overcome the privatization of politics that Lord Acton suggested is itself corruptive. His dictum is certainly confirmed when public officials themselves indulge in lawlessness, arbitrariness, kleptocracy, entrepreneurialism at public expense, spoils, immoral choices, undesired social controls, and overregulation. What the government does, the governed believe they can also do. If the government lies, cheats, and steals, so will the people.

Sociocultural

Failure to pursue the general interest may be attributable to a conflict of loyalties in which the particularistic wins, there being no commitment to the wider community but a deliberate preference for a lesser ascriptive group. Public office is used for partisan advantages. Civic virtue is lacking as is any notion of altruistic public service. Group advancement and self-gratification are the major motives for public work. Public officials cannot make "reasonably disinterested commitments . . . that benefit the substantive common welfare" (Dobel 1978, 958), and they cannot be trusted to exercise their discretion "with an entire absence of interest motive, with honesty of intention, and with a fair consideration of the subject" (Baker 1970, 31). Internal socialization and peer group pressure ensure that public officials go along with or at least keep quiet about deviance. Whistle-blowers who reveal internal wrongdoings are considered treacherous; they must be publicly discredited. Thus once corruption exists, it spreads through inaction and ready accommodation "abetted by complacency, naiveté and lethargy" (Werner 1983, 149). It can be further compounded by public maladministration, which also prevents effective counteraction.

Technological

Faulty technology and faulty administrative systems are also to blame for corruption as they permit those inclined to corruption to remain unseen and unknown, to evade detection, and to escape investigation. Mechanization lends itself to backstage manipulation by designers and technicians. Insiders can exploit legal loopholes known only to them. The ingenious and the unscrupulous take advantage of any openings and invent their own. Technology confers undue discretion on its implementers, giving them a monopoly of specialized knowledge that in turn gives them virtually absolute power to decide on their own and placing them beyond adequate public scrutiny and accountability until after the event, when it is too late to prevent abuse and misuse of such power. The greater society's dependence on technological complexity, the greater the propensity toward corruption based on monopoly and discretion without adequate public accountability safeguards.

In sum, corruption can be attributed to almost anything, even to "baseless rumors and gossip-mongering about corruption" (Shaukat 1985, 190). Any form of human interaction in the public arena can be distorted for personal gain. But while the opportunities exist everywhere, the degree of corruption varies widely among individuals, public agencies, administrative cultures, and geographic regions. For example, at the international level there is a contrast between some organizations that have been remarkably free of corruption and others in which corruption has been endemic. The former attract spirited volunteers, enthused by their humanitarian tasks, enjoying a high status and adequately compensated. In these organizations, competition for office is fierce and selection processes are painstaking. The caliber of their employees is high and their professionalism is highly regarded. Careful watch is kept on their performance for they are very much in the public eye and attract mass media publicity for their work. Other international agencies, however, operate with much secrecy and report only to themselves. They have been captured by arrogant elites who have privatized them. Other agencies have not adequately policed their field offices that operate in corruption-prone situations and are in a position to hide their corruption even from their head offices and outside auditors.

Regional Patterns

The compendium of factors contributing to official corruption indicates that where many of them are found together, a higher propensity for corruption exists, which may or may not be offset by strong countervailing factors such as open, representative government, an affluent economy, national identification and loyalty, redistributive taxation and public welfare, a strong civic culture, a jealously guarded public service tradition, legal-rational norms, competent public administration, professional integrity, and public intolerance of official misconduct. The strength of these countervailing factors makes the difference between corruption as a fact of life and corruption as a way of life, between isolated and infrequent occurrences and regularized, institutionalized, systematic corruption. Despite the unevenness of research data, several attempts at detecting generalized patterns of corruption among different geographical regions have been made, corresponding to the regions' relative wealth, political stability, social cohesion, cultural mores, administrative capability, and degree of modernization. They do reveal significant differences around the world, as might be expected using a culture-bound Western approach.

Western Europe

Western Europeans have long thought themselves culturally superior to other peoples and for centuries took their civilizing mission to other parts of the globe. They still believe themselves superior in official standards of behavior. While not free of scandal, they claim to have mastered corruption. In these countries, corruption is much the exception. They set themselves up as the standard to which other countries ought to aspire and emulate. They do exhibit high degrees of social discipline, law-abidingness, and civic virtue. They have open, democratic governments with prosperous economies where wealth is reasonably well distributed and the poor are sustained by public welfare. They are well administered. Their public employees evidence high integrity and honesty and the public is intolerant of official misconduct. In them, the mass media delight in exposing public wrongdoing and headlining occurrences of official corruption. But in recent years, their self-image has been besmirched by revelations of scandals in the highest public positions.

Australasia

The former British colonies achieved clean, honest, government possibly before the mother country and have maintained a low tolerance for corruption, although, as in Western Europe, there has been a general decline in recent years in public rectitude, with growing social permissiveness and the privatization of some areas of the public sector.

North America

Entrepreneurial politics is more prevalent and the profession of government has less status and prestige. With a public that is generally more tolerant and accommodating to corruption and the spoils system of politics that once dominated public life in North America, a lengthy reform campaign to cleanse public life has only dented systemic corruption entrenched by machine politics. Scandals occur with some frequency and a haze of sleaziness still hovers over public life generally. Nonetheless, definite limitations on corruption are imposed by constitutionalism, growing professionalism, legal-rational norms, effective public management practices, a vigilant mass media, and watchdog pressure groups.

Southern Europe

Just as Southern Europeans have endured poverty, autocracy, and instability, they have endured endemic corruption. Public resources have been scarce. Public maladministration has been rife, and public goods and services have been of poor quality. People have accommodated to this situation and have sought to get around it through extralegal channels. Despite waves of public indignation, public office has often been seen as an avenue for self-enrichment.

Latin America and the Caribbean

Many countries in the region still attribute corruption to their colonial legacy and to the example of a self-interested elite enslaving the masses. Beneath a veneer of hypocritical paternalism, elites have exploited and used autocracy to privatize public resources. In the competition for scarce goods and services, there has been no cap on the rich and no safety net for the poor except in a few states. Generally, while the protected privileged elite lives well, the masses have few rights, have little access to public office, and must pay at every step when undertaking public business. Modernization has brought an overlay of bureaucratic formalism, but underneath, public business is still conducted in a personalized manner. The state operates as a shameless machine of extraction and diversion of public resources with some dictators running their countries as personally owned fiefdoms or kleptocracies. Much of the extracted wealth is exported or goes into conspicuous consumption. But the entire region is not so corrupt. Kleptocracy has been contained by religious outrage, middle class professionalism, democratization, administrative reform, and civic virtue. There are dramatic contrasts between neighboring countries, but nowhere have the trickle-down effects of corruption satisfied enough people to avoid coercion and violence.

Sub-Saharan Africa

Postcolonial Africa also blames corruption on its colonial past, possibly with greater justification. It also contains several unabashed kleptocracies in which dictators treat their countries as private possessions, impoverish their subjects, amass huge fortunes that are secreted abroad, and enmesh everyone in corrupt transactions. Again, there seems to be no cap on the rich and no safety net for the poor. Generally the state is seen as an exploitive instrument. Office is highly prized. Almost everywhere officials have to be given treats as an extension of gift-giving and other reciprocal exchanges (Andreski 1968, 94). These officials are underpaid and have obligations to support an extended family. The plunder of public resources has been impoverishing country after country, diminishing the stock of public capital, and permitting bloated parasitical public bureaucracies to further undermine social discipline.

The Middle East

Similar conclusions are drawn for the Arab world where the extent, symptoms, and causes of corruption "vary from one Arab country to another" (Al-Saigh 1986, 83). They are linked to the environment, control systems, and public employee living standards. But the general lack of success in reducing corruption has been attributed "to the overwhelming corrupt culture which permeates all aspects of society" (Jabbra 1976, 673). Kinship binds, overriding bureaucratic legal-rational norms. Patrons protect clients who reciprocate with their support and services. Patron-client relations reinforce favoritism, nepotism, and patronage; promote illegal transactions; breed official irresponsibility; and systematize bribery.

Asia

In the Indian subcontinent, corruption is a way of life and few public officials can escape it. All the major contributory factors to corruption are present and mutually reinforcing, with the result that even the most determined efforts to fight the evil have failed miserably. But endemic corruption is also found in several other countries in Asia as diverse as Socialist Myanmar, Islamic Indonesia, Catholic Philippines, and Buddhist Thailand. Asia was the location of Myrdal's soft states (Myrdal 1968). Even so, there are varying patterns of corruption from one part of Asia to another, with some countries such as Singapore and Japan relatively clean at bureaucratic levels.

Eastern Europe

Communist society was supposed to free itself of corruption by fostering the spirit of the civic virtuous individual, altruism in the collective cause, and strict self-discipline. None of this seems to have happened in Communist regimes, which were characterized by demoralization, low productivity, a disinclination to work, high absenteeism, mass apathy, and widespread cheating. To general sources of corruption (such as autocracy, scarcity, poverty, and inequality) was added the mismanaged, distorted planned economy, which was accompanied by a huge underground network of unofficial exchanges that not only rectified some of the glaring official mistakes but also sanctioned deviant official conduct (embezzlement, misappropriation, profiteering, bribery, and deceit)—provided it achieved the desired official outcomes. The deliberate underproduction of consumer goods and the poor level of public services created a large pool of unmet demand. At the same time, there was a "widespread belief that state property belongs to no one in particular and is therefore free for the taking, as well as to public apathy about the pilferage and waste of state property" (Schwartz 1979, 428). With the downfall of Communism and the breakup of the Soviet Union, the situation has become more complex. Some countries have been able to combat institutionalized corruption better than others, but the overall situation seems, if anything, to have worsened. Corruption continues to be a way of life that few can avoid, with disasters in Romania and Albania when the state proved to be quite hollow.

Effects

Clearly, public officials who indulge in corruption gain until they are caught and penalized. For them, corruption is profitable. They can accumulate power and exercise it with fewer restrictions. They can live exceptionally privileged, sheltered lives and perhaps amass huge private fortunes. They can preserve themselves in office and predetermine succession, perhaps even creating a dynasty. They can do all the things they want to do and prevent other people from achieving anything at all. The advantages in status, wealth, and power are quite clear. But their gains are by definition unnatural advantages that otherwise would not have occurred. Their gains are made at someone else's expense, although the losers may never even realize they have been denied what should have been theirs.

Corrupt officials, knowingly or not, display contempt for other people, no matter how minor or seemingly innocent their corrupt acts. This contempt harbors within it the seeds of megalomania that, if allowed to flourish, eventually blossom into grosser and grosser acts that may lead to monstrous crimes against humanity where other people are considered expendable and other people's lives are considered meaningless and useless. All corruption is a deceit, a lie that sacrifices the common good or the public interest for something much less. It deviates from the search for the Good Society. Instead it gives comfort to social pathologies that divide, destabilize, and desensitize. Not only does it point society in the wrong direction, but it also exhausts governmental legitimacy, supports the wrong kind of public leadership, and sets the wrong kind of example for future generations. It contaminates. The following is just a sample of its adverse effects.

1. Corruption undermines political decisions, leads to inefficient use of resources, and benefits the unscrupulous at the cost of the law-abiding (Rose-Ackerman 1978).

2. Corruption involves the loss of moral authority, weakens the efficiency of government operations, increases opportunities for organized crime, encourages police brutality, adds to taxpayers' burdens, and impacts directly on the poor (Benson 1978).

3. Corruption is something everybody pays for at huge cost, direct and indirect. It is public works developments that people do not want. It is shoddy construction that becomes rapidly obsolete and therefore needs to be redone or buildings that threaten public health and safety. It is public money used to fund inflated contracts or to replace skimmed revenues. (Gardiner and Lyman 1978).

4. Corruption allows immunity for criminal acts so that the law is for sale to the highest bidder (Sherman 1978).

If unchecked, official corruption will eventually result in a "softness of state" comprising all manner of social indiscipline that prevents effective government and obstructs national development (Myrdal 1970; Nossiter 1970). It brings about a society in which little works as it should, with increasing resort made to repression to keep things from falling apart altogether. Furthermore, it leads to widespread cynicism, engendering a fatalism or hopelessness that anything can be turned around.

Despite its ill effects on the official participants and on society as a whole, corruption prevails as a way of life in many poor, autocratic societies. Does it perform any useful social functions? Can personal gains also promote public benefits? If the alternative to a corrupted society is to have none at all, then presumably a corrupted society is still better. If the government is doing evil, then official corruption may sabotage evil designs or ameliorate bad outcomes. If the economy is sluggish, then official corruption may stimulate economic investment. If the bureaucracy is inert, then official corruption may produce some action. Other extravagant claims have been made for the functionality of corruption, particularly in newly independent states:

1. Corruption aids national unification and stability, enhances nationwide participation in public affairs, helps the formation of a viable party system, and increases bureaucratic accountability to political institutions (Abueva 1966).

2. Corruption incorporates otherwise alienated groups, integrates them, and provides them with an alternative to violence (Huntington 1968).

3. Corruption strengthens political institutions, consolidates elites, and cements conservative coalitions (Scott 1972).

4. Corruption stimulates economic development by providing a supplemental allocative mechanism for investment purposes and mobilizes the bureaucracy for more energetic action on behalf of private entrepreneurs (Bayley 1966; Leff 1964; Tilman 1968).

5. Corruption humanizes officialdom, increases bureaucratic responsiveness, reduces red tape, speeds up public business, and improves the quality of public service (Dwivedi 1968).

Accepting these claims at face value, a survey of conventional wisdom nonetheless highlights some of their underlying contradictions. Politically, corruption overcomes cleavages among elites, provides opponents access to public resources, promotes national integration, and strengthens viable political institutions. On the other hand, it exacerbates ethnic and interregional conflicts and violence and undermines political legitimacy. Economically, corruption encourages capital formation, expedites transactions, and opens the economy to enterprising entrepreneurs. On the other hand, it promotes the illegal export of resources, encourages conspicuous consumption, and results in unproductive public works. Administratively, corruption contributes to flexibility and efficiency by greasing the machinery of government and cushions the impact of badly formulated policies and programs and poor decision making. On the other hand, it generates considerable distrust throughout the public bureaucracy, inhibits delegation of authority, and reduces productivity.

Detailed case studies of specific corrupt practices have disproved most of the supposed benefits claimed for them (Caiden and Caiden 1977). No substantial evidence has been offered proving that corrupt officials contribute notably to economic development and social progress; their contribution has been more marginal over the long run, and it begs the question whether much more substantial progress would have been made without such corruption. If societal needs are unfulfilled, they would be better met by legitimate and honest means rather than by corruption, whose costs to those it purportedly helps outweigh the benefits they receive. History shows repeatedly that corruption is self-defeating in the long run. It makes matters worse, not better. It postpones required changes. It widens social barriers. It undermines incentives to perform. It casts suspicions on all authority and all legitimate institutions. The weight of the evidence indicates that societies would be considerably better off if they could reduce official corruption.

Combating Corruption

Even with all the will in the world, official corruption is difficult to control. It is a complex problem involving many different factors and forces. It takes many different forms and no public agency, indeed no public official, is immune. Yet control has been achieved in many countries, and how it has been done is no mystery. Besides historical studies and contemporary cases cited in a growing literature on the subject (Clarke 1983; Klitgaard 1988; Palmier 1985), there are now annual conferences and workshops at which experts in anticorruption strategies exchange ideas and experiences. Anticorruption campaigns go beyond techniques of identifying particular forms of corruption, outlawing them, and investigating and prosecuting suspects. They now involve the whole society, not just anticorruption agencies.

Political Will

The first strategic target is political corruption—the end to all dirty tricks in politics and the creation of an ethos whereby politicians, political officials, and party functionaries are not only fair and honest but also take a dim view of official corruption in any shape or form. Political leaders must be committed to the eradication of corruption by setting a good example themselves. No favoritism in the prosecution of corruption should be permitted and no double standards tolerated. Even the most powerful should live modestly and avoid drawing attention to the privileges they may enjoy. The very high standards expected, higher than in private affairs, are necessary, for dependent upon them are the respect and confidence people place in governance and the general standards of conduct and honesty in the country as a whole. Indeed, the economic consequences of corruption have pushed international businesses to clean up their act and form pressure groups to push governments to take action against dirty business practices. Changing political values have induced international organizations and countries to start cleaning up their own acts and to sponsor anticorruption campaigns around the world.

Public Pressure

Political will needs constant pushing and prodding by a watchful public intolerant of official corruption and vigilant in safeguarding public integrity and propriety. For this, the public should know what constitutes unacceptable public behavior and where to go for assistance in combating it. Public education begins at home and continues at school and other major socializing institutions. It is continually reinforced through the mass media and public notices. Official corruption is rarely confined to public officials only; the public-at-large

participate as well. People are particularly sensitive when corruption is open
and has clear detrimental effects, as it does in public health and safety, taxation,
criminal justice, land registration, and public education. In these areas, public
opinion is easy to rally as it is in the case of foreign or externally induced corruption, which is usually confined to those with international contacts and is
therefore clearly unfair to everyone else. General public apathy can be offset by
self-appointed watchdog groups and voluntary bodies devoted to clean government.

Key Targets

Corruption is uneven. Some areas of governance are more prone to it than
others simply because they exercise the greatest influence over public decisions.
Or they operate with the highest degree of discretion, or excessive demand for
their services is unlikely to be met in the foreseeable future. Key policy makers
are always under heavy pressures to bend. Temptations are also great for any
public officials who handle large sums of public money or have dealings with
private businesses or tackle illegal goods and services. Possibly the prime target
is law enforcement. This implies that the rule of law must be upheld: that everybody should have equal access to the law; that there must be uniform, fearless,
unprejudiced enforcement; and that the public will eventually trust and identify with enforcement agencies. These achievements will do much to clean up
the rest of government and keep all other public officials honest.

Official Ethics

Codes of official ethics should be drawn up and enforced as a matter of
professional pride and personal self-discipline. But integrity can only be safeguarded if able and virtuous people are attracted to public service, and if compensation is sufficient so that they do not feel obliged to resort to corruption to
sustain a standard of living compatible to their status and rank in society. Furthermore, peer pressures to protect public service image and reputation by
suppressing revelations of internal wrongdoing should be offset by special pro-
tective measures for whistle-blowers who risk their careers, and sometimes their
lives, for daring to expose corruption. At the same time, however, the wrong-
fully accused should be shielded from malicious charges and personal vindic-
tiveness.

Strengthening Countervailing Factors

Every society exhibits certain features that encourage and foster official
corruption. Because they are embedded in the culture, they are not going to be
changed quickly or easily. They usually swamp political will, public pressure,

key targets, and public service ethics, nullifying their intentions. Unless they are tackled, endemic corruption is likely to persist. It takes generations to overcome religious doctrines, excessive demands, gross inequality, social overregulation, kinship loyalties, the absence of legal-rational norms, and all the other deep-seated contributory factors to corruption. Without ideological transformation, moral revolution, economic redistribution, political reform, sociocultural changes, legal revisions, or administrative modernization, corruption will endure.

A start has to be made somewhere, the initial steps taken and consolidated, a momentum generated, and optimism stimulated. The task seems overwhelming yet is feasible, with an array of workable strategies and tactics available. A host of suitable institutional mechanisms can be quickly assembled. A store of reliable knowledge is fast accumulating to assist in combating corruption. Even with the best will, however, corruption is too virile, too contagious, too widespread, and too costly to treat for it to be eliminated entirely. At best it can be contained and minimized, reduced from being a way of life to a fact of life, driven from intolerable to tolerable forms, from major to minor, and from consequential to inconsequential. For many countries, if that were achieved, it would be a day for rejoicing.

Note:

This chapter was originally published as "Undermining Good Governance: Corruption and Democracy" in the *Asian Journal of Political Science*, Vol. 5, No. 2 (December 1997), 1–22. Reprinted with permission. The *Asian Journal of Political Science* is a refereed biannual publication of the Department of Political Science, National University of Singapore, published under the Times Academic Press imprint of Times Media Private Limited (Trade, Reference & Academic Division). Website: http://www.timesone.com.sg/te

References

Abueva, Jose V. 1966. The contribution of nepotism, spoils and draft to political development. *East-West Center Review* 3 (1): 45–54.

Al-Saigh , Nasser M., ed. 1986. *Administrative reform in the Arab world: Readings.* Amman: Arab Organization of Administrative Sciences.

Andreski, Stanislaw. 1968. Kleptocracy or corruption as a system of government. In *The African Predicament,* edited by S. Andreski. London: Michael Joseph.

Baker, C. A. 1970. Ethics in the public service. *Journal of Administration Overseas* 10 (1): 31.

Bayley, David H. 1966. The effects of corruption in a developing nation. *Western Political*

Quarterly 19 (4): 719–32.

Caiden, Gerald. 1988. Toward a general theory of official corruption. *Asian Journal of Public Administration* 10(1): 3–26.

Benson, George, Steven A. Maaranen, and Atan Heslop. 1978. *Political corruption in America.* Lexington, Mass.: D.C. Heath.

Caiden, Gerald E. and Naomi J. Caiden. 1977. Administrative corruption. *Public Administration Review* 37(3): 301–9.

Clarke, Michael, ed. 1983. *Corruption: Causes, consequences and control.* New York: St. Martin's Press.

Dobel, J. P. 1978. Corruption of a state. *American Political Science Review* 72 (3): 958–73.

Dwivedi, O. P. 1967. Bureaucratic corruption in developing countries. *Asian Survey* 7(1): 18–36.

Gardiner, John and Theodore Lyman. 1978. *Decisions for sale.* New York: Praeger.

Greenberg, Edward. 1974. *Serving the few: Corporate capitalism and the bias of government policy.* New York: John Wiley and Sons.

Huntington, Samuel P. 1968. *Political order in changing societies.* New Haven, Conn.: Yale University Press.

Jabbra, J. G. 1976. Bureaucratic corruption in the third world: Causes and remedy. *Indian Journal of Public Administration* 22 (4): 673–91.

Johnston, Michael. 1986. The political consequences of corruption: A reassessment. *Comparative Politics* 18 (4): 459–77.

Klitgaard, Robert. 1988. *Controlling corruption.* Berkeley: University of California Press.

Leff, Nathaniel. 1964. Economic development through bureaucratic corruption. *American Behavioral Scientist* 8 (3): 8–14.

Myrdal, Gunnar. 1968. *Asian drama: An enquiry into the poverty of nations.* Vol. II New York: Twentieth Century.

———. 1970. *The challenge of world poverty: A world anti-poverty program in outline.* New York: Pantheon Books.

Nossiter, Bernard D. 1970. *Soft state: A newspaperman's chronicle of India.* New York: Harper and Row.

Nye, Joseph S. 1967. Corruption and political development: A cost-benefit analysis. *American Political Science Review* 61 (2): 417–27. Italics mine.

Palmier, Leslie. 1985. *The control of bureaucratic corruption: Case studies in Asia.* New Delhi: Allied Publishers.

Payne, Pierre S. R. 1975. *The corrupt society: From ancient Greece to present-day America.* New York: Praeger.

Philp, Mark. 1987. Defining corruption: An analysis of the republican tradition. Mennagio, Italy: IPSA Research Committee on Political Finance and Political Corruption, p. 7.

Rose-Ackerman, Susan. 1978. *Corruption: A study in political economy.* New York: Academic

Press.

Schwartz, C. A. 1979. Corruption and political development in the USSR. *Comparative Politics* 11 (4): 428.

Scott, James C. 1972. *Comparative political corruption.* Englewood Cliffs, N.J.: Prentice-Hall.

Shaukat, Ali. 1985. *Corruption: A third world perspective.* Lahore: Aziz Publishers.

Sherman, Lawrence. 1978. *Scandal and reform: Controlling police corruption.* Berkeley: University of California Press.

Tarkowski, Jacek. 1988. Centralized systems and corruption. *Asian Journal of Public Administration* 10 (1): 48–70.

Tilman, Robert O. 1968. Emergence of black-market bureaucracy: Administration, development, and corruption in the new states. *Public Administration Review* 28 (5): 437–44.

Werner, Simcha. 1983. New directions in the study of administrative corruption. *Public Administration Review* 43 (2): 146–54.

Williams, Robert. 1987. *Political corruption in Africa.* Aldershot: Gower.

3

Corruption in the United States

Richard D. White, Jr.

BETRAYAL OF PUBLIC TRUST is no rarity in American history or indeed in the annals of any nation. Corruption is an ever-present aspect of the exercise of governmental power and a persistent and often chronic handicap of political life around the world. For many countries, corruption creates a friction that grinds away scarce resources, reduces the efficiency of government machinery, and levies a cost on society that is paid in the frail currency of public trust. For other countries with a graver problem, corruption is so pervasive that it endangers the overall rule of law and threatens the survival of legitimate government and the livelihood of honest public servants. Corruption is so institutionalized in many countries that special terms for corrupt practices are routine jargon, such as *baksheesh* in the Middle East, *la mordida* in Latin America, *la bustarella* in Italy, *speed money* in India, *dash* in West Africa, and *blat* in Russia.

A Historical Perspective

Corruption has plagued the American states since the arrival of the first colonists in the New World. In drafting the United States Constitution and creating a "republic of virtue," the founding fathers were determined to combat corruption that had been commonplace under colonial governors, who permitted "places and employments, which ought not to be sold at all, [to be] sold for treble values" (Eisenstadt, Hoogenboom, and Trefousse 1979, 9). Historians suggest the early years of the republic were relatively corruption free, as America was still largely an agricultural country with reduced resources and fewer opportunities for corruption (White 1948). James Madison, the chief architect of the Constitution, hoped that such designs as federalism, the separation of powers, and checks and balances would prevent corruption in the American political system, but defects became apparent soon after ratification (Berg, Hahn and Schmidthouser 1976, 4).

The first major scandal in American history was in 1795, when the Yazoo land fraud revealed the ability of large amounts of money to influence and undermine political decisions. The fraud involved the sale of over 40 million acres covering the present-day states of Alabama and Mississippi. Officials discovered wholesale bribery of the Georgia legislature and every lawmaker, with one exception, who voted for the crooked land sale was found to be a stockholder in one of the four benefiting land companies. The scandal implicated two U.S. Senators, two Representatives, a Supreme Court Justice, led to most of the Georgia legislators being removed from office, and eventually provoked the split of the Jeffersonian Republican party.

If not a continuing occurrence, corruption at the highest level of government has recurred periodically in American political life down to the present time. Historians generally agree that the administrations of Grant and Harding were notoriously corrupt and not rivaled even in modern times by Nixon and Watergate. On the other hand, corruption labels may be exaggerated. While the Harding, Truman, and Nixon administrations have been accused of being full of corruption, this charge may be unfair as all three administrations had department heads of unquestioned honesty who ran good administrative operations in sharp contrast to other bad spots of corruption (Benson 1978). While surrounded by scoundrels, Grant was an honorable president. But even the most virtuous presidents have had corruption taint their administrations. Washington endured a land speculation scandal involving his Secretary of War and more recently Carter, a president known for high moral standards, suffered with his budget director. Meanwhile, state and local governments offer fecund opportunities for corruption. The reign of Governor Huey Long in Louisiana (1928–34) is an extreme example in which a corrupt regime controlled the state government, its legislature, and most of the state parishes and municipalities.

Another version of corruption, nepotism, has been a way of life in American government for centuries. During the Civil War at least one relative of each Lincoln cabinet member was on the federal payroll. The practice of nepotism pervaded state governments and, despite legislation, continues in many forms. In Louisiana, for example, nepotism was legal and widespread throughout Long's reign. Most pro-Long legislators had relatives, including wives and children, with state jobs. As for his own family, Long placed at least 23 relatives on the state payroll during his first year as governor (Hair 1991, 90).

The American Political Machine

A unique aspect in the history of corruption is the American political machine that flourished in many large cities around the turn of the twentieth century. The primary causes for the rise of the political machine were rapid industrialization, urbanization, and the admittance of new immigrant populations for whom family and ethnicity were the central identifications and to whom the sense of community was weak. The large immigrant populations, combined with the rewards of public employment and important monopoly privileges, provided fertile soil for the growth of party machines and their inevitable corruption (Scott 1969a, 4). The machine provided employment, legal services, economic relief, and primitive welfare services otherwise unavailable to the urban poor. Such was the case during the Boss Tweed reign of New York in the mid-1800s and the Daly machine in Chicago a century later.

The American political machine was a nonideological organization interested less in political principle than in securing and holding office for its leaders and distributing income to those who ran it and worked for it. The power of the machine boss over the voter depended upon his ability to dispense favors. He was recognized as a political leader, not because of his views on public questions, but because he was able to demonstrate day after day that his word was law (Lipmann 1930, 62). Machine politics provided immediate, specific, and concrete benefits to groups that may otherwise be thoroughly alienated from society (Huntington 1968, 59). The American machine was more like a business in which all members were stockholders and where dividends were paid in accordance with what has been invested. The machine dealt almost exclusively in particularistic rewards, providing its favors directly to individuals and families (Scott 1969a). The poor and uneducated especially supported the political machines and almost without exception, the lower the average income and the fewer the average years of schooling in a city, the more unfailing the loyalty to the machine (Gosnell 1968, 187).

While machine-style politics were associated with urban centers, the machine also emerged in the rural population (Scott 1969a, 4). Political machines were not uncommon in the rural south prior to the Second World War. Again, jobs, money, and other inducements at the disposal of the political bosses encouraged the creation of corrupt structures and processes. While there is a substantial correlation between machine politics and political corruption, not all political machines were corrupt. For instance the Byrd machine in Virginia had an above-average record of honesty (Benson 1978). Over time, however, many political machines withered away as the populations they assisted became more prosperous and acculturated, and social services became universally available or were no longer needed by the majority.

The Present Condition

Despite possessing one of the highest standards of living and one of the longest surviving democracies, the United States continues to face serious levels of corruption. But it is difficult to measure the levels of corruption or to simply ascertain whether the problem is getting better or worse. The full extent of corruption can never be known because much of what occurs never comes to light in either the courtroom or on the front page. A history of corruption in the United States cannot be written; what can be written is only a history of the *exposure* of corruption (Lipmann 1930). Even so, some scholars argue that there is a tendency to understate or de-emphasize corruption (De Leon 1993). On the other hand is the danger that exaggeration of corruption may lead to overcorrection such as needlessly stringent legislation that limits individual rights (Johnston 1983; Berg, Hahn, and Schmidhauser 1976). Another harmful result of overexaggerating corruption in the United States is that the notoriety of political corruption often leads the public to assume that the professional government bureaucracy is also corrupt. While corruption does exist in the American bureaucracy, especially in some state and local governments and among law enforcement agencies, most observers do not see corruption of the professional public service as endemic or widespread.

Commentators on corruption generally point to areas where corruption is particularly widespread, such as the states of New York, New Jersey, Maryland, and Pennsylvania and the urban center of Chicago. Meanwhile Minnesota, Wisconsin, and Oregon have the reputation for relatively clean politics (Johnston 1983, 20). But are these stereotypical descriptions indeed empirically correct, and if so, why? While corruption is difficult to measure and analyze, some data points to the seriousness of corruption in the United States. Transparency International regularly ranks the United States somewhere in the middle of its scales. Intuitively, this ranking seems accurate, as the United States is the melting pot of most of the world cultures and would embody an average of the most and least corrupt. While the country rankings are intriguing and reflect the experiences of the international business community, they are not based on a solid empirical foundation. Likewise, they imply xenophobia and may misrepresent the vast sociocultural differences between countries. Can the corruption rates of the United States, Denmark, and Nigeria, for example, truly be measured and compared, and if so, is the comparison meaningful?

Little data is available to accurately measure corruption in the United States.

One source is the Department of Justice, which publishes official statistics documenting the numbers of prosecutions and convictions of public officials for violations of federal corruption statutes. Recent data do not reveal any significant rise or drop in the level of corruption cases during the 1990s. The data are also anecdotal, only revealing federal efforts to combat corruption and ignoring prosecutions at the state and local levels, where the majority of cases predominate. Also, prosecutions are merely the tip of the corruption iceberg, revealing only those illegal acts that are discovered and brought to trial.

With little reliable data on corruption in the United States, it is difficult to accurately gauge the overall severity of the problem and to identify longitudinal trends. It is fashionable to label every political transgression as evidence of widespread corruption, but there is little baseline information on which to confirm or deny such a conclusion. Upon each new major scandal, many decry that a new wave of corruption is upon us—but corruption has always been a part of American government, and institutional memory is too short and murky to be able to discern whether the political ignominies of today are worse than those of yesteryear. From the start, a combination of insufficient reliable data and a flood of anecdotal episodes hamstrings any scholarly empirical study of corruption in the United States.

The Many Varieties of Corruption

To many, corruption is like pornography; they know it when they see it but have a much more difficult time describing it. What exactly is corruption? While scholars generally agree on the more formal definitions of corruption, the American public has wide opinions of what is right and wrong in society, politics, and business. Most agree that corruption is a significant problem, but different people have different things in mind when they use the term. Scholars generally confine their discussions of corruption to the spheres of government and politics, as corruption in the business world usually falls within descriptions of patently illegal acts such as theft and embezzlement. For this discussion, corruption indicates the unauthorized use of *public* office for private gain. Corruption is the absence of integrity in government, a misuse of power, and a cooperative, unsanctioned, usually condemned policy influence for significant personal gain in which the payment could be economic, social, political, or ideological (Johnston 1986; Warburton 1998).

Does corruption have to violate the law to be corrupt? Most agree that corruption is not equated solely with illegal behavior; in fact, corruption often involves technically legal activities, unethical use of government authority, and can occur without financial gain. Abuse of power for political purposes, such as

Watergate, can be much more corruptive than overt bribery or other illegal acts (Rogow and Lasswell 1963). By its very nature, corruption is both a normative and relative phenomenon, as the financial gain of corruption ultimately may be outweighed by a loss to our "ideatic core" (Hodgkinson 1997, 19; Friedrich 1972). In the United States, corruption involves the loss of moral authority, weakens the efficiency of government operations, increases opportunities for organized crime, encourages police brutality, adds to taxpayers' burdens, and impacts directly on poorer citizens (Caiden 1979). American corruption takes many forms, including bribery (use of reward to pervert the judgment of a person in a position of trust); nepotism (bestowal of patronage by reasons of ascriptive relationship rather than merit); misappropriation (illegal appropriation of public resources for private-regarding use), theft of materials, misuse of time, kickbacks, extortion, spoils patronage, conflicts of interest, and misuse of inside information. Activities most prone to corruption include bidding on public contracts, the use of public funds, the handling of public property, tax assessment and collection, zoning and land use, the legislative and elective processes, law enforcement, and the administration of public services prone to political exploitation (Benson 1978, 9; Nye 1967, 418).

Theories and Frameworks

While some consensus appears in describing corruption and arguments about corruption are discussed throughout American political circles, a consistent doctrine of corruption is elusive. Dobel (1978, 958) offers one of the more ambitious efforts to put corruption into a conceptual framework, constructing a theory that unifies the moral, political, economic, and social causes and patterns of corruption. He describes corruption as the moral incapacity of citizens to make reasonably disinterested commitments to actions, symbols, and institutions that benefit the public welfare. The collapse of loyalty to the commonwealth comes from the interaction of human nature with systematic inequality of wealth, power, and status. The corruption of government results in political conflict, including the emergence of quasi-governmental factions and an increasingly polarized class system. The clash of the factions leads to an undermining of the society's basic political structures and the emergence of systematic corruption in all aspects of political life. The corruption of states and the corruption of people proceed hand-in-hand.

Peters and Welch (1978, 974), agreeing that a lack of a clear definition of political corruption limits its systematic study, provide another theoretical framework. Unlike Dobel's description based on political philosophy, Peters and Welch ground their findings on empirical observations of state legislators.

They create an interactive model that categorizes corruption by its four components: the type of public official, the relationship of the beneficiary to the public official, the type of favor performed, and the nature of the payoff. For each component, propositions about perceived corrupt and noncorrupt elements are formulated and tested. Other scholars divide corruption into two categories based on levels of severity. For example, Lowi, (1981, 2) distinguishes between big corruption, which contributes to the decomposition or dissolution of the Constitution, and little corruption, which reflects or contributes to individual moral depravity.

Hodgkinson (1997) also adopts a bipolar classification, labeling corruption as falling within either primary or secondary types. Primary corruption, the less serious of the two, does not threaten the polity as a whole. While involving extreme partisanship and selfishness, those committing acts of primary corruption still accept legal and official norms. Individuals may try to get away with what they can, but they still believe in the fundamental rule of law and expect to be punished if caught. The more serious secondary corruption is where the political system encourages corruption and where there is no concern about punishment or feelings of guilt. Secondary corruption arises from the distrust of government and would include "crimes of the powerful" (Pearce 1976). Furthermore, secondary corruption has a corrosive effect on governance, which further undermines an already ailing system and, over time, leads to a culture of acceptance of corruption (Hodgkinson 1997). Hodgkinson's typology is similar to others who see differences between the more severe organizational corruption and individual corruption, often referred to as scandal (Sherman 1978). Likewise, Heidenheimer breaks down corruption by its severity, coloring corruption as black (which a majority consensus of both elite and mass opinion would condemn and would want to see punished on grounds of principle), white (the majority would probably not vigorously support an attempt to punish a form of corruption that they regard as tolerable), and gray (some elements, usually elites, may want to see the action punished, others not, and the majority may well be ambiguous) (Heidenheimer, Johnston, and LeVine 1989).

The common theme that emerges from the definitions and typologies is that the term corruption, at least in its usage within the United States, is far too broad and vague to describe accurately the many illegal, extralegal, and unethical acts that the term encompasses. The term corruption casts a wide net, snaring the most trivial acts that most would ignore, as well as those acts approaching outright treason and threatening the basic democratic process. Sorting the many types and severities of corruption becomes a difficult scholarly exercise, creating methodological problems that often overpower any attempt to measure the levels and trends of corruption in the United States.

Possible Causes

What are the causes of corruption? Explanations for corruption tend to divide along several lines that embrace systemic, cultural, functional, economic, and behavioral reasoning. The foremost theoretical question is whether corruption is the result of pathologies within the political system or the result of the rise of the occasional evil man. Most scholars who comment on the causes of corruption favor the former argument and maintain corruption is an ingrained, systemic part of the American political process. The systemic explanation disputes those who blame specific individuals as a convenient and easy way to explain away corruption while ignoring institutional defects (Berg, Hahn, and Schmidhauser 1976). The systemic explanation views political corruption as a violation of the norms of public order that are essential for the maintenance of political democracy. Thus, corruption is more realistically a byproduct of the political system rather than individual episodes of deviant pathology (De Leon 1993).

The Systemic Argument

Corruption is most likely to flourish where political institutions are weak (Huntington 1968, 59). Unreformed local government institutions—the spoils system, partisanship, district-based elections, and strong-mayor government—are archaic governance mechanisms that traditionally encourage institutional corruption. Ineffective organizations and laws, the lack of forceful auditing and internal controls, decisions involving little participation, few written records, and no specific standards for discretion can invite and abet corruption (Caiden 1979, 296). Indeed, current bureaucratic theory attributes maladministration, which includes corruption, to increasing reliance on a system fraught with bureaupathologies (Caiden 1991, 486). One empirical study of the American states finds corruption strongly related to bureaucratic factors, especially the size of the bureaucracy (Meier and Holbrook 1992, 138).

The Functional Argument

A revisionist variant of the systemic explanation is the functional interpretation arguing that corruption serves an inevitable and sometimes necessary purpose. The functional explanation contends that corruption can speed up government processes, make favorable outcomes much more likely, and cost less than legitimate forms of influence. Demand for government rewards (highway maintenance contracts, for example) frequently exceeds the supply and routine decision-making processes are lengthy, costly, and uncertain in their outcome. For these reasons, legal and official decision-making processes create a bottleneck between what people want and what they get. The temptation to get around the bottleneck—to expedite processes and make favorable outcomes more probable—is built into this relationship between government and its clients (Johnston 1982, 3). To some, the functional explanation suggests that corruption is either not a problem warranting attention and merely a "trivial sideshow of the American political circus," or so entrenched in the system that its elimination would not be worth the expense, even assuming that it could be eliminated (De Leon 1993, 32).

Functional revisionists argue that in poor countries corruption allegedly promotes economic development, political participation, policy implementation, and administrative efficiency. Robert Merton points out that the classic political machine, though corrupt, has some latent functions that are quite beneficial, especially to the impoverished seeking employment and favors in exchange for votes (Merton 1957). In lieu of an effective political structure, the political boss becomes a necessary means of centralizing power, the political machine becomes a means of securing assistance for individuals or subgroups, including the poor who need jobs and business which wants political privileges, and the machine offers an alternate route for personal advancement in vice, crime, and rackets. Merton's argument may still ring true in the American inner city where informal corruptive power has shifted from the classic political machines to other power centers, such as organized crime, sophisticated drug networks, and youth gangs.

The Cultural Argument

Some observers regard American political corruption as a cultural phenomenon, that each state or region has its own "ethos" of corruption and that corrupt politics reflect a corrupt or apathetic society. Because political culture defines acceptable political action, it should affect the amounts and types of political corruption as well as responses to corruption when discovered. In the United States, this explanation is best demonstrated by comparing corruption levels in areas with distinctly different cultures, namely the fifty American states or other distinctly different regions such as the South or Midwest (Elazar 1972; Nice 1983; Wilson 1966).

A frequently used typology for examining different cultures in the American states is Elazar's framework consisting of moralistic, individualistic, and traditionalistic categories (Elazar 1972). People adhering to the moralistic political culture are particularly intolerant of corruption and emphasize honesty and selfless dedication, a view supported by Peters and Welch (1978, 351). By contrast, the individualistic culture is somewhat tolerant of corruption, and in the traditionalistic culture, people who are active in politics are expected to gain personally from it, at least occasionally. Empirical studies using the Elazar model find political corruption is more common in traditionalistic states and less common in states with moralistic cultures, higher voter turnout, more educated populations, and less poverty. Contrary to expectations, political corruption has been found to be unrelated to crimes rates or urbanization (Nice 1983, 512). Unfortunately, the cultural explanation, while providing a more accurate description, contributes little in the way of prescription. When it comes time to making changes, many accept culture as a given. When culture changes, it does so slowly and incrementally.

The Economic Argument

Corruption is often looked upon in macroeconomic terms for it produces significant detrimental effects upon a nation's economy. Corruption hinders the creation of free markets and generates a crippling effect on economic development (Eigen 1996, 158). At the same time, some argue that corruption itself can be explained by the interaction of microeconomic forces. The economic explanation argues corruption is likely when scarce resources are allocated by a process that is vulnerable to political manipulation (Rose-Ackerman 1978). Economic theory assumes individuals are rational beings capable of assessing their interests according to costs and benefits. Specifically, microeconomists argue that if the benefits of corruption minus the probability of being caught times the penalties for being caught is greater than the benefits of not being caught, then an individual will rationally choose to be corrupt. Under such an economic backdrop, corrupt government officials regard public office as a business, the income from which they will seek to maximize. The size of their income depends upon both the market and their talents for finding the point of maximum gain on the public's demand curve. Thus, when governments allocate scarce services for which demand frequently exceeds supply, their market value often will exceed the official fees by many times, creating opportunities for lucrative and corruptive financial transactions. In such cases, market criteria supercede bureaucratic criteria (Caiden 1979, 296). The economists' solution for this type of corruption would be to raise bureaucratic costs to match market values, thereby removing an opportunity for corrupt exchanges.

The Behavioral Argument

Corruption is related to a variety of social, economic, and political forces and therefore cannot be blamed entirely on the character flaws of isolated individuals. But individual variation remains significant; not all officials in relatively corrupt states are corrupt, and not all officials in relatively honest states are honest (Nice 1983, 515). Thus, countering the systemic argument is the explanation that corruption is caused by greedy or evil individuals and not so much by the political system, its environment, or economic factors. Corruption is thus the perpetration of individual opportunists or deviants, who are figuratively and literally the exception to the rule (Hodgkinson 1997, 24). This explanation assumes corruption is an inevitable part of the human condition, buttressed by a pessimistic Hobbesian view that people are inherently bad.

This evil man theory endures. Despite the most foolproof anticorruption laws and processes, kleptocracy emerges periodically when a ruler or top official seeks personal enrichment and possesses the power to further this goal while usurping public office. Unlike the systemic and economic explanations, the behavioral argument acknowledges that corruption can be caused by irrational or nonrational reasons. The occasional pathological criminal sometimes squirms through the knothole and lands in high office and, with 87,000 separate governments in the United States, the odds of a corrupt official invading otherwise honest political systems are high. But most contemporary scholars cavalierly dismiss the behavioral explanation of corruption and they avoid it because analyzing individual behavior leads into the murky field of psychohistory.

These and other theories explaining individual behavior can help to inform the basic causes and results of corruption. Ignoring the behavioral argument can also be dangerous to democracy. When corruption is discovered, policy makers must guard against the tendency to confuse corrupt political leaders with the institutions themselves, which the leaders may have betrayed. Failure to do so can readily lead to overregulation and radical and potentially undemocratic political and constitutional reforms. In the long run, overregulation creates a vicious cycle, producing the very corruption it aims to eradicate as regulations are undermined to further organizational ends (LaPalombara 1994, 326).

Combating Corruption

While American scholars wrestle with the numerous explanations for corruption and tacitly admit it is unlikely that a single general explanation will ever be adequate (Caiden 1979, 297), they also suggest a range of policies necessary to combat and minimize the effects of corruption. Most agree that a clear and demonstrable commitment on the part of political leaders to the eradication of corruption is crucial. If the highest leadership in government is corrupt, then the rest will follow suit. Honest top leadership, however, is not enough, as policy makers must appoint trustworthy administrators and create broad coalitions both within and without government to combat corruption. A critical mass of reputable public officials and involved citizenry is necessary to maintain and build a trustworthy and effective government and to make corrupt acts the exception and not the rule.

Many anticorruption suggestions call for changes in the structures and processes of bureaucracy. Corruption is an inevitable part of the human condition and calls for practical designs to limit, discourage, and channel these tendencies (Dobel 1978, 972). The mere passage of legislation is unlikely to be effective unless it is accompanied by a score of practical measures that maximize accountability and transparency and minimize situations in which corruption is prone to occur. The adoption of comprehensive anticorruption legislation requires first, a review of legal procedures and remedies to ensure that they constitute an effective deterrent, and second, the enforcement of those procedures by strong and independent agencies of manifest integrity. The creation of ethics commissions by most states and many municipalities is an example of a positive step in this direction.

Organizational changes are necessary to ease problems of supervision and prevent concentration of corrupt power. Among the integrity instruments available are procurement practices and public financial management, administrative reform, auditing and bookkeeping practices, an independent judiciary, and widespread ethical awareness through public information and education. Bureaucratic innovations such as rotation of assignments, overlapping jurisdictions, parallel organizations, competitive bureaucracy, and the appointment of watchdog agencies are all suggestions that, when combined, lessen the opportunity, likelihood, and gravity of corruption. More specific suggestions include stringent conflict of interest provisions, revolving door strictures, and antinepotism policies (Caiden 1979, 297). Any reform of anticorruption measures, however, should be undertaken in ways that guarantee human rights and safeguard due process and fair trials.

A successful anticorruption program must identify the areas of governmental activity most prone to corruption. For example, a compensation review may be necessary to ensure that salaries of civil servants and political leaders are proportional with the responsibilities of their posts and are as comparable as possible with salaries in the private sector. If there is a wide disparity between public and private salaries, then bribery is much more likely.

Another theme highlighted by American scholars is the need for universal political education. Benson suggests that while structural reforms are necessary, the most important reform is to educate and select better people for public office (Benson 1978). Evil thrives on the apathy of the good and honest. A free press can contribute significantly by exposing specific cases, encouraging an open political debate, and ensuring accountability and responsiveness. The press, along with reforms such as sunshine legislation and freedom of information provisions, is a critical force in ensuring that the decision-making process is visible and transparent. Political participation is crucial in controlling corruption. The political and electoral processes must ensure maximum substantive participation by all citizens in all aspects of political life. Perception is another important factor, for an otherwise honest government that is perceived to be corrupt may fall victim to a self-fulfilling prophecy. The overall objective must be to change the general perception of corruption from a low-risk, high-profit activity to a high-risk, low-profit activity (Eigen 1996, 161).

The Future

No form of organization is corruption proof nor is it likely that corruption can be eliminated entirely. But it is crucial that it be minimized, for the costs of organizational or systemic corruption are intolerably high in a democracy such as the United States (Caiden 1979, 298). The United States, as a leader of the free world and as the most powerful nation, carries an additional burden to set an example of democratic and constitutional governance at its best. Corruption-free government is one of the standards that the American political system must uphold and epitomize for the developing world to emulate. But can the United States attain such a high standard where its government is looked upon as a model of honest excellence? Can corruption be reduced to an insignificant level, at which it is not a drain on effective governance and a blight on the national and international conscience?

On one hand, there is optimism. While corruption in the United States remains, there are positive signs that the situation has improved and is continuing to do so. There are no quick or easy solutions and the struggle against widespread corruption will take years. But the struggle can nonetheless be successful. Great progress has been made over the course of U.S. history in eliminating corruption. Arguably there is less corruption now than in the last half of the nineteenth century, mainly due to the demise of the centralized political machine. The Progressive era was especially energetic in efforts to combat corruption, when reformers implemented numerous measures that reduced the opportunities for and raised the costs of corrupt behavior. Civil service reforms, regulatory commissions, direct primary, initiative, referendum, and recall are examples of progressive structural reforms successful in reducing corruption.

Despite widespread criticisms of government performance, bureaucratic bashing, and negative public opinion polls, the public service continues to improve. In recent years, more council manager municipal governments have emerged, more sunshine and transparency legislation enacted, almost every state has an ethics board, and widespread classic nepotism has been reduced in most states. The bureaucracy is more representative of the public it serves, and a representative bureaucracy can be expected to be more responsive and, in the long run, be less corrupt. An increasing percentage of women now populating the public workforce is also a source of optimism, as a body of empirical research based on moral development theory suggests women, on average, have higher levels of moral development than men and again, in the long run, would be less likely corrupted (White 1999, 459). Therefore, as the percentage of women increases, especially in high political office, overall levels of corruption could be expected to decline.

On the other hand there is pessimism. Corruption remains a problem in the United States and will not disappear. Power still corrupts. If corruption increases unchecked, it may increase citizen alienation, antisystem political behavior, and withdrawal from conventional means of political participation. Corruption, graft, and jobbery continue as powerful enemies of good governance and are the midwives to oligarchy and demagoguery. Corruption still poses a threat to democracy, especially in times of strife. Corrupt public regimes flourished during the chaos of the Depression years in many American cities and states, and serious economic turmoil would be expected to increase opportunities for institutionalized corruption.

Another cause for a pessimistic view is the impact that privatization and other market-oriented reforms may have on corruption. Privatization is extolled as good for the economy and a means for more efficient delivery of public services, but it has dangers. Can a new wave of corruption be expected as private, profit-maximizing values are more deeply integrated into the public sector? Some scholars forecast that this may indeed be the case, as it is logical to assume that the importation of private sector cultures into the public sector will produce more opportunities for public greed and an increase in corruption cases. A study of transition economies reveals that privatization and market liberalization have resulted in increased corruption, although institutional reforms have proven to be adequate measures in the prevention and curtailment of corruption (Kaufmann 1997, 114). Another study found corruption in privatized government services leads to overinflated charges for products and services (Shenk 1995, 16).

Conclusion

The policy sciences in the United States have, with very few exceptions, ignored the rigorous study of corruption. Studying corruption is like drinking from a firehose; one is flooded with an overwhelming amount of anecdotal data that cannot be absorbed. There is little understanding of the patterns, frequencies, and severities of corruption in the United States. To better under-stand corruption, much more fine-grained definitions and models must be con-structed to give scholars the incisive instruments necessary to examine corrupt practices with precision. Solid theoretical foundations are needed to allow for substantive empirical research.

Why is such research into corruption so necessary? While American schol-arship has contributed significant insight into the causes of corruption, it has ignored an equally important aspect—the effect that serious corruption has on democratic governance. So little is known about the important relationship between corruption and the democratic process, or indeed if there is a signifi-cant relationship. Is corruption in the United States crippling democratic rule, as is the case in South American drug-producing countries, or is corruption merely a friction that reduces the efficiency of government as may be the case in relatively clean Scandinavian governments? Scholarship on corruption in the U.S. does not come close to answering such critical questions. While revi-sionists suggest that corruption may be so trivial as not to warrant serious atten-tion, there is little evidence to either support or refute their argument. Most agree that the United States has a corruption problem, but they are unsure how bad the problem is and whether it is getting better or worse.

References

Banfield, Edward C. and James A. Wilson. 1965. *City politics*. Cambridge, Mass.: Harvard University Press.

Benson, George, Steven A. Maaranen, and Atan Heslop. 1978. *Political corruption in America*. Lexington, Mass.: Lexington Books.

Berg, Larry L., Harlan Hahn, and John R. Schmidhauser. 1976. *Corruption in the Ameri-can political system*. Morristown, N.J.: General Learning Press.

Bicchieri, Christina and John Duffy. 1997. Corruption cycles. *Political Studies* 45 (3).

Caiden, Gerald. 1991. What really is public maladministration? *Public Administration Re-view* 51 (6): 486–93.

Caiden, Naomi. 1979. Shortchanging the public. *Public Administration Review* 39 (3): 294–98.

De Leon, Peter. 1993. *Thinking about political corruption*. New York: M. E. Sharpe.

Dobel, J. P. 1978. Corruption of a state. *American Political Science Review* 72 (3): 958–73.

Eigen, Peter. 1996. Combating corruption around the world. *Journal of Democracy* 7 (1).

Eisenstadt, Abraham S., Ari Hoogenboom, and Hans L. Trefousse, eds. 1979. *Before watergate: problems of corruption in American history*. Brooklyn, N.Y.: Brooklyn College Press.

Elazar, Daniel. 1972. *American federalism: A view from the states*. New York: Crowell.

Friedrich, Carl J.. 1972. *The pathology of politics*. New York: Harper and Row.

Gardiner, John A. and Theodore R. Lyman. 1978. *Decisions for sale: Corruption and reform in land-use and building regulation*. New York: Praeger Publishers.

Gosnell, H. 1968. *Machine politics: Chicago model*. Chicago: University of Chicago Press.

Hair, William Ivy. 1991. *The kingfish and his realm*. Baton Rouge: Louisiana University Press.

Heidenheimer, Arnold J. 1989. Perspectives on the perception of corruption. In Heidenheimer, Arnold J., Michael Johnston and Victor LeVine, eds. *Political corruption: A handbook*. New Brunswick, N.J.: Transaction.

Hodgkinson, Peter. 1997. The sociology of corruption: Some themes and issues. *Sociology 31* (1): 18–29.

Huntington, Samuel. 1968. *Political order in changing societies*. New Haven, Conn.: Yale University Press.

Johnston, Michael. 1986. Right and wrong in American politics: popular conceptions of corruption. *Polity* 18 (3): 367–91.

———. 1983. Corruption and political culture in America: An empirical perspective. *Publius 14* (1): 19–39.

———.1982. *Political corruption and public policy in America*. Monterey, Calif.: Brooks/Cole.

Kaufmann, Daniel. 1997. Corruption: The facts. *Foreign Policy* 107 (1): 114–127.

LaPalombara, Joseph. 1994. Structural and institutional aspects of corruption. *Social Research 61* (2).

Lippmann, Walter. 1930. A theory about corruption, *Vanity Fair* 35 (3).

Lowi, Theodore. 1981. The intelligent person's guide to political corruption. *Public Affairs* No. 182, University of South Dakota.

Meier, Kenneth J. and Thomas M. Holbrook. 1992. I seen my opportunities and I took 'em: Political corruption in the American states. *Journal of Politics 54* (1).

Merton, Robert. 1957. *Social theory and social structure*. Glencoe, Ill.: Free Press.

Nice, David C.. 1983. Political corruption in the American states. *American Politics Quarterly* 11(4): 507–17.

Nye, Joseph. 1967. Corruption and political development: A cost-benefit analysis. *American Political Science Review* 61 (2): 417–27.

Pearce, F. 1976. *Crimes of the powerful*. London: Pluto Press.

Peters, John G. and Susan Welch. 1978. Political corruption in America: A search for definitions and theory, or if political corruption is in the mainstream of American politics, why is it not in the mainstream of American politics research. *American Political Science Review* 72 (3): 974–84.

Rogow, Arnold and Harold Lasswell. 1963. *Corruption, power, and rectitude*. Englewood Cliffs, N.J.: Prentice Hall.

Rose-Ackerman, Susan. 1978. *Corruption: A study in political economy*. New York: Academic Press.

Scott, James. 1969a. *Comparative political corruption*. Englewood Cliffs, N.J.: Prentice Hall.

———. 1969b. Corruption, Machine Politics and Political Change. *American Political Science Review* 63 (4): 1142–59.

Shenk. Joshua W. 1995. The perils of privatization. *Washington Monthly* 27 (5).

Sherman, Lawrence. 1978. *Scandal and reform: Controlling police corruption*. Berkeley: University of California Press.

Stewart, Donald H. 1952. The press and political corruption during the federalist administration. *Political Science Quarterly* 18 (3): 426–46.

Warburton, John. 1998. Corruption, power, and the public interest. *Business and Professional Ethics Journal*, 7 (4).

White, Leonard D. 1948. *The federalists: A study in administrative history*. New York: Macmillan.

Wilson, James Q. 1966. Corruption: The shame of the cities. *Public Interest* 2 (1): 28–38.

White, Richard. 1999. Are women more ethical? Recent findings on the effects of gender upon moral development. *Journal of Public Administration Research and Theory* 9 (3): 459–69.

4

Governance and Corruption in Canada

O. P. Dwivedi and Maureen Mancuso

CANADIANS ARE OFTEN PUT OUT by their international reputation for being polite, respectful, and earnest, but on the whole rather dull. In the realm of
governmental ethics, however, this is high praise: "newsworthy" generally means
"flawed" when corruption is the subject. Canada's public service continues to
exhibit a generally high standard of ethical values and behavior—as befits a
country constitutionally pledged to "peace, order, and good government"—
and in 1999 was ranked fifth in the world for honesty in government by Transparency International (TI) and second on its Bribe Paying Index for 2000. This
is not to suggest that Canada has purged itself of official misbehavior. Scandal
remains a popular preoccupation of the news media and opposition parties.
But the pattern of corruption occurrence is one of isolated outbreaks, occur-
ring within a system that both resists the spread of malfeasance and encourages
corrective action.

Roots and Influences

At its founding, Canada inherited from Britain a well-developed meritocratic
civil bureaucracy and the ideals of altruistic public service. At the same time, it
has absorbed from its southern neighbor a Madisonian approach to government, emphasizing accountability, checks on power, and the importance of vigilance and scrutiny. As in other realms, the Canadian ethos can be simplistically
written off as a melding of British and American systems. These are undoubtedly the major influences on Canadian values, but there is more to the story.
Canada's TI ranking is noticeably higher than those of its two spiritual parents,
and in a sense Canada can claim to have gotten the best of both worlds. But in
a fusion of British tradition and American legalism, Canada is also subject to

the vulnerabilities of both.

Until the relatively recent Nolan Commission reforms (United Kingdom 1995), British political ethics were dominated by an expectation that all individuals selected for public service were by definition honorable, and would refrain from engaging in conduct that might reflect poorly on their offices (Mancuso 1995). In a fundamentally stratified society, this sense of governmental noblesse oblige had a certain degree of effectiveness in curbing unethical behavior, but it was extremely vulnerable to abuse by unrestrained individuals. In the atmosphere of the Thatcherite value shift toward unrestrained and unapologetic entrepreneurialism, Britain experienced a rash of political scandal and abuse that eventually led to a realignment (Ridley and Doig 1995). Nolan reemphasized the strong aspirational norms of the British system, but introduced more specific and prescriptive guidance and constraints in the form of rules and regulatory machinery (United Kingdom 1995).

In the United States, there has never been a shortage of rules governing official conduct: nepotism—a practice not even mentioned in the British regulatory system—is defined in the United States by an extensive and explicit enumeration of degrees of personal relationship and public involvement (Atkinson and Mancuso 1995). The question has been whether or not these rules are effective. Americans have always distrusted and basically disrespected government, and the sense that public service is a higher calling has always been overshadowed by a vision of civil servants as slow, inefficient, necessary evils (Nye, Zelikow, and King 1997). While the rule of law was an important founding principle of the country, the law evolved to deal with specific bouts of crisis and abuse. Thus, the spoils system in the bureaucracy was only eventually replaced by meritocracy after repeated episodes of cronyism, patronage, sale of offices, and at least one presidential assassination.

As continual waves of scandal have indicated, for every rule there is a loophole, and for every loophole there is both someone eager to exploit it, and someone else eager to make political hay out of uncovering and publicizing such exploitations. Many rules have unintended consequences. The dreary spectacle of the Clinton prosecution was ultimately set in motion by the Independent Counsel statute, an attempt to eliminate the possibility of political influence over investigations into the Executive Branch (Congressional Digest 1995). Instead, it institutionalized an unaccountable and uncontrollable investigative process that effectively hijacked the national agenda for over a year.

A Canadian Kenneth Starr is hard to imagine. There is a fairly extensive regulatory framework established to guide and govern the behavior of public officials, but both the uncompromising zeal and the unfettered authority of the U.S. Independent Counsel are not generally available. Nor does the Canadian system attempt to regulate ethics at the same relentlessly reductionist level. In the place of extensive, formal, prescriptive constraints, Canada provides relatively detailed but primarily aspirational guidance and admonishment to its public officials. Given that many contemporary issues have been the result of poor official judgment rather than actual criminal intent, this approach to ethical regulation has been generally successful.

Isolated vs. Systemic Corruption

The story of governmental ethics in contemporary Canada is not one of systemic corruption, but rather of mostly isolated and unorganized individual lapses and mistakes. In the 1980s and 1990s, scandals have clustered around new governments, as politicians unused to the requirements of office have confronted their new responsibilities and stepped over an ethical line, inadvertently or not. The early years of the Bob Rae government in the province of Ontario (1990–95), which featured a party (the New Democrats) with no previous governmental experience, and of the Brian Mulroney federal government (1984–93), which similarly starred a flood of political newcomers, were active times for scandals. In each case, the troublemakers and the error-prone were soon removed (or educated), and the governments carried on, somewhat the worse for wear, but not fatally delegitimized. Both were eventually defeated at the polls through legal but unpopular policies.

Historically, Canada has not always been so immune to systemic problems. Through the first half of the twentieth century, the Atlantic provinces of Newfoundland, Nova Scotia, New Brunswick, and Prince Edward Island had a well-established reputation for flagrant cronyism and the "vote early and vote often" style of politics (Thorburn 1976, 81–84). And it was only in the late 1950s and 1960s that the "Quiet Revolution" in Quebec—in part a reaction to the long and oppressive dominance of the Duplessis machine and the influence of the church—transformed a closed, introspective political culture into an active and secular one (Quinn 1975; Bourgault and Dion 1993). In recent surveys, these two regions displayed the strongest aversion to precisely the sort of influence peddling that once characterized their politics (Mancuso 1998). If there is an ethical issue that still pervades Canadian governments it is pork barreling and the distribution of government funds. Still, when people talk about political machines in Canada today, they mean parties that are continually successful at the polls through good public relations and careful organization—like the Ontario Big Blue Machine of the 1970s and 1980s led by Premier William Davis—rather than the type of corrupt regimes that persist elsewhere.

Political Culture

The original Canadian constitution, the *British North America Act* of 1867, did not provide written guidance on enduring Canadian values and culture. It could not serve "as a source of a list of regime values for administrators" (Rohr 1978, 67) because the main components of the Canadian system were customary parts of the British tradition: the role and powers of the Crown, the rule of law, the selection of the Prime Minister, the collective and individual responsibilities of ministers and the amendment of the constitution by unanimous consent of the federal government and all of the provinces. Until the adoption of the Charter of Rights and Freedoms in 1982, the principal features of the relationship between the elected government and its public service were present in the constitution only in customary form, with all the ambiguity that such a situation implies.

The Canadian cabinet has a long tradition of being larger than necessary, in order to accommodate regions or provinces that would otherwise be left outside the government. Regional considerations are present in most major issues affecting economic development, such as scientific research and development, location of federal facilities, and federal purchases. The twentieth century has featured a vast amount of "federal-provincial diplomacy" (Simeon 1972). From the beginning of confederation, the federal government has provided a per capita subsidy to each province. From 1919 to the late 1970s, it used its constitutional powers to spend for the purposes of "peace, order and good government" to entice the provinces into joint programs in areas of provincial jurisdiction such as natural resources, education, culture, and highways. Also, from 1952, the federal government began paying equalization payments to the provinces that fell below a national standard of wealth, in effect using taxes from the richer provinces to subsidize the poorer ones. Unlike the joint programs, these grants have been unconditional.

Many observers have noted that federalism as practiced in Canada prevents the federal state from having a strong role in orienting and directing social and economic life (Smiley 1987, 22). It has risen to clear preeminence in times of crisis but in peacetime, the provinces have tended to have more importance, as they have jurisdiction over natural resources, labor, education, culture, welfare, and health—most of the concerns that affect people directly in their daily lives. This has produced a "fragmented state with a fragmenting impact on Canadian society" (Cairns 1986, 56).

Social Values and Ethics

Economically and culturally, Canada has managed to avoid some of the major risk factors for systemic corruption. As a society built almost entirely through immigration, and upon a well-developed, urban-industrial economy, Canada has not had to contend with the uneasy and incomplete transference of kinship-oriented loyalties to more abstract public responsibilities that hampers professionalism in the public service of developing nations. The most problematic form of tribalism affecting Canada is language-based chauvinism. Official bilingualism—established in 1969—remains a thorn in the side of both anglophone and francophone zealots; the former see it as a conspiracy to exclude unilingual members of the anglophone majority from government office, the latter as a sop to diffuse the national ambitions of Quebec. The contentious issue of language is present to some extent in almost every debate in Canada, but for most of the population it is not a source of ethical conflict.

The generally healthy ethical state of the Canadian public sector reflects an overall societal emphasis on the importance of honesty, respect for law and order, and the sanctity of the public interest. This conventional wisdom is reaffirmed regularly in studies of public attitudes, such as that conducted by the Canadian Political Ethics Working Group. Given a choice between the abstract values of equality, compassion, honesty, freedom, and tolerance, an overwhelming majority of Canadians selected honesty as the most important (Mancuso 1998, 40). In more detailed and concrete situational questions, this same priority on honesty was also evident. Bribery, when it occurs in Canada, is far more likely to result in a quick call to the Royal Canadian Mounted Police rather than better service in a public office. Unambiguous conflicts of interest are quickly and loudly condemned (ambiguous conflicts present the problem of detection and interpretation). Similarly, other flagrant abuses are not generally tolerated and must be conducted underground and in secret.

Such secrecy provides safety only insofar as it can be maintained. Canada also has a long tradition of activist, investigative journalism in the Anglo-American style (Taras 1999). The media, wrapped in the mantle of the public's right to know, can be annoyingly energetic in its pursuit of allegations and attempts to uncover juicy political scandals. The often adversarial relationship between reporter and public official generally serves to further isolate and stigmatize unacceptable political behavior, although it can be problematic in itself when it begins to interfere with objective reporting of information. A too-sensationalistic press can overstate the prevalence and scope of official misconduct and lead to public disenchantment with politics and those involved in it.

Often, when a scandal breaks, it seems that Canadian media outlets are so excited to find something local to cover that they significantly overreact. At the same time, their reaction is quite measured compared to the frenzy that characterizes the contemporary American press. The almost complete penetration of American media into Canadian homes—some 90 percent of the Canadian population lives close enough to the border to receive American broadcast television—means that foreign obsessions like political interns and the definition of simple words can have large but undeserved impact on Canadians' perceptions of their own political culture and institutions. Thus, Canada has been fighting and only partially resisting this sort of cultural transference from the United States.

Public Values and Ethics

Within the political realm, much attention has been paid to the values and ethics of those who actively contribute to the activity of Canada's governments. Former federal Deputy Minister of Justice John Tait focused on the values that defined the fundamental ethos of the public sector (Tait 1996). His report was part of an attempt to reinvigorate a civil service in the midst of significant evolution and facing important challenges. The economic doldrums and high deficits of the late 1980s and early 1990s led to a period of retrenchment and reorganization within the public sector. Many departments whose employees had perhaps unwisely come to expect lifetime tenure were subjected to layoffs and downsizing. A new, more entrepreneurial approach to public sector administration—the New Public Management paradigm—had provoked a cultural shift within the public service and seemed to be in conflict with some of its traditional priorities and concerns (Dwivedi and Gow 1999, 125–59).

Meanwhile, these internal challenges were mirrored by external changes. As in many other countries, the civil service's reputation for both probity and competence was under siege from a growing sense of public cynicism about government and politics in general (Pharr, Putnam, and Dalton 2000). The historic level of respect and deference displayed by Canadian citizens to their public officials seemed to be in steep decline. With this disengagement came a decline in public understanding of the political process, especially of the sometimes sophisticated maneuvers that characterize Westminster-style responsible government. Compared to the relentlessly available and more aggressively personalized political system of the superpower next door, parliamentary democracy requires both subtlety and finesse to practice and appreciate. During this period virulently antigovernment rhetoric dominated political discussion on the North American airwaves, and Canadians heard their government-run healthcare system regularly excoriated as ineffective, beyond repair, and virtually Communist (by representatives of for-profit, American healthcare conglomerates).

In the face of these challenges, Tait proposed a process of rededication to civil service goals and values, and periodic reassessment of achievement (Tait 1996, 53). He specifically identified four core clusters of values crucial to the Canadian public service. Democratic values are those that relate to the civil service's function in a parliamentary system of responsible government, including accountability and respect for the public interest. Professional values have to do with norms of excellence, continuous improvement, effectiveness, and service to the public. Ethical values are principles like integrity, honesty, and impartiality that are common to all parts of society, but which take on special importance in the context of the public trust carried by civil servants. Finally, people values emphasize concern for others and the importance of respect, civility, communication, and benevolence.

Many of these same values are applicable to and important in the roles of elected officials as well, but whereas civil servants can ideally concentrate their energies on serving the public interest, politicians must also confront the less idealistic concerns of electability, fund raising, and campaign promises. These activities often involve behavior that is, if not unethical, at least calculated and manipulative. Accordingly, politicians tend to have a more negative public image than civil servants, and comparisons to used car sellers abound. But politicians, ephemeral and ideological in contrast to the neutral permanence of bureaucrats, are ultimately the ones who bear electoral responsibility for governmental actions. When they fail to meet public expectations, they cast doubt upon the whole process of government, which they visibly represent to the public.

Where the civil service emphasizes values like professionalism and accountability, elected officials focus more on what Tait calls people values and the skills of communication and compromise. Successful politicians must be able to win over not only their natural supporters but their adversaries as well, both in the general public and within the legislature. Politicians, who are the crucial link in accountability between voter and government, probably harm themselves most severely with continual efforts to avoid blame and claim undeserved credit. While public servants make the myriad tactical choices involved in policy implementation, politicians, as proxies for the public will, make the strategic decisions. Effective political leadership often requires using this decision-making power in unpopular but ultimately beneficial ways. Of course, it is sometimes difficult to discriminate between fearless leadership and stubborn arrogance.

Such arrogance is a value that Canadian politicians seem able to supply in great abundance. With some of the strictest party discipline in the world, and a long history of parliamentary majorities, governments have often seemed to eventually think of themselves as no less permanent than the civil service. After a few terms in office, public support is taken for granted rather than continually earned. The eventual result has been some truly spectacular party collapses in key general elections. Another practice perceived as arrogance is the handling of campaign promises. While these have always been suspected of insincerity, the public clearly prefers that they be both made and taken seriously (Mancuso 1998). Voters appear frustrated with grandiose platforms that are taken apart and only implemented piecemeal during the years between elections (Hyde 1997). Recent campaign props such as the federal Liberals' "Red Book" and the Ontario Conservatives' "Common Sense Revolution" have successfully mined this demand for documented and accountable policy proposals, although it is not clear whether either resulting government has been any more faithful to its stated aims.

Regulating Ethics

Achieving ethical politics is greatly facilitated in a system that can emphasize and develop strong ethical values, but ultimately some form of explicit guidance is needed to deal with actual and potential violations. As noted above, in the balance between admonition and prescription, Canada has tended to follow a middle course between British obligation and American legalism. Still, the actual rules that apply to a given situation are often hard to determine, for several reasons. Canada's decentralized federation grants the provinces extensive powers and areas of exclusive jurisdiction: each provincial government has its own variations on ethical regulation and management. Some unacceptable practices, such as bribery, constitute actual criminal offenses, and are codified in the Criminal Code. Because this is an area of federal jurisdiction, it is relatively consistent and consistently applicable across the country, but only the most severe violations are actually criminalized. Many activities, such as MPs entering into government contracts, are prohibited by ordinary Acts of Parliament, and thus apply in varying degrees according to the language of each Act. Relevant legislation dates from the nineteenth century but additions are relatively recent.

Other important strictures do not have the actual force of law but instead derive from the Standing Orders of Parliament or the various provincial assemblies. An MP's obligation to disclose a financial interest in the subject of legislation or parliamentary debate is actually a rule of the House of Commons and is technically enforced by the Speaker's office rather than any police or investigative agency. Another source of rules is the Prime Minister's Office (PMO) itself: such decrees are enforced within the government through the PMO's discretionary powers of appointment and removal. An example is the "Conflict of Interest and Post-Employment Code for Public Service Holders 1994," which applies to cabinet ministers (but not other parliamentarians) and senior civil servants such as deputy ministers. Other public servants are also subject to a two-tiered code (one level for core officials and one for the wider public sector) that shares many of the same principles as the PMO's Conflict of Interest Code. This code is administered as a condition of employment. In general, criminal code provisions are the most specifically prescriptive. The quasi-legal Standing Orders and PMO decrees tend to be more aspirational in tone and content, reflecting their more subjective mode of effect and enforcement.

The 1994 Code specifically references the office of the Ethics Counselor of Canada, which was brought into being simultaneously. The counselor administers the code, receives the declarations and statements of interest it requires, and generally offers advice and guidance to those subject to it. Unlike similar positions in other jurisdictions—even within Canada—the ethics counselor is only partially independent and remains a prime ministerial appointee. The declarations collected are not made public. The counselor's function is primarily advisory rather than investigative, and the office has no direct powers of sanction, other than access to the prime minister. In contrast, British Columbia's Ethics Commissioner plays a more active role and has been involved in cases that led to the resignation of a provincial premier (Greene and Shugarman 1997). But the Ethics Counselor does have some authority with which to discourage undesirable activity, although control over parliamentarians remains weak.

Significant breaches of noncriminal regulations have historically been dealt with through ad hoc royal commissions of inquiry, such as the 1986 Parker Commission that looked into allegations of conflict of interest in the affairs of the Industry Minister. That commission established the importance of avoiding not only actual and potential conflicts but also apparent conflicts, and it has become a modern touchstone for the assessment of incidents and accusations. Other provisions round out the regulatory system: the Auditor General of Canada has the authority to conduct inquiries and analyze behavior, but no coercive power. An assortment of freedom of information acts and transparency laws combine to restrict the opportunities for keeping questionable activities secret from the public.

Ultimately, for all but the most blatant, criminalized transgressions, responsibility for punishing misbehavior falls under the discretion of the government. In a sense, the various codes of ethics simply codify and formalize the kinds of activity considered likely to embarrass the government and erode its level of public support. The principle of electoral retribution is thus the fundamental ethical regulation in a system of responsible government. Dismissal, demotion, political exile, and other forms of sanction are manifestations of the omnipresent concern for reelection.

Conclusion

For a number of reasons, Canada is not an ideal place to study public sector corruption in action. Sociocultural norms of obedience and fair play conspire with a relatively resilient regulatory stance to produce significant disincentives to those in public service who would misuse their offices. Most cases turn out to be the result of individual opportunistic transgressions, rather than systematic subversions of political relationships and institutions. There remain some areas of systemic vulnerability, particularly in the managing of conflict of interest, patronage, and perhaps most important, the ethical gap between the public and their government. But Canada has so far been rather fortunate that its strong ethical traditions, active investigative press, energetic party competition, and reasonably engaged electorate have all contributed to maintaining an approximation of the good government and good governance its founders sought to attain.

References

Atkinson, Michael, and Maureen Mancuso. 1992. Edicts and etiquette: Regarding conflict of interest in Congress and the House of Commons. *Corruption and Reform* 7(1): 1–18.

Bourgault, Jacques, and Stephanie Dion. 1993. Public sector ethics in Quebec: The contrasting society. In *Corruption, character and conduct*. Toronto: Oxford University Press.

Cairns, Alan. 1986. The embedded state: State-society relations in Canada. In *State and society: Canada in comparative perspective*, edited by K. Banting, Vol. 31 of the Royal Commission on the Economic Union.

Congressional Digest. 1999. 78 (5).

Dwivedi, O. P., and James Iain Gow. 1999. *From bureaucracy to public management*. Peterborough, Ontario: Broadview Press and the Institute of Public Administration in Canada.

Hyde, Anthony. 1987. *Promises, promises: Breaking faith in Canadian politics*. Toronto: Viking.

Langford, John W., and Alan Tupper. 1993. *Corruption, character and conduct*. Toronto: Oxford University Press.

Mancuso, Maureen. 1995. *The ethical world of British MPs*. Montreal-Kingston: McGill-Queen's University Press.

Nye, Joseph S., Philip D. Zelikow, and David C. King. 1997. *Why people don't trust government.* Cambridge, Mass.: Harvard University Press.

Parr, Susan, Robert Putnam, and Russell Dalton. 2000. Trouble in the advanced democracies? A quarter century of declining confidence. *Journal of Democracy.* 11 (April): 5–25.

Ridley, F. F., and Alan Doig, eds. 1995. *Sleaze: Politicians, private interests and public reaction.* Oxford: Oxford University Press.

Rohr, John. 1978. *Ethics for bureaucrats.* New York: Marcel Dekker.

Simeon, Richard. 1992. *Federal-provincial diplomacy: The making of recent policy in Canada.* Toronto: University of Toronto Press.

Smiley, Donald V. 1987. *The federal condition in Canada.* Toronto: McGraw-Hill Ryerson.

Thorburn, Hugh O. 1976. Election day in New Brunswick. In *Political corruption in Canada: Cases, causes and cures,* edited by Kenneth M. Gibbons and Donald C. Rowat. Toronto: McClelland and Stewart.

United Kingdom. 1995. *Report of the committee on standards in public life* (The Nolan Committee).

5

France's Elf Scandals

Douglas Andrew Yates

SCHOLARS OF POLITICAL AND ADMINISTRATIVE corruption in France and francophone Africa owe much to critical journalism, particularly the satirical *Canard Enchaîné*, *Le Figaro*, *Le Monde*, and *Liberation*, but the facts tend to be sporadic and longitudinal analysis is rarely quantitative. During the 1990s, a specialized scandal press has exposed institutionalized corruption at every level with the Dossiers Noirs series concentrating in France's sub-Saharan sphere of influence, an institutionalized neocolonialism of "Françafique" (Glaser and Smith 1994; Verschave 1998) where corrupt persons and practices are illustrated. But important academic studies exist, especially the theoretical work of Jean Francois Bayart (1989) and others concerning *la politique du ventre* describing the rent-seeking behavior of former French colonies exploiting their oil and mineral exports which has been influenced by international criminal organizations. Although the often criminal practices known as the Elf scandals are part of *la politique du ventre* in Africa, this chapter concentrates solely on the French side of Elf Aquitaine, which provided the money needed by countries such as Congo, Gabon, and the Cameroons for their governance and the period when that state oil company was directed by Loïk Le Floch-Prigent, its only head who had not been a member of the elitist Grands Corps, the cream of French education.

Le Floch

Loïk Le Floch-Prigent was born in a small town in Brittany after the ravages of the Second World War had taken their toll. Its fishing villages and peasant farms were not the motors of industrial development, and the ravages of war had only served to destroy what little industrial base the region had. His child-hood was therefore that of a son of a modest provincial doctor. While this did not prevent such boys from rising up through the ranks of French society, it was practically impossible for them to do so without leaving their regions and mak-ing the pilgrimage to the *grandes écoles* in Paris. He imagined himself as a great man, boyish dreams that never left him on his rise to the top. Le Floch was not admitted to Polytechnique. Instead, he had to settle for second best, the Institut Polytechnique de Grenoble which would have been enough to ensure him a second-class career in France. Those who went to second-tier schools tended to spend their careers forever beneath the graduates of the *grandes écoles*. It did not take him long to realize this. In 1968 he went to America, as many French-men do who wish to escape the rigid social structure of the *grandes écoles* in France. He enrolled in a midwestern mining college and studied mining sci-ences. When he was through, he returned to France and found a low level job in the Ministry of Industry's scientific and technical research bureau, the DGRST.

At work, Le Floch earned the respect of his peers and had the reputation of someone who was a good listener. Despite his second-class diplomas, he did manage to climb to the number three post in the service. But that was where his ascent stopped. His personal appearance became a trademark that he would carry throughout his career. He sported a Breton beard and had a strong dis-like of ties, particularly in hot weather. During the hot summer months he would often go to the office bare-necked, and on the worst occasions, wore thongs on his feet. Such fashion impairment set him apart from the *grands corpsards* of Polytechnique who tended to dress professionally, even well. Le Floch looked more like a provincial civil servant and was treated like one when it came to promotion. The class bias of the *grands corps* prevented such outsiders from rising too high in the ministries.

While working at the DGRST, Le Floch had the good fortune to make the acquaintance of Pierre Dreyfus, a socialist who had been the president of the national automotive giant Renault. In 1981 Dreyfus appointed Le Floch as his cabinet director. This was a turning point in Le Floch's career because the so-cialists had taken power. M. Herrand's rise to power gave the socialist presi-dent, among numerous powers inherited from De Gaulle and his Gaullist suc-cessors, the power to appoint the heads of all national industries in France's swollen public sector. Le Floch worked like mad to please his patron Dreyfus. Dreyfus gave Le Floch the dossiers of steel and textile restructuring, to which Le Floch dedicated himself tirelessly. "Loïk was capable of picking up his phone at any hour and calling anyone," estimated one of his associates at the time. "I think Dreyfus was bluffed by his inflated side." In 1982 there was a cabinet re-shuffle and Jean-Pierre Chevenement demanded the Ministry of Industry.

Mitterrand therefore called in Dreyfus to offer him a post somewhere else. "Nothing for me," replied Dreyfus, "but on the other hand, there's a cabinet director . . ." and then he proposed Le Floch to serve as the new president of the huge state enterprise Rhône-Poulenc. Mitterrand was surprised by Dreyfus's candidate. Le Floch was a total unknown, and Rhône-Poulenc was one of the largest state enterprises in France. "You are always reproaching me for never proposing anyone but *enarques*, polytechnicians, or members of the *Corps des Mines*," responded Dreyfus. "Le Floch has another pedigree, and the head of Rhône-Poulenc is vacant."

In the world of corporate executive suits, Le Floch was a stranger in paradise. The first friend he made at Rhône-Poulenc was its general director, Serge Tchuruk, an industrialist of the classical variety in France, with diplomas from the *grandes écoles* and a network of personal connections throughout the business world. Tchuruk was the first man who introduced Le Floch to Alfred Sirven, a flamboyant lawyer and ancient Gaullist who had fought in the French Resistance, with a good law degree and personal contacts on the left and right. "Sirven is a good man," Tchuruk said and almost at once Le Floch took to him. What probably appealed to Le Floch most was how Sirven seemed to know everyone who was anyone. But Sirven was more than just a contact. He was the consummate intermediary, which was precisely what Le Floch needed at that moment, surrounded by hostile and snickering elites.

In 1986, the year that the Gaullists won the legislative elections and started the first period of "cohabitation" between the political left and right, Le Floch was suddenly fired. Jacques Chirac, the new prime minister, under pressure from the economically liberal Edouard Balladur, fired Le Floch without warning. It was an abrupt and rude departure, particularly for Le Floch, who had nothing to fall back on. The usual procedure was to offer the outgoing president some kind of post. But Chirac's advisor, Jacques Friedman, did not even do that. "All you have to do," Friedman told Le Floch in a moment of negligence, "is return to your *grands corps* of origin." Apparently he did not even know that Le Floch had no such origin. The years 1986 to 1988 were terrible for Le Floch. He had known paradise and then lost it. He became bitter and depressed. Janine, his first wife, left him and they were divorced. This was when Alfred Sirven stepped in to help his old boss. Sirven lent the keys to his vacation home in the Orne to Le Floch and showed a remarkable loyalty to the outcast Breton. Not to be forgotten were his backroom dealings to try and find a post for his disconsolate friend. Rumor has it that it was Sirven who lobbied friends of Mitterrand to give Le Floch another post. When the next legislative elections were held, and the Socialists recaptured their majority in the national assembly, Le Floch found himself well positioned for a new post. Sirven had learned an

important lesson from this long and painful experience. It was important to
have friends on the political right, as well as the political left.

Le Floch Joins Elf-Aquitaine

In 1989 Le Floch was parachuted into the Presidency of the Société Nationale
d'Elf-Aquitaine, the country's premier public enterprise. Informal resistance
from within the hierarchy ensued immediately. Not only had Le Floch broken
the unwritten code against non-*corpsards* running Elf, but his second wife, Fatima
Belaïd, was of Algerian ancestry. Like his degrees and clothes, Le Floch's apartment was not quite up to the social demands of a French corporate president.
The portrait that was painted of Loïk and Belaïd by insiders and *corpsards* was
that of a *parvenu*, a person who acquires wealth or power but who fails to conform to established forms, customs, and habits of the class into which he has
risen. Le Floch was an upstart, without any of the cultural background or social
experiences that they considered necessary. He and his wife were, in short, too
vulgar to rule.

It is important to keep in mind that Loïk Le Floch-Prigent did not invent
the institutionalized corruption of Elf. He merely inherited it. But under his
presidency the entire process went out of control. The image of corruption that
usually comes to mind is personal enrichment and the acquisition of certain
conspicuous luxuries. Certainly Le Floch became corrupt in this sense of the
word. When he was appointed president in 1989, it was a little like he had won
the lottery. He and Fatima immediately moved out of his modest apartment in
the 17th arrondissement (of Paris), and into a large sumptuous company suite in
the heart of the 16th arrondissement, which is one of the wealthiest in Paris.
Fatima wanted to hold lavish dinners for the *grands hommes* and *grandes femmes* of
France. They hosted grandiose receptions where show business types rubbed
shoulders with government ministers, all on company salaries, of course. But
the highlight of this period, socially speaking, was when they were invited to
President Mitterrand's private flat. When they were not dining with the rich and
famous, there were plenty of other opportunities to profit from Le Floch's new
job. Belaïd never missed an opportunity to travel with her husband on company
jets when he visited Africa, the Americas, or Asia. Le Floch made sure to purchase a special Flacon 900 private jet, at an estimated price tag of 1.2 billion
francs, which became their second residence. The combination of the couple's
new found wealth and bad taste led some critics to call him *Le Plouc Fringant.*

But this kind of personal moral corruption was nothing compared to the
financial havoc wreaked by Le Floch's business friends. The name that first
comes to mind is Maurice Biderman. Le Floch met Biderman when he was

working for Dreyfus at the DGRST. Biderman got his start in business from his uncle, a Sentier rag merchant. When Le Floch first met him, in 1982, Biderman was already worth 1.5 billion francs. He had made his reputation under President Valery Giscard d'Estaing as someone who could save businesses that were going bankrupt. Using massive government subsidies, Biderman bought out these failing enterprises and prevented the politically disturbing social conflicts that would have erupted. Le Floch invited Biderman to become an advisor in the restructuring process of the industry in which Biderman had emerged as a major player. This favor was returned in 1986, when Le Floch found himself out of work. Biderman appointed Le Floch to serve on the board of directors of his company. It was during this period, in 1988, that Biderman first introduced Le Floch to Jacques Chirac. Biderman had connections with the Gaullists and invited the two men to dine at his home. Thanks to Biderman, Le Floch started to make personal contacts on the political right. In 1989, it was Le Floch's turn to reciprocate. The year Le Floch assumed the presidency of Elf, Biderman's business was failing. He asked Le Floch to bail him out. So in 1990 Le Floch arranged for Elf to buy Biderman's business for hundreds of millions of francs, all with the benediction of the socialist government. Three years later Elf was still dumping money into the failed firm, withdrawing 150 million francs from the inexhaustible Elf Gabon to pay for Biderman's restructuring.

Biderman demonstrated to Fatima that her ambitions were too small. So she plotted with Le Floch to give her a little something to do with all her spare time. In 1990, less than a year after he had been parachuted into the presidency of the company, Le Floch held an Elf management reunion with three hundred of the top cadres gathered at the Théâtre Champs-Elysées in Paris. During his speech he announced, to everyone's surprise, that he had decided to create a new charitable foundation, with an endowment of fifty million francs, called the Fondation Elf. But what really shocked his audience was when he announced its first president—Fatima!

No expenses were spared for Fondation Elf's new headquarters. A building on the rue Dumont-d'Urville was purchased and transformed into a little embassy. This was when her expense account began to become dangerously excessive. When her credit ran out, Le Floch pressured the banks to extend more credit. Fatima's credit cards were maxed out at such "charitable" locations as Yves Saint Laurent, Nina Ricci, and Virgin Megastore. The cost of these shopping sprees in 1991 alone was 1.5 million francs. Rumors began circulating about the Le Floch's extravagant lifestyle, discretely at first, then more loudly.

Alfred Sirven did not like the influence that Fatima wielded. Le Floch had named Sirven to the number two post at Elf, albeit with the seemingly innocuous title of *conseiller du president* in charge of general business affairs. Sirven jealously guarded his partnership with Le Floch and resented the manner in which the newcomer Fatima had so rapidly enriched herself at the company's expense. While Le Floch traveled around the world mastering the geopolitics of a major international oil company, Sirven arranged the little details that clinched the deals. Le Floch and Sirven were a deadly and successful team. Sirven placed himself, in short, in the center of all Elf's affairs. This would cost him dearly when those affairs turned into scandals. A well-chosen example was when Le Floch wanted to meet Guy Dejounay, the president of the Compagnie Générale des Eaux (one of the largest industrial enterprises in France). Sirven arranged the details, and the meeting was a success. To repay host Dr. Raillard for his hospitality, Sirven helped to sell his house to Elf for an estimated 18 million francs even though he continued to live there! Sirven did not understand how much that the long-time Elf executives, particularly the *corpsards* and members of the inner networks, resented the way he was spending company money. These insiders would later become court witnesses against him.

Corruption Escalates

Sirven and Biderman began dipping into the African funds. Biderman's failing company had already cost Elf dearly, but the real trouble began when Le Floch decided to draw 150 million francs out of Elf Gabon's inexhaustible cash box to pay for Biderman's restructuring. The source of the problem was André Tarallo. By the time Le Floch came to power in 1989, Tarallo had constructed a chain of offshore fields extending from Angola, to Congo, to Gabon, past Equatorial Guinea to Camaroon, and terminating in Nigeria. The Gulf of Guinea became to Elf what the Persian Gulf was to other major international petroleum firms. Tarallo's real power in the company was based on the fact that Africa provided the bulk of Elf's production in almost total secrecy. Institutionalized corruption in the African oil enclaves generated billions of francs in "lost" money for well-connected insiders. These oil rents provided the major source of liquidity available for the clandestine networks that inhabited the company. Tarallo was in charge of the African oil operations and money—the money that Le Floch's friends were using to fund their European escapades.

For the first two years of Le Floch's presidency, 1989–91, André Tarallo reigned as a kind of independent force within the company, surrounded by loyal engineers, politicians, and a group of executives at every level. His connections within the French government went all the way to the Elysées. They also went to the Gaullists, fellow Corsican Charles Pasqua, and his former ENA classmate, Jacques Chirac. Tarallo was untouchable. But during those same two years Alfred Sirven attempted to wrest control of the African cash cow from

Tarallo. Besides diverting 150 million francs from the Elf Gabon to Biderman, Sirven also began to use the secretive Swiss banking system to divert dirty money from African sources. Sirven penetrated Tarallo's Gabon. He also courted Pasqua and Corsican networks. Tarallo continually resisted these infringements, through his contacts at headquarters. Tarallo's base of action was not in Africa nor even in Paris, but in Corsica. Using the countless millions of francs of African oil rents that were under his control over a quarter-century, Tarallo had purchased a sumptuous villa outside his hometown of Bonifacio. The Corsican Mafia, with connections at the highest levels of government, provided the milieu for Tarallo's discrete transactions. With an official salary of only 25,000 francs per month, it was difficult for Tarallo to explain to the court how he had acquired this estate. But the ninety million franc villa was, of course, only the tip of the iceberg. It was simply a location from which suitcases full of cash amounting to untold hundreds of million of francs were carried off private jets and into European villas and Swiss bank accounts.

Ethical considerations aside, André Tarallo held the keys to the Elf cash box, and these were precisely what Sirven wanted. The result was a struggle for power and money at the very heart of Elf. On the one side of this battle stood Tarallo and those who had risen to power within the group over the past quarter-century, including *enarques* and *corpsards* who were loyal to his cause. On the other side stood Le Floch, Sirven, and the other vulgar *parvenus* who had been parachuted into Elf's corporate hierarchy, and who wanted to take what they considered to be the perquisites of power. Then, in 1991, at age sixty-five, Tarallo was forced (by French labor law) to retire. The balance of power shifted, and Sirven took the keys to the cash box.

The end of the Cold War opened a new frontier to the large multinational oil companies: the oil and gas operations in the collapsed Soviet empire. Not only was the former Soviet state petroleum company looking for new partners to invest capital and technology in the vast expanses of the Siberian wilderness, but the newly independent republics of Central Asia and the Caucasus were ready to invite Western oil firms to develop their untapped mineral wealth. In Eastern Europe the former Communist refining and distribution networks that had been satellites to the Soviet oil industry were being privatized, providing additional opportunities for foreign investors who might be interested in capturing these new car-driving European consumer markets.

Loïk Le Floch-Prigent happened to be the president of Elf at a unique moment in the history of world oil. Although much has been made of the scandals that emerged out of his aggressive moves to penetrate these ex-Communist markets, few writers have given him any credit for moving the company in this direction. It was Le Floch who first broke with the company's traditional vertical strategy of oil supply and started its current horizontal strategy of oil supply, and in doing so, commenced a new era in Elf's long history of achieving French energy independence. In pursuing a horizontal strategy, Le Floch started to pull Elf out of its privileged African domain and into the unprotected world of international business competition over oil resources, where the French government's influence was only that of a middle power. The Elysées had no sphere of influence in these republics, which had been under Moscow's control for the previous half-century. Out there in the new Eastern frontier, business was going to have to be conducted without the overwhelming influence that France enjoyed within its African sphere. Le Floch quickly understood that the business of competing for oil concessions was not an affair for gentlemen practitioners. Fortunately, he was not burdened by an overly restrictive sense of business formalities. He was totally fluent in the language of political corruption, party contributions, professional kickbacks, and secret transfers of funds. With his business partner Alfred Sirven to help him with the details, Le Floch successfully navigated the uncharted waters of post-Communist regimes, where the new spirit of capitalism had been tainted by the ageless quest for personal enrichment.

In 1991 Le Floch negotiated with the Russian state oil company to purchase crude oil from the former Soviet Union. When these talks ground to a standstill, he called Sirven to help grease the wheels. Sirven in turn called André Guelfi, an international business consultant, to propose the job. Guelfi personally knew former apparatchiks, including mayor Anatoli Sobtchak, and could, with a few well-placed phone calls, get the negotiations moving again. In no time at all he closed the deal between Elf and Russia, and for this service, he received $12 million, twenty million francs in cash, and a 3 percent commission on every barrel of oil produced under the terms of the contract. In 1992, Le Floch used Guelfi to clinch another deal, this time an exploration contract in the oil-rich Central Asian republic of Kazakhstan. While this deal was being negotiated, Guelfi lobbied Le Floch to try to cut a deal with the government in Uzbekistan. Le Floch was interested, but he had to convince the French government to allow Elf to invest although it had few contacts there. If Le Floch was going to penetrate this new Eastern market, he was going to need someone who could get things moving. Once again, he called upon André Guelfi, who knew President Karimov personally, and who also had indirect contacts with Mitterrand. Guelfi flew his private jet to Uzbekistan to negotiate a deal with Karimov. Then he flew back to Paris and contacted Françoise Sagan, a writer who was a close friend of Mitterrand. Guelfi convinced Sagan to write a letter to the French president persuading him to open relations with Uzbekistan. She wrote the letter. Mitterrand made an official state visit to the central Asian republics, including a stopover in Uzbekistan. In 1993, Le Floch signed an accord with Uzbekistan. For his services Guelfi received 3 percent of every barrel of oil that was to be produced under the terms of the contract.

In 1991, the East German refining and distribution network Minol was being privatized. As Minol was strategically located between Soviet oil production and German oil consumers, Le Floch decided to make this acquisition another part of his horizontal strategy. He intended to buy only Minol service stations. But Mitterrand, who invited Le Floch to lunch at the Elysées, announced at the table during one of those lunches that he wished Elf would buy more than Minol's service stations: "My friend Kohl," he explained candidly, "would like Elf to take the Leuna refinery at the same time." Le Floch understood that the president's wish was tantamount to command, and he immediately started negotiations to acquire the refinery. Alfred Sirven was the go-between and 256 million francs were deposited in a secret bank account in Liechtenstein, on the Swiss border, out of which "honoraria" were withdrawn. A close associate of Kohl, Holgar Pfahls, ensured these payments were made to German officials. In 1992, Le Floch personally met with Kohl to discuss the deal. Fifteen days later a protocol was signed between Elf and the German government.

Each of these moves into the East eventually erupted into scandal although at the time each was perceived as good business. The moves were a logical extension of a larger corporate strategy pursued by Elf during the Le Floch presidency. When André Guelfi was asked to explain his contribution to these scandals, he said, with an air of defiance, that political kickbacks of this kind were not unusual. This is the way business is done in the real world, he suggested, and realists ought not to be scandalized by such revelations.

But two French magistrates were scandalized. Acting upon a complaint filed in 1993, Eva Joly and Laurence Vichnievsky used their broad judicial powers to arrest, question, and detain most of the individuals involved in the Elf scandals. Nineteen people have been interrogated by Joly and Vichnievsky. Most are being tried. Some have already served time in preventative detention. Loïk Le Floch-Prigent, for example, served six months in such detention on charges of *abus des biens sociaux* when he refused to cooperate with Joly and Vichnievsky. His wife, Fatima, who cooperated with the magistrates rather than serve time in preventative detention, had to pay 2.5 million francs (and faced up to five years in prison) for her wrongdoings. André Tarallo also was charged, and he faced ten million francs in fines and possible imprisonment if convicted. Alfred Sirven fled French justice in 1993 but was extradited from the Philippines in 2001. Maurice Biderman was freed on twenty-five million francs' bail. André Guelfi faced charges for tens of millions of francs paid in the Luena scandal. They and others were facing stiff fines and prison sentences for their involvement. The total amount of money improperly diverted in the Elf affair has been estimated to be between three and four billion francs. This represents around half of the company's annual profits. This has not prevented Elf from remaining one of the largest and most profitable French enterprises. In 1999, Elf was bought out during a hostile takeover by the other French oil company, TotalFina. That takeover ended the independent existence of Elf but not the Elf scandals that threaten to reveal serious wrongdoing of senior public officials in past governments.

Conclusion

Clearly, African oil money had a corrupting effect on the French and their business partners in Europe. It also had an effect on the Africans involved, not so much corrupting them as providing large amounts of money to preexisting power circles. Oil money was simply processed through *la politique du ventre* to permit government leaders of the African oil enclaves to build state capacity, construct power bases on clan-based distribution systems, and reinforce their personal hold on power—all within the larger context of French domination— just as Omar Bongo dominated Gabon, Sasson-Neguesso Congo-Brazzaville, and Paul Biya the Cameroons. Throughout his trial, Floch-Prigent maintained that he was just a cog in an institutionalized corruption machine involving the political and administrative elites of France who profited from an elaborate network of kickbacks and bribes well known to insiders and meticulously documented by them and who also used the public enterprises to provide "ghost jobs" for cronies with dirty hands.

References

Bayart, J.-F. 1989. *L'État en Afrique: La politique du ventre.* Paris: Fayard.

Bayart, J.-F., S. Ellis, and B. Hibou. 1999. *The criminalization of the state in Africa.* Oxford: James Currey.

Beblawi, H., and G. Luciani. 1987. *The rentier state: Nation, state, and integration in the Arab world.* London: Croom Helm.

Canard Enchaîné. 1998. Elf: L'empire d'essence. Paris: Les dossiers de Canard Enchaîné.

O'Brien, Donald, and B. Cruise. 1991. The show of state in a neo-colonial twilight: Francophone in Africa. In *Rethinking third world politics*, edited by James Manor. London: Longman.

Péan, Pierre. 1988. *L'Argent noire: Corruption et sous-développment.* Paris: Fayard.

Yates, Douglas. 2000. The Elf scandals. *Scripta Politica et Economica* 19 (2): 15–26.

6

Tackling Corruption in Central and Eastern Europe

Tomasz Anusiewicz, Tony Verheijen, and Antoaneta L. Dimitrova

CORRUPTION HAS BECOME AN increasingly serious problem in the countries of Central and Eastern Europe as it has become in all the countries of the former Soviet Union. The issue of growing corruption in the region became a matter for political and academic debate in the mid-1990s but only in recent years have the complexity of the anatomy of corruption in the region and its unique features been recognized. Governments, civil society, and international organizations have now started addressing the issue in a more coherent and serious way. It is currently fashionable to speak up about corruption, which in some countries has become the focus in good governance activities. For instance in Slovakia, a major effort to devise a national anticorruption strategy has been undertaken. As yet, there are few examples overall of successful actions taken, although the Stability Pact Anti-Corruption Initiative adopted in February 2000 promises OECD assistance in the fight against bribery in southeast Europe.

Regardless of the generally acknowledged seriousness of the problem, it has been difficult to forge an informed and objective debate on corruption in the region. Discussions on corruption are either fought along partisan lines or alternatively between politicians and civil servants, often through the mass media. It is therefore important, both from an academic and from a professional point of view, to generate a more objective debate about possible causes and solutions. Lower ethical standards and corruption are global problems that will require new solutions and approaches. In this context, the ongoing crisis in Central and Eastern Europe presents an additional and unexpected opportunity, as systems undergoing change may be able to adjust easier to new approaches and avoid the mistakes of the past. Approaches and techniques from established democracies might not always be applicable for countries in transition, which may need to take emergency measures to save what confidence is left in their administrations. Traditions of nepotism existing in some countries have to be addressed, while a culture of transparency, which may have no roots in some post-Communist societies, may need to be introduced.

Context

The following section is based on Leslie Holmes' general classification of possible causes of corruption and analyzing corruption as a feature of the transition to democracy (Holmes 1993). He identified cultural, general psychological, and system-related causes.

Cultural Causes

In some countries patronage and corruption are accepted facts of life. Not helping relatives or ethnic group members to obtain a job would be considered inappropriate behavior in the general context of such a culture. In these cases corrupt behavior would be almost automatic, and hardly classified as trying to obtain inappropriate private benefits, even though this behavior contradicts the basic principles of Western public administration. Cultural causes have some relevance to a study of unethical behavior in the context of Central and Eastern Europe and other countries of the former Soviet Union. For instance, a recent study on politico-administrative relations in Kyrgyzstan and other Central Asian states (Dukenbaev 2000) highlights the importance of tribal relations in explaining the prevalence of cronyism in politico-administrative relations and appointments in public administration. Cultural causes have also been used to explain corruption in Balkan countries, but earlier studies have shown that in fact this is not a key cause of corruption in most Central and Eastern European countries (Verheijen and Dimitrova 1996).

Psychological Causes

Psychological causes of corruption are closely interrelated with the lack of understanding of the principles guiding the behavior of civil servants in democratic governance systems. The move from a Communist political system, in which the civil service was under strict Communist Party control, toward a democratic system, in which civil servants are expected to be professional and impartial, has left civil servants in a state of uncertainty. This uncertainty factor has led civil servants to stick to established patterns and loyalties, which sometimes have little to do with the proper behavior of a civil servant and lead to (often unintentional) corrupt behavior. In this context, it is therefore hardly surprising that loyalty to other members of the organization has often taken on added importance. The impression of the all-pervasiveness of corruption, reinforced by the media and by politicians, is a second potential psychological cause of corruption as it might well lead civil servants who, under normal circumstances, would not dare or find the moral cost of corruption too high to get involved, to follow the example of their fellow officials.

Systemic Causes

Several types of system-related causes for corruption can be extracted from the literature on this subject, namely the impact of modernization, inequality and inequity, factors related to the economic system, and factors related to the political and legal system. Some Central and Eastern European countries underwent rapid modernization of the economy and the society in the early years of Communism (Mihailescu 1993). From rural, agrarian societies with relatively closed communities and a high level of social control, these countries changed in a relatively short period into industrialized, urbanized societies, in which social control played only a very limited role. This modernization has been one-sided, partial, and distorted. The development of the complexity of Western societies was blocked by Communist power; civil society was atomized. As a reaction to the pressures of one-sided modernization, cleavages occurred between various groups of East European population, often between rural and urban areas. The current process of democratization, and the imposition by elites of a set of democratic values that do not match social realities, have brought further confusion and exacerbated urban-rural cleavages. The lack of social control created by a stable and to a certain extent uniform basis of values and beliefs has weakened administrative ethics.

The principle of egalitarianism has strong roots in several Central and Eastern European countries. Often the attitude prevails that the new rich must have made their financial gains in a (partially) illegal way. Civil servants may conclude that they too can try to obtain benefits in an illegal way. The lack of moral restrictions on corrupt behavior reinforces this type of reasoning. In addition, civil servants may feel that their prospects for material improvement are rapidly diminishing. In the conditions of reorientation to a market economy and correspondingly increased interest in material values, the lack of economic incentive can be a serious cause for corruption.

Other causes for corruption include the hardships of the economic transformation. An important reason for corrupt behavior is the relative poverty of civil servants in Central and Eastern Europe. Civil servants are often in a disadvantaged position. Their promotion possibilities are limited by the reduction of the number of civil servants. Their salaries have always been relatively low and they are now even worse off as it is more difficult for them to make additional money by holding several jobs as many others are doing under the pressure of economic austerity. This last point is especially valid in countries that have adopted a civil service law. The difficult economic situation combined with the disadvantageous position of civil servants creates almost an imperative to use their position to gain inappropriate and in some cases illegal private benefits.

The fact that civil service morale is so low and that many civil servants are apparently using their position to get personal material benefits can be explained by looking at the awkward situation in which most civil servants find themselves in their country's current legal and political situation. Under the former regime, civil servants (here used to indicate those directly employed in ministries of the central government) had a high degree of job security. Often civil servants could obtain certain limited benefits from their job and, in general, having a job in the civil service was well regarded. This situation has changed dramatically. The institutional uncertainty described earlier as an attribute of democratization—in the form of political struggle, institutional fights for power, and a legal system in transformation—is taking a heavy toll on the civil service. One consequence of political struggle and polarization is the increase of political appointments and an almost total destruction of job security. The desire to control the civil service has become almost an obsession for politicians. As a consequence, hiring and firing civil servants practically at random has become an accepted practice, which does not foster their commitment.

Transition and Corruption

Recent studies of transitional economies and of democratization in general are beginning to acknowledge the two-fold relationship between democratization and public administration reform. On the one hand, democracy cannot be consolidated without a well functioning state and a "usable" bureaucracy that is able to implement the decisions of a democratically elected government (Linz and Stepan 1996, 20); on the other hand, democratization can bring corruption in the short term by temporarily weakening the state and loosening social inhibitions. Exploring the link between this weakening state authority and the rise of corruption seems particularly relevant in the context of Eastern Europe. By questioning authority in general, democratization can bring confusion about standards of morality in general and promote antisocial behavior.

While the unending stream of allegations and reports on corruption coming from Central and Eastern Europe have brought corruption to the attention of analysts, there may be few remedies to offer. The problems of changing state institutions while simultaneously redefining statehood and implementing austere economic restructuring programs based on strict financial discipline may be simply too overwhelming. Some handicaps may be the unavoidable mutual obstructions that occur with the unprecedented triple transitions in the region. To give a concrete example: The passing of the law on the civil service may be an essential prerequisite for clarifying the rules of the game and thus curbing corruption. But in many transitional countries, such law has found little political support among legislators who have early understood the immediate political advantages of the absence of such legislation. This is a case of the players adjusting the rules of the game as they go, with detrimental consequences (Offe 1991).

Administrative Corruption

Looking at the classical definitions of bureaucracy and politico-administrative relations, as outlined above, and comparing them to public administration systems in Central and Eastern Europe, the character of public administration in the region is far removed from Western theoretical models. In the first place, a number of specific characteristics of the previous regimes (totalitarian and authoritarian) and of the bureaucracies under these regimes are making the task of defining the limits, prerogatives, and structure of the emerging civil services in post-Communist countries particularly difficult. Furthermore, all public administrations in the region are in a state of flux: they are part of an institutional structure that is experiencing a great deal of institutional uncertainty, characteristic of transition periods. Third, the economic transformation, taking place simultaneously and interdependently with the process of democratization, is imposing restrictions on the actions of political actors and the extent to which they can commandeer resources to rebuild public administration.

Under the Communist regime, the administrative system was immobile yet relatively transparent. Civil servants would keep their posts for a long time, both in high-level and in lower-level administrative positions. Also there was a relatively clear division of responsibility for different administrative tasks. In cases of misbehavior, the responsible civil servant could be traced relatively easily. Civil servants knew that if found guilty of substantial forms of corruption, they could risk losing their position and the privileges associated with it. This relative transparency prevented major forms of corruption. Of course the highest level officials were an exception to this rule; they were relatively free to decide whatever they wanted. Those who enforced the rules did not abide by them.

Corruption occurred especially at the low levels of the administration. Lower level civil servants were often prepared to circumvent administrative procedures in return for favors from clients. The legal system under the Communist regime was extensive, detailed, and to a large extent unpublicized. If civil servants in lower levels had followed the letter of the law this would certainly have obstructed the system. Thus, this form of corruption could actually be considered legitimate. If administrative rules and procedures were too detailed and inefficient, avoidance of specific procedures could be defended. The borderline between flexibility and corruption lay in this case between voluntary avoidance of procedures by an official in return for equal services offered by a client and asking for bribes to avoid certain procedures. Extortion by officials in return for avoidance of specific regulations also occurred, but there are good reasons to assume that this was the exception rather than the rule.

But if one looks at the long-term consequences of the existence of such a system, a potentially disastrous picture emerges. The authoritarian or totalitarian regimes that prevailed in the region until 1989 did, by virtue of the total domination of the state over its citizens, ban private economic interest. The abolition of substantial private property practically eliminated the distinction between state employees and private enterprise. In the countries of "really existing socialism" everyone was an employee of the state. At present, this creates confusion as to who has the (dubious) rights and obligations of a civil servant.

The democratic transition in Central and Eastern Europe separates private and public organizations. But at the same time in many countries there is still no significant differentiation between employment conditions of private employees and public servants. The three candidates to join the European Union (Slovenia, the Czech Republic, and Slovakia) do not yet have civil service laws, while the law in Latvia has yet to be fully implemented. At present, different behavior is expected from civil servants, especially those occupying high-level positions, than from owners and managers of private enterprises. This behavior is difficult to define, as the distinction between public, semi-public, and private bodies and their respective organizational cultures is not yet developed. One can well imagine that the absence of clearly defined statutory rights and obligations can lead to the continuing occurrence of cases of corruption in the civil service.

Another factor "necessitating" corruption was the state of the economy. The failing Communist distribution system led to the development of a second, underground, or black economy (Hosking 1979). Goods and services that could not be obtained through official channels could be obtained through secondary channels. This helped ease the dissatisfaction of the people and limited the delegitimizing effect of a failing distribution system. Some forms of corruption in the Communist past even helped to humanize relations between street-level bureaucrats and their clientele. If street-level bureaucrats had followed exactly the often contradictory rules of the Communist legal system, it would have been almost impossible for citizens to obtain the services they needed. Bypassing the impossible rules and regulations, citizens could obtain services from street-level bureaucrats by giving them incentives to break those official rules. In this way citizens and civil servants became reluctant accomplices. As long as civil servants did not demand excessive compensations for their extra efforts, this type of behavior might actually have been beneficial to the administrative system, providing a form of politically stabilizing redistribution.

While this degree of petty corruption necessary to keep the system working might be ignored, the role of the administration in upholding that system has to be highlighted as part of state-citizen relations. The administration was very much part of the system of oppression, if only because there was a certain degree of merging of bureaucratic structures with the Communist Party apparatus. The role state institutions played in suppressing the civil society in the former Communist countries has led to universal mistrust of them. Alienation of the citizen from the state and suspicion toward the state and civil servants can be observed in all Central and Eastern European countries (Jowett 1993). The lack of a cooperative relationship between the citizens and the new administrations leads to cynicism on both sides and opportunistic motivation for the civil servants, who are not seen as fulfilling the role of mediator between the state and the citizens in the classic Weberian sense.

Last, but not least, the democratization process in the region is unique in that it is proceding simultaneously and is often associated with economic transformation on an unprecedented scale. Restoring private property rights and transition from a planned to a market economy will be essential in the long run for the reemergence of civil society in the region and the success of democratization. But in the short run it is creating instability and social unrest. Not only are policy makers forced to take unpopular measures in the form of austerity programs, which limit their base of popular support by attracting inevitable popular dissatisfaction, but they are also constrained by the amount of resources that can be allocated to reform of the civil service. Furthermore, liberal free market ideological reorientation arrived in the region, often in the company of views on public administration regarding limiting the power of the state, privatizing state agencies, and performance-related pay. The simultaneous introduction of concepts of this kind can be very dangerous in the conditions of institutional uncertainty mentioned earlier. In practical terms this often translates into an underpaid civil service, whose members have hardly gotten used to the distinction between state and private interests when they are invited to think of themselves as service providers in a free market.

Examining the causes for corruption, a number are associated with the previous Communist regimes and the characteristics of the civil service under them. Transition to democracy has in a way served to reveal the accumulated alienation between the bureaucrat and the citizen, while at the same time removing the tenets of the structure existing before, along with its checks and balances. The new openness and transparency, together with the new media freedoms, have also inevitably served to reveal corruption where it may have existed in a hidden form before. In the general enthusiasm for market reforms at the beginning of democratization, few understood how necessary the preservation of a stable and reliable civil service was for the success of economic reform and political transformation. Without a civil service code and a clear definition of their new role, the new civil servants, as impartial mediators between the political elites and the citizens, failed to replace the old bureaucrats. Political polarization penetrated the civil service, and the lack of a stable appointments system and job security left the civil servants in the middle of a political battleground.

The general deterioration of ethics as well as the shock and confusion accompanying the economic and societal transformation have left the civil servants in a moral wasteland, in which there is very little to prevent and much to encourage corruption. Economic hardships and low salaries have contributed to this process. Politicians have done very little to alleviate this situation. Instead, civil servants have often been pawns in the power game or scapegoats to be accused of corruption and inefficiency when reforms have not had the desired effect. While some of the above-mentioned causes for corruption, especially the ones concerning the relations between the civil servants and their clients, are the legacy of the past system and will take years to change, others stemming from instability and uncertainty can partially be reduced by taking a number of concrete measures. Mobilizing the political will to do that will be a difficult task, as many new and old politicians in the region are comfortable with the present situation.

Combating Corruption

Corruption in Central and Eastern European states can be tackled only through the adoption and implementation of broadly accepted, coherent political strategies, combined with efforts to rebuild mutual respect between civil service and politicians on the one hand and the public on the other.

Using Civil Society

The role of civil society in fighting corruption is crucial. Although there might be cases of governments inviting nongovernmental organizations to cooperate in coalitions to fight corruption at national and local levels, they are rare. It has often been at the initiative of civil society activists to undertake the research, analyze the problem, and propose and implement programs of action. There are several examples of such grassroots initiatives to improve transparency and accountability in their countries and worldwide. Transparency International (TI) national chapters are the most extensive international network in this field. In Slovakia, TI spearheaded the creation of the National Program to Fight Corruption, the implementation of which has now been started. In Albania, the Albanian Center for Economic Research has undertaken a project to identify barriers keeping businesses in the informal economy from entering the formal business sector. In Bulgaria, the Center for the Study of Democracy and its Coalition 2000 program involved a number of NGOs working in cooperation with government institutions and individuals to combat corruption. The goals of Coalition 2000 included promoting public awareness, establishing mechanisms that supported anticorruption efforts, and serving as a watchdog organization. In Poland, the nongovernmental Program Against Corruption, an initiative of the Batory Foundation and the Helsinki Foundation for Human Rights, initiated its activities at the beginning of 2000. The Polish program aims to form citizen groups to hold local governments accountable through monitoring their governance practices.

As illustrated above, civil society can act as pressure group, demanding accountability and transparency from governments. Civil society mobilization, promotion of groups, organization of city and commune anticorruption centers, partnerships with local governments, monitoring of public services, coalition building to defend victims of corrupt practices, and support of public appeals are of great importance for the successful struggle against corruption on the local level, but also add up to substantial effects on a national scale. But the levels of enhancement, organization, and self-management of civil society still remain relatively low in most countries of the region.

Using the Media Constructively

Although independent media, where they exist, are supposed to play a key role in fighting corruption, journalists usually show a very limited interest in investigative journalism, due to the amount of labor, time, and risk involved. More often, journalists undertake investigation and publicize cases of corrupt practices upon political orders. They use corruption scandals as covers for sensational stories that increase newspaper sales, and so attract more advertisers and cash to the editors, or even to themselves, making them vulnerable to corruption. Therefore, codes of ethics for journalists should be created, publicized, and respected.

Freedom of Information

In most (if not all) countries of the region, national constitutions provide for free access to information and freedom of expression. The practice is often far from ideal. In Poland, practically any authority can block access by using legislation such as the personal data protection act. The obvious need is comprehensive free access to an information act. A successful example in this area is a Slovak initiative of a coalition of 120 nongovernmental organizations and its campaign of sending postcards with the slogan "what is not secret must be public" to parliamentarians, collecting over 100,000 signatures and producing a Web page. A law on freedom of information came into force in June 2000. There is also a draft law on freedom of information and an associated campaign led by the Center for Freedom of Press Monitoring in Poland and the Adam Smith Center, as well as a draft law and campaign led by the Center for Independent Journalism in Moldavia.

Changing Politicians' Attitudes

Politicians should be convinced that using alleged corruption in the civil service as an instrument to fight political battles is counterproductive: the opposition will have to work with the civil service next. Corruption will only increase the already existing alienation between politicians and civil servants and create more antiheroes. A more constructive approach would be to publicize positive images of outstanding civil servants, an approach little used in this region.

Reintroducing Administrative Control and Incentives

Civil servants at the highest level have to actively support efforts to fight corruption and to consistently train newcomers to respect the ethical rules of the administration. Organizations should seek to formulate a new code of ethics with the help and involvement of every employee. All newly appointed top-level civil servants should sign a declaration of intent to uphold the principles in the code. Only then can a gradual change be achieved. Middle-level civil servants should be encouraged to fight corruption in the lower ranks of the administration by a consistent rewards policy. Top-level civil servants themselves should guard the ethical standards in the middle ranks of the administration. Opposing elements should be identified, isolated and, if they cannot be convinced to change, dismissed. This change in administrative mentality cannot come about if the employment conditions of civil servants are not dramatically improved. Job security should be granted and civil servants given appropriate financial support to meet new employment criteria. Most importantly, salaries should be increased.

Conclusion

Only an inclusive approach, built on a combination of several of the measures highlighted here, is likely to lead to a reversal of the current trend of increasing corruption in Central and Eastern Europe. The complex causes of corruption in the region, with the intertwining of traditional causes and transition-related causes, make it difficult to develop a watertight approach in combating corruption. Furthermore, normalization of economic and political conditions in the region remains the key condition for any anticorruption initiatives to succeed in the long term, and this condition is unlikely to be fulfilled soon in a large number of states in the region. The worrying trend of economic decline in parts of the region and the ensuing political insecurity mean that corruption is likely to remain a problem for the region, evidenced by the somewhat defeatist attitudes currently shown in Russia where, as noted in the *Washington Post Weekly*,

Scientists [have] pleaded with Putin to do something about corruption in the customs service, whose employees regularly compel scientific institutes to pay bribes they cannot afford for the delivery of important supplies and instruments purchased abroad.

"It's impossible to do anything," Putin replied . . . "The customs service is too criminalized." (23 October 2000, 22)

The situation may not be as bad elsewhere in the region although the situation in Ukraine and possibly Belarus is still described as being where "public-spiritedness is weak, corruption rampant, the press docile" (*Economist* 20 January 2001, 43) and where public protests have mostly fizzled. However, as countries seeking to enter the European Union must first reduce their corruption, some improvement can be expected in them, thereby creating pressures to conform elsewhere in the region.

References

Dimitrova, A. and Verheijen, T. 1998. In *Professionalization of public servants in Central and Eastern Europe*. Bratislava: NISPAcee.

Dubenbaev, A. 2000. Political-administrative relations. Paper presented at the 8th NISPAcee Conference, 13–15 April, Budapest.

Holmes, L. 1993. *The end of Communist power*. Oxford: Blackwell Publishers.

Hosking, G. 1979. *History of the Soviet Union*. London: Fontana.

Jabes, J. 1998. *Professionalization of public servants in Central and Eastern Europe*. Bratislava: NISPAcee.

Jowett, K. 1993. The new world disorder. In *The global resurgence of democracy*, edited by L. Diamond, and M. Plattner. Baltimore, Md.: Johns Hopkins University Press.

Linz, J. and A. Stephan. 1996. Toward consolidated democracies. *Journal of Democracy* 7 (2).

Mihailescu, I. 1993, "Mental Stereotypes in the First Years of Post-Totalitarian Romania," *Government and Opposition* 28 (3): 315–24.

Naim, M. 1995. The corruption eruption. *The Brown Journal of Public Affairs* 2 (2).

Offe, C. 1991. Capitalism by democratic design. *Social Research* 58 (4): 865–92.

Schopflin. 1991. Post Communism: Constructing new democracies in central Europe. *International Affairs* 67 (2): 235–50.

Verheijen, T. and A. Dimitrova. 1996. Private interest and public administration. *International Review of Administrative Sciences* 62 (2): 197–218.

Zielonka. 1994. New institutions in the old east bloc. *Journal of Democracy* 2 (2): 87–104.

7

Corruption and the Lack of Accountability in the Middle East

Joseph G. Jabbra and Nancy W. Jabbra

THE GROWTH OF GOVERNMENT activities in the Middle East after independence was accompanied by an increase in the size and importance of bureaucracy. With full control over the public purse, the state in that part of the world became responsible for charting social and economic development policies and for running the bureaucracy required for their implementation. The challenge of Middle Eastern bureaucracies to transform societies rapidly from traditional to modern entities has contributed to their size and vested them with an intense concentration of powers. In turn, their size and acquired powers have increased the opportunity for corruption, unethical conduct, and misuse of public office for personal profit—thus the need to establish appropriate safeguards and proper checks and balances to protect Middle Eastern societies from bureaucratic abuses.

One way of doing so is to ensure that in carrying out their official responsibilities, Middle Eastern public servants are accountable for their actions and behavior. It is the duty of public servants to answer and account for their actions and behavior when requested by their superiors and other entitled people, in accordance with legitimate rules and regulations governing their position. Thus, accountability in the public service becomes a fundamental prerequisite for preventing the abuse of delegated power, for ensuring its direction toward the achievement of national goals, and for implementing government policies efficiently, effectively, prudently, and with probity (Royal Commission on Financial Management 1979, 21).

Sample Formal Accountability Mechanisms

A preliminary and formal examination of Middle Eastern public bureaucracies reveals two kinds of control mechanisms relating directly to the principle of accountability. The first is internal and governed by the pyramidal structure of the bureaucracy whereby each administrative layer is accountable to the next higher one. The second is external and comprises political, administrative, juridical, and nonofficial watchdogs that strive to make sure the bureaucracy is accountable, efficient, productive, and not corrupt.

Egypt

Government departments and central agencies in Egypt are accountable to their ministers. In turn, the ministers are accountable individually to the cabinet and collectively to the national assembly for the actions and behavior of public employees working within their ministries. In reality, the cabinet is responsible to the president of Egypt, whose office wields enormous powers. Cabinet committees and central agencies monitor the accountability of public employees. Ministerial committees coordinate and account for the execution of public policy in planning, legislation, organization and administration, economic affairs, human resources, and local administration. Independent central and control agencies (for example, the Central Agency for Training, the Central Agency for Organization and Administration, the Central Auditing Agency, and so forth) perform the same functions (Ayubi 1980, 200). Administrative vigilance is also provided by the Council of State, the Administrative Parquet Department, the Administrative Inspection Department, the Ministry of State Department, and the Secretariat of the President.

The Council of State, established in 1946, is the supreme administrative court. Patterned after the French Council of State, it consists of a judicial section and a consultative section on administrative regulations and their interpretation. Created in 1954, the Administrative Parquet Department oversees procedures of control and investigation of administrative violations and hears complaints and calls for disciplinary action against public officials. The Administrative Inspection department inspects the work of public officials and ensures the proper application of laws and the correction of any errors in administrative, technical, or financial procedures. Finally, the General Secretariat of the Presidency serves as a channel of communication and liaison between the president's office and the various ministries and is directly involved in administrative control activities (Metz 1991, 229–60).

Iran

The 1979 postrevolutionary constitution stipulates that the president's office holds the highest official power next to that of the Faqih, the just and pious jurist, recognized by the majority of the people as best qualified to lead the nation. In effect, the president is the head of the state in this Islamic republic. He must be a Shiite Muslim and a man of political and religious distinction. He appoints the ministers who are confirmed by the Legislative Assembly, heads the Council of Ministers, supervises the work of his ministers, and coordinates the decisions of the government (Articles 133 and 134). The president and his cabinet are responsible and accountable for the activities of the Iranian public service, the establishment and implementation of government policies, and the execution of the country's laws. The Iranian Legislative Assembly has the right to question the president or any individual minister about policies, and the president is required to appear before the Legislative Assembly within one month of the request; ministers must appear within ten days (Articles 88 and 89). If the deputies are dissatisfied with the information given during such questioning, they may request the Majlis to schedule a vote of confidence on the performance of the minister or the government as a whole. The constitution also provides for the Council of Guardians, which is charged with examining all legislation passed by Parliament to ensure that it conforms to Islamic law. Article 156 of the constitution provides for an independent judiciary (Metz 1989, 195–203).

Israel

The separation of powers between the executive and legislative branches in the Israeli political system generally follows the British model. While the president is the titular head of state, the cabinet is the top executive policy-making body and the center of political power in the nation. The cabinet consists of the prime minister and an unspecified number of ministers. The cabinet takes office upon confirmation by the Knesset (legislature), to which it is collectively accountable for all its acts. The prime minister's resignation results in the resignation of the entire cabinet but resignations of individual ministers do not have this effect. Cabinet posts are divided among coalition partners through behind-the-scenes bargaining, and a strict merit system regulates the recruitment, appointment, promotion, transfer, termination, training, and discipline of government employees. Civil servants, especially in the senior grades, are prohibited from engaging in partisan politics by the civil service law of 1959.

The Israeli civil service is headed by a commissioner (appointed by the Cabinet and directly accountable to the minister of finance) who has full responsibility for all personnel matters. In practice, these matters are left to the discretion of the various ministries. Israeli civil servants automatically belong to the Civil Service Union whose agreement is required for conditions of government employment.

The Knesset supervises and provides direction for the government. It has the power to approve budget allocations, question cabinet ministers, provide a public forum for debate of government-related issues, and conduct a wide range of administrative inquiries. It reviews government policies and supervises the activities of Israeli public servants through the office of the state controller (who is also the ombudsman), which is completely independent of the government and is accountable to the Knesset alone. In exercising supervisory responsibilities, the state controller checks on the legality, regularity, efficiency, economy, and ethical conduct of public institutions. The checks are performed by continuous spot inspections of the financial accounts and activities of all ministries, the armed forces and security services, local government bodies, and all organizations subsidized or managed by the state (Metz 1990, 179–99).

Lebanon

Ministers are accountable for their departments to the cabinet, which in turn is accountable to Parliament collectively and individually for the bureaucracy. Members of Parliament are required to monitor the bureaucracy and apply pressure on the cabinet to account for and explain any irregularities in the behavior of public servants. Such parliamentary pressure serves to bring about much needed administrative reforms. Administrative watchdogs play a similar role. For example, the Civil Service Commission (created in 1959) is in charge of developing and maintaining a strong, capable, and accountable civil service; its responsibilities include equipment, training, promotion, transfers, and retirement matters. In addition, it hears complaints from civil servants in relation to transfer requests and disciplinary matters involving penalty or dismissal.

The Central Inspection Administration (created in 1961) sets and administers inspection policies aimed at improving procedures, reducing costs, and increasing efficiency. Its jurisdiction extends over all divisions of the administration. The Council of State serves as a court of appeal and *cassation* for administrative cases assigned by a special law to other courts. In 1965, a general disciplinary council for public officials was established to deal with all administrative infractions, again with certain exceptions. Finally, open hearings, interest groups, and organized citizens' participation and pressure attempt to keep public servants accountable and prevent them from using their public office for personal gain (Collelo 1989).

Saudi Arabia

The King exercises his supervision and control of the Saudi bureaucracy through the Council of Ministers and his private offices. The Council of Ministers (established in 1953), a powerful, central, and dynamic institution, is responsible to the King for all its activities and those of the bureaucracy that serves as its agent. Central and independent agencies are accountable directly to the king. Although their heads possess ministerial powers, they do not normally participate in the deliberations of the Council of Ministers. The following will serve as illustrations: The Civil Service Board, established in 1977, attends to civil service matters (for example, personnel, salary, position classification) in all ministries, public agencies, and corporations, and strives to ensure accountability and high quality performance among public employees (Al Mazrua 1980, 290).

The General Bureau of the Civil Service reports to the Civil Service Board and has a mandate to enhance the accountability and efficiency of Saudi public servants. It supervises closely the execution of civil service laws, regulations, and resolutions and carries out research, especially in the area of position classification, compensation, allowances, and awards. The Institute of Public Administration (created in 1971) provides training for Saudi public servants and enhances their accountability. The High Committee for Administrative Reform (established in 1963) spearheads administrative reform, reorganizes existing government agencies, creates new departments, and develops new and effective work systems and methods to improve efficiency and accountability among Saudi public servants (Al Mazrua 1980, 327–33).

The Central Department for Organization and Management (established in 1966) is mandated to foster efficiency and effectiveness in the Saudi public service, make Saudi public servants accountable for their actions and behavior, monitor the execution of reform recommendations adopted by the High Committee for Administrative Reform, and initiate needed administrative development. Finally, the Grievance Board, created in 1954, represents an extension of the traditional practice of direct accessibility to the king by any citizen who has a grievance against the bureaucracy (Al Ghamdi 1982, 142–44; Metz 1993, 191–204).

Turkey

The Turkish Constitution of 1982 provides for the accountability and integrity of the administrative process. Article II stipulates that the Republic of Turkey is a "[d]emocratic, secular, and social state governed by the rule of law." The constitution divides the powers of the state among the three branches of government and vests executive authority in the president as head of state whose responsibility is to ensure the normal functioning of government. The Council of Ministers (Cabinet) joins in equal responsibility for the implementation of public policy and for the actions of subordinates. The 1982 constitution guarantees judicial independence and prohibits any government agency or individual from interfering with the operations of the courts and judges. It also establishes Turkey's centralized administrative system. Since the early years of the Turkish republic the public bureaucracy has played an important role in politics (Metz 1996, 236–51).

Obstacles to Accountable Bureaucracy

The above brief description of the formal structure of government in the Middle East suggests that accountability prevails in public transactions and that public bureaucracies therefore are corruption-free. But a more detailed and systematic analysis shows that despite the existence of formal control mechanisms, accountability does not fare well among Middle Eastern public servants. In fact, two types of obstacles thwart formal control mechanisms intended to promote accountability and integrity in bureaucracy: administrative and structural, and sociocultural and behavioral.

Administrative and Structural

Overcentralization   Overcentralization of administrative structure and overconcentration of authority characterize the bureaucracies of the overwhelming majority of Middle Eastern countries. First, dictatorial superiors and top managers are usually associated with passive subordinates. Second, the large span of control and lengthy lines of command cause loose control and distortion of orders. Third, subordinates rely to excess on their superiors and send them minor administrative problems for resolution; as a consequence, senior public servants become occupied by administrative minutiae instead of spending their time on more important matters. This results in, fourth, underemployment of subordinates and underutilization of their talents. Fifth, citizens waste time and money by having to travel to crowded offices in order to finalize their transactions. Finally, influence peddling and corruption tend to thrive in such an environment.

The Egyptian administrative system, for example, is heavily centralized, with authority concentrated in the hands of top bureaucrats. In fact, centralization in government organizations became the preferred Egyptian solution for any problem of coordination. Egyptian officials are always trying to concentrate more power in their own hands through all means available, not excluding hypocrisy, bribery, backbiting, double-dealing, and deception. Palmer, Yassin, and Leila (1985, 323–37) concluded that the sources of centralization in the Egyptian bureaucracy were rooted both in the pragmatic realities of bureaucratic life and in the broader dimension of Egyptian culture. Similar illustrations exist in many other Middle Eastern countries including Lebanon and Saudi Arabia (Metz 1996, 64).

Outmoded Systems   A major obstacle to accountability in Middle Eastern bureaucracies has been outmoded systems and procedures and outdated technical and physical facilities, resulting in an unsystematic flow of information, poor coordination, lack of comprehensive planning, difficulty of control and supervision, red tape, and inefficiency—all providing an environment conducive to corruption, misuse and abuse of power. In many of them, outmoded technical systems and procedures are still being used in financial administration and program training. Typewriters, calculators, and computers are not always available, and physical and storage facilities are substandard. Government buildings lack central heating and adequate lighting and furnishings. The offices of many directorates are dispersed throughout the capital city, contributing to low morale among public servants and making supervision and accountability difficult to enforce and acts of corruption easy to commit (Ayubi 1982, 292).

Even wealthy Saudi Arabia has not been able to overcome such difficulties or establish satisfactory antibureaucratic corruption measures. Experts have continued to complain about the lack of science and technology, management by objectives, scientific management, and organizational development (Al-Khaldi 1983, 44–45). Moreover, working conditions, filing systems, office layouts, maintenance services, and typing and copying facilities are still inadequate. Lengthy, cumbersome, and outdated procedures continue to hamper the normal flow of work and do not encourage efficiency and accountability (Al-Hegelan 1984, 12). Even in recruitment, the methods used to advertise positions are inadequate and ineffective: Often vacancies are not advertised at all and even when they are, they do not specify qualifications or duties and responsibilities; the same applies to entrance examinations and assessment for transfers and promotions (Binsaleh 1982, 130). This situation points to a serious lack of accountability and nurtures an unhealthy environment conducive to patronage, nepotism, and bribery.

Expansion   Expansion of the bureaucracy need not lead to a lack of accountability of public servants. In fact, it can be a logical consequence of government's
increasing involvement in providing more services to society. But the emergence of the state in the post–World War II era as the chief employer in developing countries caused a rapid, unexpected, and unplanned expansion of the
bureaucracy, which hampered the development of a strong sense of accountability and integrity among public servants. The situation made proper control,
coordination, and supervision extremely difficult to achieve; it also caused overstaffing and underemployment, lack of clearly defined lines of responsibility,
and in some cases lack of qualified personnel, all leading to instances of serious
bureaucratic corruption. Control, coordination, and planning have been inadequate (Al-Sadhan 1980, 80). As a result, a total state of confusion would at
times cripple public agencies and departments, bringing administrative transactions to a standstill and further increasing opportunities for corruption (Ayubi
1982, 326).

Overstaffing   Overlapping and lack of qualified personnel as a result of overstaffing do not form a good environment for the development of accountability
among public servants. On the contrary, they encourage corruption and abuse
of power. Promotion policy has contributed significantly to overstaffing, with
promotions made annually between ranks regardless of whether there were
vacancies for those promoted. Overstaffing results from the steady pressure on
the government to provide employment for university graduates and from the
bargaining attitude of top officials, who exaggerate their personnel needs in
order to increase their prestige and opportunities for promotion. According to
Ayubi (1980, 247), sectoral and geographic overstaffing contributes to bureaucratic inflation, idleness, cynicism, and disguised unemployment in Middle
Eastern bureaucracies and thus creates a hostile environment for accountability among public servants. The government of Saudi Arabia has approached
this problem in three ways. First, it began hiring non-Saudis, largely from the
Arab countries; second, the Institute of Public Administration trained public
employees. Third, and most seriously, it tried to substitute for the lack of qualified personnel by overstaffing government offices with people who did not have
the proper training to serve the public responsibly. The problem has been further compounded by a mismatch between the qualifications of public employees and the requirements of their positions. Overstaffing has been exaggerated
by frequent overlap and duplication of administrative responsibilities (Binsaleh
1982, 24; Al Khaldi 1983, 193).

Rigidity and Complexity of Rules   Public servants subject to rigid and complex rules seldom take initiatives, nor can they be accountable for their actions and behavior. In the bureaucracy of Lebanon, rigidity stems from overcentralization of authority and a legalistic approach to administrative decision making and procedures that does not allow much room for innovation. In fact, rigidity has led to a tendency among Lebanese public servants to avoid responsibility, especially when faced with new problems not foreseen and regulated by law. Similarly, the laws governing bureaucratic behavior in Egypt and Iran have been rigid and confusing (Attrabi 1982; Murad 1983, 31). The Saudi bureaucracy also has suffered from rigidity and complex rules and regulations. Matters have been subjected to lengthy and time-consuming procedures involving the approval of several officials, each of whom may go through a similar exercise. The concept of accountability has been mostly ignored in Saudi bureaucracy so that its officials have tended to be cautious, rigid, and routinized (Al-Ghamdi 1982, 286; Al Hegelan 1984, 12; Alnimir and Palmer 1982, 93–104).

Salary Structure and Turnover   One of the most sensitive and complicated issues in public personnel administration is salary structure and turnover. It has a direct effect on an employee's efficiency, accountability, integrity, and moral conduct. It also influences the government's ability to recruit and maintain qualified, accountable personnel. For example, the low salary structure for public employees in Lebanon has always led to two serious results: first, competent people receive more attractive salary offers from the private sector and avoid or leave public service; second, those who join or stay are afflicted with low morale and forced to look for other sources of income (including bribery) to compensate for their low salaries. Automatic salary increases that have been granted indiscriminately and not on merit are another major contributor to employees' unwillingness to work harder or to show more innovation and accountability in carrying out their responsibilities. Salaries for Egyptian bureaucrats have been low and the relative deprivation of Egyptian bureaucrats has produced in many officials an obsession with obtaining higher salaries. Despite improvements in the compensation scale for Saudi public servants, the problem of inadequate salaries continues to contribute greatly to the problems of turnover and low standards of personal integrity in the Saudi public service. Rising expectations, rapid social transformations, as well as economic and inflationary pressures continue to tempt government employees to seek different sources of income by going into business or joining corporations and doubling their salaries. Low salaries and rising expectations lead to laxity in moral standards and personal integrity, and to corruption, graft, and profiteering.

Sociocultural and Behavioral

Traditional customs, attitudes, and behaviors that are deeply embedded in Middle Eastern society and that may affect public service accountability negatively and lead to corruption include nepotism and favoritism, patron-client relationships, corruption, avoidance of responsibility, and lack of adequate training.

Nepotism and Favoritism   The family continues to rival the state as the focal point of loyalty and security in Lebanon, Egypt, Saudi Arabia, Iran, Turkey, Iraq, and Israel. In fact, accountability to one's family often takes precedence over accountability to the state and thus leads to the practice of nepotism and corruption. Moreover, loyalty to the family is paralleled by a strong devotion to one's village and friends, thus leading to favoritism. Neither nepotism nor favoritism is conducive to accountability and integrity among Middle Eastern public servants. For example, family, friendship, and geographical ties among Lebanese bureaucrats are strong. Especially in the case of less qualified employees, nepotism was a major hindrance to the principle of accountability; bureaucrats who owed their appointments to family or friends were likely to delay, derail, or obstruct regular administrative procedures in order to repay their debt. Moreover, because of loyalty to family, the Saudi public servant, for example, practiced nepotism and was partial in assigning jobs and distributing benefits.

The Patron-Client Relationship   Unethical, corrupt, and irresponsible practices in the bureaucracy may result from a strong patron-client system. In the Middle East as well as in most developing countries where identification with the national community and its laws is still weak, protection is sought outside the family through ties with powerful protectors or patrons (Jabbra and Jabbra 1983, 133). This system of relationships has encouraged the development and institutionalization of attitudes of disrespect for accountability and integrity among Middle Eastern bureaucrats and their clients. Patron-client relationships, patronage, and influence go hand in hand with corrupt and unethical conduct and "indicate a very poorly developed social conscience for which personal profit and private loyalty take precedence over public duty" (Vankatappiah 1968, 275). Many examples still abound throughout the Middle East.

Laxity and Avoidance of Responsibility   In the past, Lebanese bureaucrats often came to work late, showed little interest in their jobs, went home early, and took maximum advantage of loose regulations affecting leave with pay. In addition, laxity characterized the upper levels of the bureaucracy. Although top bureaucrats were expected to be leaders and pacesetters, their behavior did not much differ from that of their subordinates, except that they signed more documents. The same was true in Egypt. Although some public servants were committed to their jobs, the attitude of the majority toward hard work was lax. Egyptian public servants arrived late and by noon many of them were getting ready to go home (Ayubi 1982, 299). Moreover, a significant number did not go to work at all, and few higher officials were punctual. When at work, Egyptian public servants seemed to do everything other than attend to their jobs (Ayubi 1980, 293). Obviously there was little accountability in this context and few seemed to care much. While supervisors vied to concentrate more power in their hands, subordinates tended to shun responsibility and send all transactions to their superiors for clearance, thereby avoiding responsibility and refusing to settle conflicts or take risks (Palmer, Yassin, and Leila 1985, 331–33). More responsibility meant more work. The situation was not much different in Saudi Arabia (Al Khaldi 1983, 95–96; Alnimir 1982, 95). Public servants, in general, lacked enthusiasm and the desire to innovate. Their avoidance of responsibility was clearly illustrated by their unwillingness to move to areas where their skills were most needed and their unwillingness to work at least temporarily in an uncomfortable rural environment. They were dissatisfied with the salary structure and were often fatalistic.

Lack of Accountability and Corruption

Because it means the use of public office for personal gain, corruption can flourish among public servants in the Middle East if accountability and integrity are lacking. Corruption in many Middle Eastern countries has been reinforced by a weak commitment to the public interest and the common good; changing economic status of public servants, which makes their salaries insufficient to satisfy their rising expectations and love of ostentation; a confusing network of government institutions and regulations; and an oversupply of graduates seeking a limited number of available positions, thus opening the door for bribes. All these factors have given public servants a golden opportunity to cultivate the art of bribery and corruption by systematically using public office to promote and protect their private interests.

For example, although it has been difficult to collect hard facts about corruption in Saudi Arabia, one could identify several factors that accounted for its prevalence (Alnimir 1982, 93–104). First, the Saudis' public spirit and loyalty to the public interest was weak because of their commitment to parochial and particularistic values. Saudi public servants were expected to use their public position to maximize their personal interest. "It is in keeping with old practice in the area for officials at all levels to take advantage of their position to enrich themselves. Those that do not do so would be regarded as stupid and eccentric" (Lipski 1959, 178). Second, Saudi public servants were overimpressed by the achievements of their counterparts in Europe and North America. Their rising expectations about consumer goods caused many Saudi public servants to seek extra financial resources by methods not sanctioned by law. Third, overcentralization of authority in the hands of a few officials also facilitated corruption. The lack of an effective system of control and supervision and the lack of accountability made corruption easy. In the early 1960s, the government of Saudi Arabia, in an effort to control corruption, issued a form titled "Where did you get this?" on which government employees were to list all their property so that the government could compare their income with their holdings. Unfortunately no one bothered either to fill out the forms or to collect them, and the regulation was forgotten. Similar illustrations can be found in Lebanon, Egypt, Iran, Iraq, Jordan, and Morocco. While there have been reforms since then, not much has changed, as any reading of Middle Eastern daily newspapers indicates.

New Process of Socialization

This analysis and specific illustrations sustain the premise that lack of accountability and integrity among public servants in Middle Eastern countries is a major source of corruption that imposes a heavy financial burden on them and hinders their economic, social, and political development. Above all, it stifles the growth of bureaucratic integrity and professionalism that are sorely needed in those countries. For accountability to prevail in the bureaucracies of the Middle East, the obstacles to its implementation must be eliminated. Their elimination is based upon the understanding that they are imbedded in the social settings of Middle Eastern bureaucracies. Thus, the relationship that binds bureaucracies to their social settings makes it difficult to reform the former without changing the latter.

A truly accountable and corruption-free public service in the Middle East will be attained only when the bureaucratic behavior patterns shown in this chapter to be antagonistic to accountability are greatly modified. Since these patterns are rooted in and nourished by the general social setting within which the public service has to operate, reform measures must be directed at guiding a new socialization process—involving the family, peer groups, secondary groups, and the mass media—among the public at large and within the civil service through a well-thought-out code of conduct focused on upholding the law, objectivity, fairness, impartiality, efficiency, and effectiveness, and avoidance of unethical practices and conflict of interest. Along with establishing a code of ethics, Middle Eastern governments must strive to pay their public servants adequate salaries, lest they be tempted to use unethical practices to supplement their low wages. Governments also must establish sanctions commensurate with breaches of the code of ethics, publicize these sanctions, and implement them swiftly and impartially when either citizens or bureaucrats are at fault. In commenting on the visit of Secretary of State Colin Powell to the Middle East in February 2001, political scientist Augustus Norton of Boston University remarked, "Millions of people in the Middle East hate their governments because they are corrupt, unresponsive and are not meeting the basic needs of the population in virtually every country . . . People do want to walk into a government office and meet with responsive officials whom they don't have to bribe with half their salaries" (*Los Angeles Times* 24 February 2001, A8).

References

Abdo-Khalil, Zeinab M. 1983. Public sector administration in Egypt. Ph.D. diss., Claremont Graduate School, Los Angeles.

Al-Ghamdi, Abdullah A. 1982. Action research and the dynamics of organizational environment in the kingdom of Saudi Arabia. Ph.D. diss., University of Southern California.

Al-Hegelan, Abdulrahman Abdelaziz. 1984. Innovation in the Saudi Arabian bureaucracy: A survey analysis of senior bureaucrats. Ph.D. diss., Florida State University.

Al-Khaldi, Abdullah M. 1983. Job content and content factors related to satisfaction in three occupational levels of the public sector in Saudi Arabia. Ph.D. diss., Florida State University.

Al-Mazrua, Suliman A. 1980. Public administration trends and prospects in the context of development in Saudi Arabia. Ph.D. diss., Claremont Graduate School, Los Angeles.

Alnimir, Saud Mohammed. 1981. Present and future bureaucrats in Saudi Arabia: A survey research." Ph.D. diss., Florida State University.

Alnimir, Saud and P. Palmer. 1982. Bureaucracy and development in Saudi Arabia: A behavioral analysis. *Public Administration and Development* 2 (1): 97–98.

Al-Sadhan, Abdulrahman M. 1980. The modernization of the Saudi bureaucracy. In *King Faisal and the Modernization of Saudi Arabia*, edited by Wellard E. Belwig. Boulder, Colo.: Westview Press.

Attrabi, H. A. 1982. *Egypt, Problems and Solutions*. [Arabic] Cairo: Madbouli.

Ayubi, Nazih M. N. 1980 Bureaucracy and politics in contemporary Egypt. London: Ithaca Press.

———. 1982. Bureaucratic inflation and administrative efficiency. *Middle Eastern Studies* 18 (3): 18–19.

Binsaleh, Abdullah Mohammed. 1982. The civil service and its regulation in the king-
    dom of Saudi Arabia. Ph.D. diss. Claremont Graduate School, Los Angeles.

Chackerian, Richard, and Suliman Shadukhi. 1983. Public bureaucracy in Saudi Arabia:
    An empirical assessment of work group behavior. *International Review of Administrative
    Sciences* 49 (3): 319–22.

Collelo, Thomas. 1989. *Lebanon, a country study.* Washington, D.C.: Department of the
    Army.

Jabbra, Joseph G. 1976. Bureaucratic Corruption: Causes and remedy. *Indian Journal of
    Public Administration* 4 (4): 673–91

Jabbra, Joseph G. and Nancy W. Jabbra. 1983. Public service ethics in the third world: A
    comparative perspective. In *Ethics in the Public Service: Comparative Perspectives,* edited
    by Kenneth Kernaghan and O. P. Dwivedi. Brussels: International Institute of Admin-
    istrative Services.

Lipsky, G. A. 1959. *Saudi Arabia: Its People, Its Society, Its Culture.* New Haven, Conn.: HRAF.

Metz, Helen, ed. 1989. *Iran: A country study.* Washington, D.C., Government Printing
    Office.

——. 1990. *Israel: A country study.* Washington D.C.: Government Printing Office.

——. 1991. *Egypt: A country study.* Washington D.C.: Government Printing Office.

——. 1991. *Jordan: A country study.* Washington, D.C.: Government Printing Office.

——. 1993. *Saudi Arabia: A country study.* Lanham Md.: Bernan Press.

——. 1996. *Turkey: A country study,* fifth ed. Lanham, Md.: Bernan Press.

Murad, Magdi Wahba. 1983. The Egyptian public sector: The control structure and effi-
    ciency considerations. *Public Administration and Development* 3 (1).

Palmer, Monte, El-Sayeed Yasin, and Ali Leila. 1985. Bureaucratic flexibility and devel-
    opment in Egypt. *Public Administration and Development* 5 (4).

Royal Commission on Financial Management and Accountability Final Report. 1979.
    Ottawa, Ont., Canada.

Tawati, Ahmad Mohamed. 1976. Civil service of Saudi Arabia: Problems and prospects.
    Ph.D. diss. West Virginia University.

Vankatappiah, B. 1968. Misuse of Office. In *International encyclopedia of the social sciences,*
    11.

8

Governance and Corruption in West Africa

Dele Olowu

CONSIDERABLE NEW INSIGHTS have been gained into the nature and forms of corruption in West Africa since the first studies appeared in the early 1960s. Initially, research on corruption in African countries generally and in West Africa especially tended to focus on petty corruption by individual civil servants. Later, it included the political forms of corruption by politicians and ruling parties. By the 1990s, research on corruption in this region highlighted the universal nature of corruption in the public, private, and even civil society organs. It also highlighted the critical difference between institutionalized, grand corruption orchestrated by the heads of states and petty corruption by the majority of the poorly paid public officials. The latter was the first to receive attention but in the last two decades, there is a better understanding of the relationships between these two forms of corruption and a clearer appreciation of which is the chicken and which is the egg (Johnston 1992; Caiden 1992; Bayart 1993; Moody-Smart 1997; Chabal and Daloz 1999).

This chapter focuses on institutionalized forms of corruption in West Africa and links it to current and ongoing research on governance improvement in the region. Governance patterns reflect different degrees of state institutionalization in the region, and the degree of state institutionalization and legitimation constitute indicators of institutionalized corruption in countries of the West African subregion. This is based on the assumption that the state is a moral agency with specific goals that it pursues on behalf of society. If so, then it is possible to focus on states at different stages of state institutionalization in the subregion to illustrate the argument. Four case studies have been selected in the subregion: Sierra Leone and Nigeria under Abacha, and Ghana and Nigeria under their current civilian administrations.

Context

This chapter begins by exploring the extent to which a relationship exists between the degree of state institutionalization and governance quality as defined by institutionalized forms of corruption. According to Transparency International, countries in the region seem to be more corrupt than Africa's other regions, with Nigeria and Cameroons considered the world's worst. Initially, research on corruption in West Africa took on a moralistic tone, but it took on cultural, economic, and institutional dimensions as other parts of the continent were included (Ekpo 1979; Rasheed and Olowu 1993; Hope and Chiculo 2000). Only with the relatively recent revival and popularization of the concept of governance has it begun to dawn on researchers that there might be a relationship between the processes of state formation and institutionalized forms of corruption rife in the region and in many other African countries (Chabal and Daloz 1997).

Modern state formation in Africa predated colonialism but the colonial experience refashioned and redirected that process. To that extent, state formation is a relatively recent phenomenon, dating back to the end of the Second World War. In fact, the first sub-Saharan African (SAA) independent state only attained political independence in 1956. Understandably, these states lack critical state attributes. Some scholars stress power (coercive capacity), authority (the legitimizing capacity), and participation (responsiveness capacity) attributes while others focus on state autonomy from internal and external actors (Almond and Powell 1966; Ottaway 1999). Migdal (1988) integrates these into four key capabilities: (1) societal penetration—capacity to implement state rules and policies over the whole territorial space, (2) societal regulation—capacity to regulate social relationships, (3) extractive capacity—ability to extract resources from citizens and (4) allocative capacity—ability to authoritatively and intelligently allocate resources in a way that enhances the respect and legitimacy of the state. The absence of these attributes means that a state's capacity to govern—exercise the authority to actualize societal goals—is limited. The poor socioeconomic performance of many countries in SSA has been blamed on bad governance: "Underlying the litany of Africa's development problems is a crisis of governance. Because countervailing power has been lacking, state officials in many countries have served their own interests without fear of being called to account" (World Bank 1989, 60).

Governance is taken to mean the quality of the fundamental rules of politics that regulate the relationship between the rulers and the ruled. Good rules promote cooperation among individuals and groups in society to achieve societal goals. Bad rules discourage such efforts or activities. Good governance can therefore be deemed to exist where and when the quality of the rules encourages cooperation, healthy competition, and contracting among individuals and institutions in the realization of societal goals (Ostrom 1990). If corruption is defined as the departure from the norms of good governance, no state could officially condone or promote corruption. The ability of a country to tackle corruption is a function of two crucial factors, namely, the effectiveness of its anticorruption strategies and the determination of the political leadership to pursue anticorruption activities (Quah 1999). But even these are products of state institutionalization.

During the 1990s, African countries began to put in place governance improvement programs aimed at ensuring that state power was used to promote public rather than the private interests of those who wielded power. Such governance improvement efforts can be viewed as forms of anticorruption strategies. Four of these strategies will be studied: democratization, decentralization, public sector reforms (with special focus on privatization, and wage reform), and the creation or revitalization of anticorruption agencies.

Institutionalized corruption is the result of weak institutionalization of the state in Africa. Besides promoting networks of patronage politics, weak institutionalization also results in the emergence of shadow states. In such states, competition for power often takes place outside the state rules and most of these activities—involving those who wield power as well as those excluded from power—constitute forms of institutionalized corruption. It is therefore possible to classify countries by the extent to which state systems are institutionalized. The greater the degree of state institutionalization, the higher the level of good governance and the less the degree of institutionalized corruption, and vice-versa. Three types of countries are recognized. The first model includes states that are very weakly institutionalized. These are states in which the top political leadership uses the apparatus of the state to seek personal rather than public goals. In moderately institutionalized states, these attributes would be more nuanced. Finally, in highly institutionalized states, the leadership would attack all forms of corruption on a bold front. Sierra Leone and Nigeria under the military (especially the Abacha era) are used as examples of Model 1 (uninstitutionalized state), Ghana under Rawlings (both as military and civilian leader) is Model 2 (partially uninstitutionalized state), and Nigeria under its current civilian regime is classified as closer to Model 3 (fully institutionalized). These are not pure types. It is instructive that Nigeria is included under two models. This underscores the close linkage between state institutionalization and regime characteristics and also highlights the possibility of a country moving from one model to another depending on the actions and activities of its political leadership and the response of nonstate actors (Hyden and Bratton

1992). The three countries—Ghana, Nigeria and Sierra Leone—are all former
British colonies and share a common British governance heritage.

Model 1: Sierra Leone as a Shadow State

Sierra Leone, independent in 1961, early enjoyed a robust Westminster-
type democracy of government and opposition but it rapidly became a shadow
state when the military struck and a countercoup was needed to restore the
democratic process. President Siaka Stevens systematically destroyed democratic
institutions and imposed presidential one-party rule.

... The All People's Congress foisted a very corrupt, greedy and exploitative ruling class
on the people and in the process, also ensured their unprecedented impoverishment ...
By the time the APC was overthrown in 1992, it had subjected the people to twenty-seven
years of misrule, economic mismanagement, unprecedented hunger, diseases, ignorance
and of course, a delibitating civil war. . . . One of the most enduring legacies of the APC
and its cronies was the acceptance of corruption as a way of life by the rank and file in
the country. Corruption was elevated to a national way of life . . . (Sesay 1999, 300).

President Stevens used money and an elaborate network of secret services to
instill fear in the people and to undermine the country's once vibrant economy.
He manipulated the parliament and the constitution to handpick his inexperi-
enced successor, Joseph Momoh, so that Stevens and his cronies could enjoy
their wealth without the possibility of reprisal.

Momoh was overthrown by a military coup of young army officers who came
to protest the nonpayment of their salaries. The systemic corruption that characterized governance in Sierra Leone has been extensively researched (Riley
1983; Kpundeh 1995; Reno 1995). Widespread corruption in the public sector
was indeed responsible for the country's economic decline. The country's many
scandals—kilowatt (1974/1975), vouchergate (1982), milliongate (1984)—were
well documented, as were the activities of illegal diamond miners in collusion
with government authorities (Kpundeh 2000; Reno 1999). It was therefore no
surprise that the military took over in 1992.

But the story of Sierra Leone's first coup is itself a lesson in state failure.
Misrule under Stevens and Momoh had not only left Sierra Leone destitute, it
had transformed it into a country in which practically all forms of state attributes were poorly formed. The country's rich resources—diamonds, rutile,
and others—were mined illegally by groups of adventurers who contracted
with local patrons, in collusion with state actors who benefited tremendously
from such deals. These effectively created a shadow state that has haunted

Sierra Leone for much of its postindependence history. These gangs of commercial operators had sponsored parallel state structures that mined and traded in diamonds outside the state. Senior government officials were also deeply involved in this for their personal, rather than state or public interests. The result was continuing weakened state capacity to the point that it could not even pay state salaries.

As elsewhere in the subcontinent, the new military rulers accused the previous government of massive corruption, patronage politics, and lack of transparency. But not long after they came to power, they too became enmeshed in a much grander scale of corruption. Kpundeh (2000: 202) for instance reports that "immediately following the 1992 coup, military personnel were discovered mining diamonds in exchange for Belgian and Romanian weapons." This was but the tip of the iceberg. Reno has systematically uncovered the nature of the warlord politics that were tied to the illegal trade in diamond mining in the eastern portions of Sierra Leone from the early independence era. The state was starved of crucial resources and state regulation of the economy was used to sabotage rival private ventures (Reno 1999, 116). The bulk of state revenues went into the pockets of politicians and their associates and helped underwrite patronage networks. Under Momoh, the state acknowledged the activities of illegal miners (estimated to provide job opportunities for some 50,000 young men), and relied on them to bail the state out of its financial straits.

Momoh attempted to tackle this problem of rogue state officials associated with his predecessor, who worked with clandestine businesspeople to deprive the state of formal revenue. He invited a number of foreign firms to take over mining operations in different parts of the country. This required that the government provide security to these firms. The result was that the government alienated the army of young men who worked in illegal mines (estimated at 25,000). These now became ready recruits for insurgents from Liberia who saw Sierra Leone's gold mines as sources of finance for their war against the Liberian government. In March 1991, rebels of Charles Taylor's guerillas invaded the most valuable areas of Sierra Leone's mining areas and named Foday Sankoh governor of Sierra Leone. The latter's organization received ammunition from Taylor and in turn provided Taylor's organization with Sierra Leone's rich mining regions. The displaced miners became ready recruits for the civil war that increasingly engulfed Sierra Leone from 1991. Momoh increased the army from 3,000 to 14,000 troops but did not have the resources to equip or pay them. A group of young army officers led by Valentine Strasser, a noncommissioned officer, came to protest the nonpayment of salaries for months and the poor supply of arms and ammunitions to fight off the rebels. These officers found an easier option was to depose Momoh's ruling clique rather than to persuade it to pay their salaries.

The military were never able to confront the fundamental problem of Sierra Leone politics, namely the existence of illegal mining activities that deprived the state of huge resources and legitimacy. If anything they simply aggravated it. The enlarged army took 75 percent of state spending, leaving little for social services or infrastructure. Even then, military units organized their own mining operations and often attacked people and rival miners. Economic collapse heralded the attack of the rebels on the capital city of Freetown in April 1995. This led ultimately to a situation in which the government of Sierra Leone had to contract the repulsion of rebel advances to a private mercenary organization, the Executive Outcomes of South Africa, which had had considerable experience in Angola. Executive Outcomes worked in collaboration with the local militia organizations, the *kamajors,*to drive the rebels from Freetown. The government retained them, and their presence facilitated the peaceful transfer from military to civilian rule in 1996.

The problem of how to pay for the huge expense of its foreign mercenary organization was resolved by allowing it to mine diamonds from the areas it liberated from the rebels. The presence of Executive Outcomes also brought a number of other investors and multilateral agencies back to Sierra Leone. This led to a spate of privatization that included the central bank, the state-owned bank, the oil refinery, and the port. Sierra Leone has thus become locked into a vicious cycle in which weak state capacity led to state collapse, which is revived only by an increasing dependence on foreign participation in the economy and governance. As soon as Executive Outcomes left in 1997, the rebels found their way back into the country and plunged it into another round of civil war. The country has only recently reemerged with the assistance of ECOMOG and United Nations forces.

Model 1: Nigeria Under the Military Governed by Manipulation and Greed

The Nigerian military first came to power in a coup in 1966. Its major complaint, as elsewhere in the region, was the excessive corruption of the civilian regime that it had replaced. In 1979, the country returned to civilian rule but this lasted only four years before the military struck again in 1984 and remained in office until 1999, the inauguration of the country's fourth republic. By the time the military had left office, the institution had become a study in state greed as it had subjected the economy and society to systematic corruption. By 1985, corruption had become the bedrock of Nigeria's political culture as a government report commented:

Corruption has become a household word in Nigerian society from the highest levels of the political and business elites to the ordinary person in the village. Its multifarious manifestations include the inflation of government contracts in return for kick-backs, frauds and falsifications of accounts in the public service, examination malpractices in our educational institutions including the universities, the taking of bribes and perversion of justice among the police, the judiciary and other organs for administering justice . . . various heinous crimes against the state in the business and industrial sectors in collusion with multinational companies such as over-invoicing of goods, foreign exchange swindling, hoarding, and smuggling . . .

But the worst phase of military corruption came under the last of the military rulers, General Sanni Abacha, who inherited a legacy of corruption from his predecessor, General Ibrahim Babangida, who was eased out of office by a combination of military and political forces (Osaghae 1998). Alex Gboyega (1996, 3) has systematically documented corruption that under General Babangida reached "unprecedented levels in incidence and magnitude." He systematically undermined critical national institutions. He created many offices to pave the way for politically ambitious officers to occupy positions that became a source of huge wealth for them. "Armed forces officers lucky to be appointed to essentially political positions treated their offices as personal estates to be administered entirely at their discretion and mostly to their benefit and comfort" (Gboyega 1996, 7). Indeed, the reform of all the country's civil services in 1988 politicized top positions and thereby was designed to institutionalize sycophancy among state officials.

Serious allegations of graft and embezzlement made against military and political officers were treated with levity by the Babangida administration. But these allegations pale when compared with the brazen corruption in the country's major industry and revenue earner—oil. Proceeds from crude oil were never accounted for as two stabilization accounts were created to make it easy for the president to make extrabudgetary expenditures to shore up his regime. A coup by young army officers in 1990 was met with gifts for military personnel and the judiciary. Several companies were given mining rights even when they did not have any experience, skilled staff, or capital. Licenses for lifting oil were given by political officeholders to their cronies against regulations. But the more serious menace was the illegal "bunkering" (lifting) of oil by strongmen against which the government was powerless. The Ministry of Finance allocated money with a "greasing of palms." As if these were not enough, in March 1993 Babangida passed a decree that released properties of officials (mostly military) who had been found guilty of improperly enriching themselves at public expense to these corrupt officials. Several retired and serving officers had huge stolen state resources returned to them in this way.

All of the above might be considered mere child's play compared to what happened after General Abacha took over power from his crony, Earnest Shonekan, whom Babangida had left in office in November 1994 as leader of an unelected and unpopular interim government when he had stepped aside. General Abacha systematically dismantled all vestiges of public accountability. All democratic structures were abolished as these stood in the way of his self-succession plan. He worked tirelessly toward this goal, and official corruption was one of the most important strategies for attaining it. In revelations that came to light after his sudden death in July 1998, one of the families fronting for him had been given US$700 million for an unspecified assignment. Another US$600 million deposited in a Luxembourg bank by members of the Abacha family has been frozen (*Economist*, 9 September 2000; *Tell*, 22 May 2000) while the current Nigerian government seeks to recover some US$4 billion laundered abroad.

Abacha and his cronies systematically pillaged the country. Three areas were particularly noteworthy. The first was the use of economic reform to punish enemies. Privatization and financial sector reforms were used to benefit cronies of the government and punish those who were critical of it. For instance, privatization led to a number of lucrative companies being sold cheaply to high profile members of the administration. Second, the economy was returned to its pre-1985 state through command and manipulation. Economic liberalization programs initiated by Babangida were reversed, thereby returning the country to the import licensing and fixed exchange rate regime, which became a source of huge profits for those associated with the government. The government made appointments to local governments a presidential prerogative and created six states in 1996 just to boost the president's self-succession plan. Finally, the government embarked on a program of state violence—assassinations and crimes against its perceived enemies. Violence increased as several enemies of the government were gunned down in the streets, bombs were planted in the houses of those who opposed the government, and the political process itself was rigged.

Corruption and the systematic degradation of national institutions under Abacha was largely responsible for the massive brain drain, decline in salaries and economic performance, drug trafficking, and the collusion between high level government officials and international fraudsters in what was known as "419 syndicates." A local magazine published a list of some 2000 crooks associated with this scam and the government officials with whom they worked. The magazine revealed that governments of the United States, Canada, and many European countries had formed special police squads to tackle Nigerian fraud-related activities. Their work was complicated by the fact that culprits often involved high-level government officials.

Model 2: Ghana and Democratic Reawakening Under Rawlings

Ghana under Flight Lieutenant Rawlings took the most drastic actions against corruption in West Africa when in 1979 it executed three former military heads of state (Generals Affifa, Acheampong, and Akuffo) plus five other senior military officers and incarcerated several officials and businesspeople. But that did little to diminish pervasive corruption in practically every aspect of economic activity. Rawlings and his group struck again, calling "for a holy war against corruption, privilege, inequality and a . . . revolution to transform social and economic order in Ghana." (Ayee 2000, 187). The Rawlings government—first as a military government and later as a civilian, democratically elected government—went to great lengths to tackle corruption head on. Its main strategy has been to create several anticorruption agencies to make corruption easier to detect and punish, such as:

- The Peoples' Defense Committees and the Workers' Defense Committees to identify and try corrupt practices (1982), later transformed into Committees for the Defense of the Revolution (CDR);

- Public tribunals that awarded long and draconian sentences against those found to be corrupt (1982);

- Citizens Vetting Committees (CVC), renamed in 1984 as Office of the Revenue, to investigate the source of their wealth;

- National Investigation Committee (NIC) also created in 1982 to investigate corruption and turn cases over to the Special Public Prosecutor;

- The 1992 constitution provided for an official code of conduct that required public officers to declare their assets and liabilities and avoid conflict of interest situations. A Commission for Human Rights and Administrative Justice (CHRAJ) was empowered to investigate and enforce these provisions.

- A Serious Fraud Office (SFO) was created to investigate and prevent activities capable of causing financial or economic loss to Ghana.

But in spite of these multiple organizations corruption has persisted. Many have been ineffective because of the absence of a principled anticorruption ethic in society, the poor resources made available to them, and the absence of effective anticorruption strategies (Rasheed and Olowu 1993; Olowu 2000).

Besides the creation of these anticorruption agencies, Rawlings made efforts to reform the public service through privatization and wage reforms, and through decentralization and democratization. The record of these efforts has not been impressive. Democratization was constrained by the fact that the ruling party controlled most of the means of communication and had the lion's share of government-provided campaign financing. The government prevented party politics at the grassroots, another constraint on its widely publicized decentralization program. Ghana's decentralized 110 district assemblies were expected to be autonomous and provide opportunities for grassroots development and participation. But several agencies that were expected to have become a part of the local bureaucracy remained with the central government. Moreover, the District Assembly secretaries (deployed civil servants) made critical decisions for local governments and were not accountable to the assemblies since all local power was vested in them as the president's men. This did not prevent them from engaging in corrupt practices.

Model 3: Democratic Reawakening in Nigeria

Believing that a major cause of the country's persistent underdevelopment was the problem of corruption, Nigeria's fourth republic president, Olusegun Obasanjo, immediately declared war against it. A panel comprising not government officials but civil society actors has been appointed to probe all uncompleted projects, supplies, and services in order to investigate past governments and their leaders dating back to 1976. This gesture has set a new tone for politics in the country; sacred cows are being touched. A new anticorruption law makes both the giver and receiver of bribes liable to imprisonment. An independent anticorruption commission with enormous powers, patterned after the Hong Kong model, has caught a number of public leaders. Several of those associated with the looting that took place under Abacha were made to refund their ill-gotten gains and many of their foreign bank accounts were frozen.

Four strategies constitute the cornerstone of the anticorruption drive of the present government. They are democratization, decentralization, public sector reform (comprising privatization and wage review), and anticorruption agencies. All of these are aimed at changing the culture of politics in Nigeria.

Democratization has made governance more transparent. Many corrupt activities of past governments have come to light as a result of this as well as the deliberate activities of the present government in encouraging national and international media to cover governance issues without any constraints.

Furthermore, the president is directly accessible by the Internet and e-mail. This strong fillip given to the media has made it difficult for corrupt activities to be hidden. The media have also been particularly helpful in unearthing information on the false declarations of qualifications by those who become leaders under the new dispensation.

Democratization also gave greater impetus to horizontal and vertical decentralization. Under the military, the executive also functioned as the legislature. The judiciary was repressed by ouster clauses contained in much of the legislation. Democratization has conferred much greater autonomy and independence on these two other branches of government. Moreover, it has also stimulated much more elaborate patterns of intergovernmental relations as the states and local governments have become more independent, although this has also multiplied corruption opportunities.

A third strategy is public sector reform with two important components—the resumption of the country's privatization of its several public enterprises that had been stopped by the Abacha administration—and wage review. Since parastatals were one of the major sources of corruption in the past, this part of the public sector reform is critical. The Babangida administration put in place a policy of privatization in 1986 but this was reversed by the Abacha regime. A more transparent policy and implementation framework is being put in place and the feeling is that the government is going in the right direction. Salaries in the public sector had declined to an all-time low under the Abacha government. The gap between pay in the public and private sector was wide and public sector pay was no longer considered a living wage (Otobo 1999). The new administration gave a five-fold increase in salaries for public officials in 2000 by fixing a new minimum wage. Wage review has thus helped in some ways but has failed to address the reality of how to attract and retain quality civil servants.

Finally, all of the above have been complemented by an anticorruption law and the establishment of several anticorruption agencies similar to those in Ghana.

The above should not be construed to imply that corruption has vanished from Nigeria with democratization. Far from it. An article in *West Africa* (9 October 2000) uncovered much corrupt activity in the executive branch. The Ministry of Finance still demands that state governments and ministries pay huge bribes monthly before their statutorily allocated funds are released to them. This is done in the open. With so many allegations against ex-President Babangida of illegal enrichment and mismanagement of state funds (including the Gulf War oil proceeds of US$4 billion), no probes have been instituted against him yet.

Conclusion and Lessons from the Models

This chapter has tried to make a distinction between the petty corruption common in West Africa and the systemic corruption that occurs at the highest levels of governance. This is not to discount the importance or cost of the former. The *World Development Report 2000/2001* devoted to attacking poverty cites the additional cost (up to 87 percent) of the incessant road blocks and bribes extorted by customs, police, and transport officials on West African roads. These are real. Nevertheless, emphasis has been focused on the more institutionalized forms of corruption here because this promotes the culture of corruption reflected in petty forms.

Several lessons emerge from the cases reviewed above. The first is that the process of state building or state institutionalization is proceeding at different rates in West Africa. The quality of political leadership and their political goals affect the pace of state institutionalization. Where the leadership is pursuing private instead of public interests, institutionalized corruption results. Second, direct anticorruption activities—including the creation of several anticorruption agencies—is not in itself an effective strategy. In the absence of adequate resources and institutions to champion and enforce anticorruption programs in societies where there is no principled anticorruption ethic, the effect of such agencies is bound to be limited as the Ghanaian experience under Rawlings demonstrates. On the other hand, when anticorruption activities complement other strategies—democratization, decentralization, and public sector reform (privatization and wage reform)—the effect can be positive as the recent Nigerian experience shows.

Of the four strategies, the least developed is decentralization. States are required to put in place effective decentralization strategies but without developing effective systems of local governance, starting with the region's burgeoning cities, the culture of graft and patrimonialism in the formal public sector will persist. Notions of trust, accountable performance, and citizenship are likely to be easier to actualize in such face-to-face contexts than in the larger, artificial state contexts. By building nations and states upward around subjectively defined communities and neighborhoods, some of the worst forms of patrimonialism may be eschewed. Most countries initiated democratic decentralization programs in the 1990s but only a few have actually transferred all three key essentials of effective decentralization: responsibilities, resources, and accountability systems to the localities. The development of effective systems of accountability at community levels, backed up by state leaders and state institutions to promote public and not private interests will most likely be a prerequisite to the reduction of institutionalized corruption in central governments.

References

Almond, G. and G. Powell. 1966. *Comparative politics: A developmental approach.* Boston, Mass.: Little Brown Co.

Ayee, J. R. 1999. Ghana: The continuing search for cures in the fight against corruption. In *Corruption and development in Africa. Lessons from case studies,* edited by K. R. Hope and B. C. Chikulo. London: Macmillan.

Bayart, J. 1993. *The state in Africa: Politics of the belly.* London: Longman.

Caiden, G. 1992. From the specific to the general: Reflections on the Sudan. Special Issue of *Corruption and Reform* 7 (3): 205–14

Chabal, P. and Jean-Paschal Daloz. 1999. Africa works: Disorder as political instrument. Oxford: James Currey.

Ekpo, M. U., ed. 1979. *Bureaucratic corruption in sub-Saharan Africa.* New York: University Press of America.

Gboyega, A., ed. 1996. *Corruption and democratization in Nigeria.* Ibadan: Fredrick Ebert Foundation.

Gyimah-Boadi, E. 1999. Ghana: The Challenges of Consolidating Democracy. In *State, conflict and democracy in Africa,* edited by R. Joseph. Boulder, Colo.: Lynne Rienner Publishers.

Hope, K. R., and B.C. Chiculo, eds. 2000. *Corruption and development in Africa: Lessons from country case studies.* London: Macmillan.

Hyden, G. 1999. The governance challenge in Africa. In *African perspectives on governance,* edited by G. Hyden, D. Olowu, and H. W. O. Okoth-Ogendo. Trenton: Africa World Press.

Hyden, G., and M. Bratton, eds. 1992. *Governance and politics in Africa.* Boulder, Colo.: Lynne Rienner Publishers.

Johnston, M. 1992. Micro and macro possibilities for reform. In *Corruption and Reform* 7 (3): 189–205.

Joseph, R. 1999. Autocracy, violence and ethno-military rule in Nigeria. In *State, Conflict and Democracy in Africa,* edited by R. Joseph. Boulder, Colo.: Lynne Reinner Publishers.

Kpundeh, S. 2000. Controlling corruption in Sierra Leone: An assessment of past efforts and suggestions for the future. In *Corruption and Development In Africa: Lessons from Country Case Studies,* edited by K. R. Hope and B. C. Chiculo. London: Macmillan.

Migdal, J. S. 1988. *Strong states and weak societies: State-society relations and state capabilities in the third world.* Princeton, N.J.: Princeton University Press.

Moody-Smart, G. 1997. *Grand corruption: How business bribes damage developing countries.* Oxford: World View Publishing.

Olowu, D. 1988. Bureaucratic morality. *International Political Science Review* 9 (1): 215–29.

Olowu, D. 1993. Ethical violations in Nigeria's public services: Patterns, explanations and remedies. In *Ethics and Accountability in African Public Services,* edited by S. Rasheed and D. Olowu. Addis Ababa, United Nations Economic Commission for Africa.

Olowu, D., A. Williams, and K. Soremekun, eds. *Governance and democratization in West Africa.* Dakar: CODESRIA.

Osaghae, E. E. 1998. *Crippled giant: Nigeria since independence.* London: Hurst and Co.

Ostrom, E. 1990. *Governing the commons: The evolution of institutions of collective action.* Cambridge: Cambridge University Press.

Ottaway, M. 1998. *Africa's new leaders: Democracy and state reconstruction?* Washington, D.C.: Carnegie Endowment.

Otobo, E. 1999. Nigeria. In *Public administration in Africa: Main issues and selected country studies,* edited by L. Adamolekun. Boulder, Colo.: Westview Press.

Quah, John S. T. 1999. Corruption in Asian countries: Can it be minimized? *Public Administration Review* 59 (6): 483–94.

Rasheed, S., and D. Olowu, eds. 1993. *Ethics and Accountability in African Public Services.* Addis Ababa: United Nations Economic Commission for Africa.

Reno, W. 1995. *Corruption and state politics in Sierra Leone* New York: Cambridge University Press.

———. 1998. *Warlord Politics and African States.* Boulder, Colo.: Lynne Rienner Publishers.

Riley, S. 2000. Western policies and African realities: The new anti-corruption agenda. In *Corruption and development in Africa: Lessons from country case studies,* edited by K. R. Hope and B. C. Chiculo. London: Macmillan.

Sesay, A. 1999. Paradise lost and regained? The travails of democracy in Sierra Leone. In *Democratization in West Africa,* edited by D. Olowu et al. Dakar: CODESRIA.

World Bank, 1992. *Governance: The World Bank's experience.* Washington, D.C.: World Bank.

———. 1989. *Sub-Saharan Africa: From crisis to sustainable growth.* Oxford: University Press.

———. 2000. *World development report 2000/2001.* Oxford: Oxford University Press.

Wunsch, J. S., and D. Olowu, eds. 1990. *The failure of the centralized state: Institutions and self governance in Africa.* Boulder, Colo.: Westview Press.

Zartman, W., ed. 1995. *Collapsed states: The disintegration and restoration of legitimate authority.* Boulder, Colo.: Lynne Rienner Publishers.

9

Understanding Corruption in the South African Public Sector

Victor Grove Hilliard and Henry F. Wissink

IN THE PAST DECADE SOUTH AFRICA has undergone profound political and constitutional changes resulting in a decline of morals and values to such a magnitude that corruption, maladministration, and financial mismanagement have become major issues tainting the public sector. Public perception is that it has grown worse, not better, since the African National Congress (ANC) assumed office in 1994 (Mattes and Africa, 1999). Many South Africans use just about any excuse to justify unethical behavior, and everything that goes wrong is blamed on the legacy of apartheid or the new regime's inexperience. Obviously, there are other and more compelling reasons for corruption—political, economic, social, and cultural. In the final analysis, all four dimensions are interrelated and interact to exacerbate corruption. This makes it difficult to hold the line and prevent further deterioration in official conduct.

Causes

Although the many contributory causes of corruption are dealt with in a compartmentalized manner, they are interlinked and cannot be treated in isolation.

Political

Historical Legacy   No event in South Africa can be seen in isolation from the historical setting in which it has occurred. South Africa experienced racial discrimination for more than four decades, particularly black Africans who were marginalized from, and deprived of, the socioeconomic and political benefits that whites, as a minority, had liberally enjoyed (Hilliard and Wissink 1999b, 223–24). Then in 1994 came radical change. A new ruling elite has emerged in postapartheid South Africa and is struggling desperately to close the socioeconomic gap between rich and poor. This has led to much resentment because the dispossessed are, generally, not reaping the benefits of the postapartheid era. The masses still see a handful of people—now not only whites but also elite blacks—enjoying the spoils while the majority are still largely disadvantaged and envious and expect a speedy transformation of their needy situation.

Black Exclusion   For forty-six years (from 1948 until 1994), blacks were excluded from mainstream politics in South Africa. Effectively, blacks were disenfranchised. Furthermore, the apartheid policy caused most blacks to become migrants, thereby forcing them to return to their own homelands or Bantustans that were created and controlled by the Nationalist government to further the apartheid ideology. The essence of the apartheid policy was that blacks were seen and treated as sojourners or transient workers in white urban areas. They belonged with their own people in their own homelands; they had no right to reside among whites who reaped the country's greatest economic benefits.

The Bantustan or homeland policy caused much poverty. The homelands were not economically viable states, but forlorn places with little infrastructure and industry to support a growing black population. Additionally, migrant labor policies and influx control (to prevent blacks from entering white areas without carrying a pass or reference book) were applied with tenacity throughout the country. Expectations were raised in 1994 that the quality of life of the average black person in South Africa would improve, but these expectations have largely remained unfulfilled. Job creation has been on the decline and South Africa's low economic growth rate has been insufficient to accommodate the country's unemployed. Another problem has been the lack of sufficient international investment in South Africa. Thus, any job is to be prized and sought after, particularly those in the public sector.

Racial Superiority   The greatest drawback of apartheid was its master race concept. This meant that whites, notably white Afrikaners, regarded themselves as superior to other persons. No mixing of races or biracial marriages were permitted under apartheid. It may take decades to heal and restore the dignity and feelings of self-worth of black South Africans. In postapartheid South Africa, blacks have gained political power but less economic empowerment. Many blacks still have to eke out a daily existence with little hope of reaching the economic heights of many of the whites and their elite compatriots. This has bred resentment and prompted considerable grassroots pressure for the redistribution of wealth. As wealth cannot be redistributed without it first being created and because the process of wealth creation is slow, unsavory tactics are used to exploit and "ride" the system—hence the incidence of large scale corruption, maladministration, and financial mismanagement.

The Liberation Struggle   During the dark days of apartheid, many became involved in the liberation struggle that was harmful to both perpetrators and victims. Even to this day the Truth and Reconciliation Commission (TRC) is still busy with the many atrocities that occurred under the apartheid regime. As South African society is highly traumatized, many of those oppressed by the apartheid system feel that it is justified to beat the system and to take as much as they can to compensate for past deprivation.

Rapid and Radical Political Change   Some citizens have adjusted well to change while others have not. Since 1994 South Africa has become a secular state. This secularization has generated a new community in which it is difficult to reach consensus on what constitutes right and wrong behavior and ethical and unethical conduct. Many citizens are confused about the basis for acceptable norms and values. This will take time to sort out and the development of ethical codes of conduct may not necessarily rectify this situation. Another matter of major concern is the tendency of the new ANC government to continue to centralize and concentrate power just like its Nationalist predecessor. It contends that the centralization of power is needed to speed affirmative action appointments and has introduced several pieces of legislation weakening the powers of local authorities. This resembles the tactics of previous white governments to control public affairs using extensive executive power and deprive people of direct control of and participation in local administration.

Economic

Deprivation and Joblessness   A prime cause of corruption is social deprivation. For years black Africans have been the dispossessed enduring tremendous hardship. The large-scale joblessness (some 40 percent of the labor force) has exacerbated the problem. The new ANC government has been unable to stimulate sufficient job creation programs, and joblessness has actually increased. Since 1994, about one million jobs have been lost. Thus, economic power and privilege are still concentrated in the hands of a few. It is possible that no more than 400 whites effectively control up to 80 percent of the South African economy (Venter 1998, 15).

Lack of Infrastructure   In many parts of South Africa, basic or rudimentary infrastructure is still lacking. The country lacks tarred roads, sewage systems, reticulated and purified water, and electric power. The vast majority still lives in abject poverty and looks at the wealthy minority with great envy. The end then begins to justify the means, and any manner of acquiring wealth becomes the accepted norm. Once again the whole problem boils down to the fact that political promises cannot be fulfilled due to severe financial constraints. The country has lost its postapartheid charm and is seen as just another African country in need.

Restricted Tax Base   Coupled with deprivation (and other problems associated with corruption) is that the tax base in South Africa is inordinately narrow. Although an estimated six million people are liable for taxation, two million contribute upwards of 90 percent of the central government's taxes. This small minority resents contributing the bulk of the government's finances. What makes matters worse is that there is a growing disparity between benefits received for taxes paid. Those who pay the most taxes receive the least benefits. Taxpayers feel aggrieved that money is ostensibly being squandered on a host of unnecessary luxuries and superfluous projects such as salaries for consultants, perquisites, and inflated salaries for public functionaries but little goes to good governance and to bolstering the economy of the country. This has resulted in many ways to circumvent the laws, especially tax legislation. People generally resist paying taxes if there is no quid pro quo.

Migrant Labor Policies   The migrant labor policies of the erstwhile Nationalist government had many unintended spin-offs. They destroyed many family units. They helped to spread the HIV/AIDS epidemic, which is now a serious threat to the work force. Furthermore, they also resulted in many "fatherless" children left behind in the homelands, the cities, and neighboring countries. They forced South African blacks to carry reference books when they moved about the country and also resulted in blacks being "deported" to their homelands if they were illegally or unlawfully found in white areas. This system has led to considerable resentment and bitterness with adverse impacts on productivity and immigration policy. Illegal aliens, some of whom are carriers of the HIV/AIDS virus, are infiltrating South Africa by obtaining falsified documents such as passports, identity books, and work permits.

Lack of Training and Development   One major shortcoming has been a lack of training and development for the new guard. When the ANC-dominated government came to power, there was scant mentorship and little training and development, especially in the areas of public administration and public service ethics. It serves little purpose to have numerous codes of conduct in place when new public functionaries lack the necessary education and training. But little provision was made for this and inadequate training and development remains an obstacle.

Social

Breakdown of Authority   Generally, the family as a place of security and of nurturing in society is crumbling. Respect for authority is declining and lack of discipline is on the rise spreading from the family to the schools to other areas of civil society. Disciplining children is frowned upon. The notion that anything goes in terms of conduct and morality appears to be undermining the very fabric of society. Already, some portions of the population have departed from the basic principles of honesty (Hanekom, Rowland, and Bain 1990, 157).

Too Few Good Role Models   With notable exceptions embodied by Nelson Mandela and Helen Suzman, South Africans have seen very few good ethical role models if one considers the atrocities that the previous regime and its henchmen committed. In the past, South African leadership styles were not exemplary. The Nationalist regime ignored international opinion and adopted a paternalistic, top-down approach to governing and managing the country. Much of this sort of managerial style has now been discarded by the new ANC government, which advocates a large dose of bottom-up management and openness and transparency in governance and administration. However, older attitudes linger within the public bureaucracy.

Social Fabric Torn Asunder   In retrospect, apartheid almost destroyed South African society. It severely compartmentalized society. The divisions created were racially-based—blacks, Indians, coloreds, and whites were all allocated their own group areas. Sadly, towns and cities were fragmented and even after the group areas were abolished in the early 1990s, the profile of South African towns and cities has not changed appreciably. Not only was the segregationist policy reprehensible but it led to a considerable amount of duplication and overlapping of services and an administrative system so unwieldy and bizarre that it requires radical overhaul.

Redefinition of Value Systems   South African values have been particularly
shaped by the diversity of the population and by institutionalized racism. There
was the gross violation of human rights under the previous Nationalist Party
regime. Now, human rights are a prominent component of the new ANC regime. Unlike the past, no one particular religious group can unduly influence
the government. On the other hand, freedom of belief results in a lack of consensus on the basic elements that should constitute a code of conduct and a
good work ethic for South Africa. Some groups emphasize communalism, the
principle of sharing, and the African principle of *ubuntu* (togetherness). In
other words, they focus on collectivism, or a form of socialism, and what the
group instead of what the individual should be achieving in society. Other groups
emphasize individualism, capitalism, and the profit motive. This causes con-
flicting values in society because one group aspires to wealth, while another
group aspires to the redistribution of wealth without first finding mechanisms
to create the wealth to spread around. The wealth generators may not feel guilty
about cheating the authorities because they vehemently disagree with a policy
of redistribution of wealth.

Cultural

Low Productivity   Productivity is low in South Africa because of an ineffective leadership style, worker insecurity due to affirmative action, trade union
pressure for less work and more pay, crime and violence, crippling taxation,
incorrect advice about which careers to pursue, and expensive, uncompetitive
labor costs. But it also appears that there are many others as well, including
training deficiencies: a wrong choice of school subjects, inadequate vocational
guidance, a lack of work experience, a chasm between theory and practice, too
much specialization, and training geared to uphold the old apartheid order,
focusing on and catering to the needs of society on a racial basis (Hilliard and
Wissink 1999a, 7–10). There has also been a huge brain-drain in South Africa.
It is estimated that, on average, a thousand highly skilled inhabitants per month
leave the country officially; unofficially these statistics could be much higher.
This has left a large vacuum and a dent in the labor market that has resulted in
many untrained persons entering the labor market without proper mentoring
opportunities. Many skilled public servants have left the public service with
lucrative severance packages, while many of the new guard are less experienced. The severance packages have turned out to be a fiasco and have merely
exacerbated the low productivity in the South African public service. The new
ANC government wanted to get rid of deadwood, but unfortunately the effect
was that much of the best talent left the public service and began their own

businesses or left the country for better job prospects and a safer future for their families.

Rebellion Against Authority   Although the white minority forms only a small portion of the South African population, it is nevertheless a force to be reckoned with. It still has the power to subtly undermine the new ANC government. Indeed, South African public servants talk openly about sabotaging the new government. But not only are minorities becoming recalcitrant. Some dissidents involved in the armed struggle also have difficulty submitting to the new government. Tensions run high in many areas of the public service, the schools, and particularly the military.

Inflated Competence   Together with unrealistic expectations, many new incumbents are unwilling to start at the bottom and to submit to training and development to climb up the ranks. They want to be speedily promoted right to the top of the hierarchy. Unfortunately, those who are unwilling to submit to the rigors of climbing the ranks and want the spoils of the system immediately have difficulty grasping that there are deficiencies in their judgment, training, and development. These errors of judgment and hasty decisions contribute to maladministration, the aspiring toward instantaneous wealth, and, eventually, corruption.

Nepotism and Cronyism   South Africa's diversity has had a significant effect on how inhabitants view wrongdoing. In some cultures, nepotism is not considered a serious matter. When the new black majority government came into power, affirmative action was adopted for the black majority and many qualified exiles returned ready to govern. So now the rules governing merit appointments are being set aside and blacks are beginning to receive preferential treatment through nepotism, cronyism, and string-pulling. The public service is becoming racially more homogeneous but is increasing the opportunities for collusion and the formation of cliques and cabals within the public sector. The Nationalist regime used secrecy, cliques, and cabals to further its cause. Now the new ANC government seems to be emulating many of the previous regime's policies and practices (Hilliard and Wissink, 1999b, 224). Clearly, an excessive preoccupation with secrecy in the public service is a recipe for corruption, irrespective of who is in power (Hilliard 1992, 14).

Loss of Traditional Values and Norms   Both blacks and whites have lost much of their original culture and traditions in Africa. Both groups have sacrificed something to become blended into a very cosmopolitan, diverse nation.

Blacks have moved to the towns and cities of South Africa in search of work although many cannot find jobs. Needing shelter and infrastructure, they began to squat and to erect informal dwellings, living in filth and squalor in many black townships. So South Africa now has a large population living off crime and it seems that the government is unable—or has lost the political will—to contain lawlessness because so many have to resort to crime in order to survive. Those who do happen to get into positions of power try to capitalize. The new government has to keep a close watch on bribery, corruption, and fraud, particularly on kickbacks, cronyism, and nepotism, more so as current public service managers in the post-1994 era are beginning to close ranks and try to cover up their misdemeanors. This sort of collusion will only further taint the public service.

Possible Remedies for Corruption

The challenge of corruption in South Africa is formidable. The possible remedies for corruption are many but not one particular remedy can be said to be better than another. In fact, a multipronged approach is needed to combat corruption and unethical conduct. The means used in South Africa may not necessarily correspond with those used in Western democracies for some will have to be home grown.

Upholding the Public Interest

All public servants should champion the public interest. This entails empathy and respect for future generations—impartiality, avoiding conflict of interest, and avoiding (the appearance of) impropriety. Public servants should not use their public position to pursue personal agendas (Lewis 1991, 46). Public servants have a responsibility (obligation) to serve the public interest. It is a question of whether the interests and the welfare of more inclusive populations other than self, family, clan, or tribe are served (Cooper 1990, 69). This is tricky considering the manner in which the Nationalist Party applied the apartheid policy that was used to further the cause of a language (Afrikaans), of an ideology (segregation of racial groups), and even of a religion (Calvinism). This practice lasted for 46 years. So the ANC has to be exceptionally careful that it does not fall into the same trap of favoring its own kind at the expense of other groups in society or at the expense of being politically incorrect.

Obsession with political correctness could be the downfall of South Africa. In terms of the *Employment Equity Act*, 1998 (Act 55 of 1998), race, gender, and disability come into the employment equation. For instance, blacks receive preference over whites, and women preference over men for jobs. But does this mean that black women should be preferred to white women? These sorts of dilemmas are now hounding public employers. In many cases, where an appropriate candidate cannot be found through the normal recruitment channels, head-hunting is the order of the day. Notwithstanding the need to redress the imbalances of South Africa's past, it must be remembered that the general welfare of the nation should always come first, and that efficiency and effectiveness should be the prime motives for transformation.

Building Moral Character and Imagination

An ethical population has to be created from the existing multiracial, multicultural, and multiethnic society. But ethics is not just about law-keeping and abiding by the rules and regulations of an organization. Morality and ethics run far deeper. They encompass virtue and integrity. They require critical thinking and principled reasoning. It is important for South Africa to employ honest public servants from the outset. If the public service is saddled with a dishonest corps of officials, it will be extremely difficult to correct the situation at a later stage. Today, therefore, there is considerable emphasis on virtue ethics linked to the maintenance of the public interest (Hilliard and Lynch 1999, 93). Virtues are predispositions to behave in a way that encourages the pursuit of the internal goods of a practice and protects them from external goods such as money, fame, power, and organizational aggrandizement (Cooper 1990, 165). These virtues are a central concern to public administration and public administrators, as only virtue keeps public officials on track.

Enforcing Codes of Conduct

South Africa has numerous codes of conduct for public functionaries. One such code is the "code of conduct for the public service," chapter M of section 41(1) of the *Public Service Act*, 1994. While codes of conduct are useful tools for enforcing moral rectitude, they should not be regarded as the be-all of public service ethics. In fact, many codes of conduct are "nice-to-have" documents with little practical value unless properly enforced. Lewis (1991, 153) emphasizes that codes of conduct must have prosecutorial enforcement properties to maintain public integrity. Even at the agency or administrative level, disciplinary actions must be taken against those who violate codes of conduct. Otherwise, codes of conduct become merely statements of good intentions.

Demanding (Public) Accountability

One of the most important principles of the 1996 Constitution contained in section 195(1)(f) is that public administration must be accountable. Accountability is an important concept and principle in the new, postapartheid dispensation. It helps minimize corruption and other malpractices. Therefore it is essential that public accountability or public answerability is demanded from every public official, elected or appointed. All should be accountable to higher authority, as they are implementers of public policies. But things can go awry and public functionaries can err. Therefore there should be continual public alertness to hold officials accountable for their actions. When accountability is neglected, corruption takes its toll. So public officials should always be under scrutiny and aware of constant public scrutiny to ensure that the right things are done—more so than that things are done right. Sticking to the rules can actually result in public officials doing the wrong thing, as when before 1994 they implemented the apartheid policy without question. The ANC has to ensure that as it goes in a different direction, it too does not relax its guard and weaken public accountability measures and mechanisms.

Conclusion

This chapter has dealt with the possible causes of and remedies for corruption within South Africa, whose highly complex society has been aggravated and highly fragmented by apartheid. Although apartheid is now part of history, it still influences society in a very profound manner, especially in the realm of public ethics. Despite globalization South Africa has to attract international investors again. For the purposes of international investment and trade alone, the incidence of corruption has to be reduced and the faith of the international community rekindled. Thus, the fight against official corruption has to be intensified lest irreparable harm is done to the country, which will set it back many years and further disillusion its people.

References

Amstutz, M. R. 1999. *International ethics: Concepts, theories, and cases in global politics.* Oxford: Rowman and Littlefield.

Cooper, T. L. 1990. *The responsible administrator. An approach to ethics for the administrative role.* San Francisco: Jossey-Bass.

Hanekom, S. X., R. W. Rowland, and E. G. Bain. 1990. *Key aspects of public administration.* Johannesburg: Southern Publishers.

Hilliard, V. G. 1992. Corruption in the public sector: Causes and remedies. *Boardroom* 4: 10–21.

———. 1994. Dealing with diversity in South Africa. *Boardroom* 2: 11–13.

Hilliard, V. G., and T. D. Lynch. 1999. Entrenching ethical and moral behaviour in the South African public sector. *Administratio Publica* 9(1): 83–102.

Hilliard, V. G., and H. F. Wissink. 1999a. Developing a model to address training deficiencies in a post-apartheid public service. *Politeia* 18 (1): 5–19.

———. 1999b. Alternative administration: A Southern African perspective. In *Bureaucracy and the Alternatives in World Perspective*, edited by K. M. Henderson and O. P. Dwivedi. New York: Macmillan Press.

Hilliard, V. G., and N. D. Kemp. 1999. Citizen participation crucial to good governance and administration in South Africa. *Politeia* 18 (3): 40–67.

Hilliard, V. G., and E. H. B. van Biljon. 1999. Devising a pathway for productivity improvement in the South African public service. *SA Journal of Labour Relations*. 23 (4): 30–49.

Lewis, C. W. 1991. *The ethics challenge in public service. A problem-solving guide.* Jossey-Bass: American Society for Public Administration.

Mattes, R. and C. Africa. 1999. Corruption—the attitudinal component: Tracking public perceptions of official corruption in South Africa, 1995–1998. Ninth International Anticorruption Conference, Durban, South Africa.

Venter, A., ed. 1998. *Government and politics in the new South Africa.* Pretoria: J. L. van Schaik.

10

Combating Corruption in the Asia Pacific Region

Jon S.T. Quah

CORRUPTION IS A GROWTH INDUSTRY, judging from the proliferation of case studies in Asian countries in recent years. But in spite of the plethora of such research, there is still a paucity of comparative study on corruption and its effects on governance in Asian countries. While corruption is a serious problem in many Asian countries, the perceived level of corruption in these countries varies according to the effectiveness of their governments in curbing corruption. Singapore is perceived to be the least corrupt Asian country while Indonesia is considered to be the most corrupt.

What is corruption? What is the linkage between corruption and governance? Corruption is defined as "the misuse of public power, office or authority for private benefit—through bribery, extortion, influence peddling, nepotism, fraud, speed money or embezzlement" (UNDP 1999, 7). If governance refers to "the exercise of political, economic and administrative authority to manage a nation's affairs" (UNDP 1997, 9), can minimizing corruption contribute to good governance? Or is combating corruption to improve governance an impossible dream? This chapter contends that it is possible to improve governance in an Asian country if its government is committed to curbing corruption. To illustrate this contention, the three major patterns of corruption control in Asia will be analyzed to ascertain their various levels of effectiveness.

Pattern 1: Anticorruption Laws Without an Independent Agency (Mongolia)

This first pattern of corruption control is the simplest and also least effective, as it consists of anticorruption laws that are not implemented by a specialized anticorruption agency. The best illustration of an Asian country following this pattern of corruption control is Mongolia, which began its fight against corruption recently with the transition from a command economy to a market economy (Qhah, 1999a). The most important anticorruption law in Mongolia is the Law on Anti-Corruption (LAC), which was enacted in April 1996. The LAC requires all Mongolian public officials to declare their incomes and assets and those of their families within a month of assuming their positions, and thereafter to submit their annual declarations during the first two weeks of February of each year. Those who fail to submit their declarations will be fined between US$6 and US$29. Those officials who do not monitor the declarations will be fined between US$24 and US$35. Moreover, officials who do not declare gifts or foreign bank accounts must pay fines of between US$35 and US$47. Finally, corrupt officials will be discharged or displaced according to the procedure provided in the law.

To supplement the LAC, the Criminal Code of Mongolia has three articles concerning bribery. Article 195 states that officials found guilty of receiving bribes can be suspended from their positions or imprisoned for six years. Article 196 stipulates that bribe-givers will be imprisoned for up to four years or must perform public works for 18 months. For recalcitrant bribe-givers, the penalty is a jail sentence of three to ten years. The third article, Article 197, imposes the same penalty of imprisonment for up to four years or performing public works for 18 months for those convicted of mediating the taking and giving of bribes.

The LAC is ineffective. So far only three members of parliament from the ruling Democratic Union coalition have been jailed (in October 1999) for taking bribes in connection with a casino tender. The LAC has two weaknesses. First, the responsibility for implementing the LAC has not been assigned to a specific agency, as Article 5 indicates that all state organizations are required to perform four common duties to prevent corruption. The experiences of the Corrupt Practices Investigation Bureau (CPIB) in Singapore and the Independent Commission Against Corruption (ICAC) in Hong Kong confirm the effectiveness of employing an independent agency in implementing the anticorruption laws in both city-states (Quah 1995). The second weakness of the LAC is that the penalties imposed on officials for failure to submit or monitor their annual income and assets declarations are ineffective deterrents as the fines are low and there is no imprisonment.

Because Mongolia does not have an independent anticorruption agency, corruption offenses are handled by the Criminal Police Department (CPD), which investigates these cases and refers them to the Investigation Department (ID). The CPD and ID investigate complaints of corruption against public officials and if there is evidence to substantiate these complaints, the cases are handed over to the General Prosecutor's Office (GPO). From the GPO, cases are processed by the *aimag* courts, the Capital City Court and the Supreme Court. This procedure for processing corruption offenses is defective—it provides opportunities for corruption among the officials involved as they can interpret the law differently. For example, a case seen as bribery by the police can be viewed as a smuggling offense by the GPO, and as illegal crossing of borders by the courts. Since judicial salaries are low and "one out of three judges does not have an apartment" (McPhail 1995, 45), the courts are perceived by the public to be corrupt as individuals can bribe the poorly paid judges to make decisions in their favor.

Pattern 2: Anticorruption Laws with Many Agencies (India, Philippines, China)

The second pattern of fighting corruption is the implementation of the anticorruption laws by many agencies in democratic countries like India and the Philippines and in a Communist country like China.

India

In India, the fight against corruption began in 1941, when the British colonial government created the Delhi Special Police Establishment (DSPE) to "investigate cases of bribery and corruption in transactions" involving the War and Supply Departments (Palmier 1985, 30). The DSPE was expanded in April 1963 to form the Central Bureau of Investigation (CBI). The Prevention of Corruption Act (POCA), which was enacted in March 1947, is implemented by the CBI, the Central Vigilance Commission (CVC), the state anticorruption bureaus, and the state vigilance commissions. The CBI's role is to investigate cases of bribery and corruption, but it can only do so in a state with the consent of its government. This requirement became problematic after the decline of the Congress Party as some state governments withdrew the consent given by their predecessor "whenever they felt that an investigation taken up by the CBI was politically embarrassing or uncomfortable for them" (Narasimhan 1997, 255–56).

The CVC was formed in February 1964 to supplement the CBI's role in curbing corruption. The CVC's four functions are: (1) to investigate any transaction in which a civil servant is alleged to act for an improper purpose; (2) to examine complaints against civil servants for using their powers for improper or corrupt purposes; (3) to request reports from ministries, departments, and public enterprises to enable it to check and supervise their vigilance and anticorruption work; and (4) to request that the CBI investigate a case, or to entrust the complaint, information, or case for inquiry to the CBI or the ministry, department, or public enterprise concerned (Narasimhan 1997, 264–65).

S. S. Gill has written, "Looking to the number of agencies created to tackle corruption, it would appear that the government was in dead earnest to eradicate this malady." But, he lamented, "This elaborate and multi-layered apparatus to control administrative corruption has hardly made a dent on the situation" (Gill 1998, 237–38). The CBI was also perceived by the public to be "a pliable tool of the ruling party, and its investigations tend to become cover-up operations for the misdeeds of the ministers." Its ineffectiveness was further reflected in its low conviction rate as only 300 of the 1,349 cases (22.2 percent) in 1972 and 164 of the 1,231 cases (13.3 percent) in 1992 resulted in conviction. Gill also accused the CBI of going "only after the small fry" as only one gazetted officer was dismissed in 1972 and two officers in 1992. The CBI's record in investigating the various megascams was also dismal as there were no convictions. Indeed, according to Gill, Prime Minister Narasimha Rao's tenure "exposed the utter ineffectiveness and servility of official investigating agencies." As the CBI deflected the investigations and targeted only the small fry, the courts "had to repeatedly reprimand the CBI for its deliberate slowness and biased attitude" (Gill 1998, 122).

In view of the CBI and CVC's ineffectiveness, it is not surprising that in 1999 India was ranked seventy-second with Colombia, among the 99 countries surveyed by Transparency International. India's poor corruption ranking was also confirmed by the Hong Kong–based Political and Economic Risk Consultancy (PERC) 2000 annual survey, which ranked India as the second most corrupt country in Asia after Indonesia (*International Herald Tribune*, 23 March 2000, 16).

The Philippines

The Philippines is the Asian country with the greatest number of anticorruption measures; it has relied on seven laws and fourteen antigraft agencies since its fight against corruption began in the 1950s. The first anticorruption law was the Forfeiture Law of 1955, which authorized "the state to forfeit in its favor any property found to have been unlawfully acquired by any public officer or employer." But this law was ineffective as there were no convictions even four years after its passage. The Anti-Graft and Corrupt Practices Act or the Republic Act (RA) No. 3019, which was passed in April 1960, identified eleven types of corrupt acts among public officials and required them to file every two years a detailed, sworn statement of their assets and liabilities. The third anticorruption law, RA No. 6028, which provided for the creation of the Office of the Citizens' Counselor, was passed in August 1969, but it was not implemented.

The remaining four laws were the Presidential Decrees (PD) issued by President Marcos after the establishment of martial law in September 1972. PD No. 6 identified twenty-nine administrative offenses and empowered heads of departments to dismiss guilty officials immediately. This resulted in the sacking of nearly 8,000 public officials. In November 1972, PD No. 46 prevented public officials from receiving and private individuals from giving gifts on any occasion, including Christmas. Finally, PD No. 677 and PD No. 749 were amendments to RA No. 3019, requiring all government employees to submit statements of their assets and liabilities every year, instead of every other year, and providing immunity from prosecution for those willing to testify against public officials or citizens accused of corruption (Alfiler 1979, 326–27).

The number of anticorruption agencies in the Philippines can be attributed to the frequent changes in political leadership as such agencies were either created or abolished by the president. Between May 1950 and January 1966, five anticorruption agencies were formed and then dissolved as there were five changes in political leadership during that period. President Marcos created another five anticorruption agencies during his two decades in power because the first three agencies were ineffective and lasted between eight months and two years (Quah 1982, 168–69). In July 1979, Marcos formed the *Sandiganbayan* (special antigraft court) and the *Tanodbayan* (ombudsman) by issuing PD No. 1606 and PD No. 1630, respectively.

President Corazon Aquino assumed office in February 1986 and she established the Presidential Commission on Good Government (PCGG) to identify and retrieve the money stolen by Marcos family members and their cronies. Unfortunately, Aquino's anticorruption stance was viewed cynically by the public. Two of her cabinet members and her relatives (referred to pejoratively as "rela-thieves") were accused of corruption. The PCGG was also a target for charges of corruption, favoritism, and incompetence, and by June 1988, five of its agents faced graft charges and thirteen more were under investigation. In May 1987, Aquino established the Presidential Committee on Public Ethics and Accountability (PCPEA) to respond to increasing public criticism. But the PCPEA was ineffective: it had limited resources and inadequate staff and funds. Thus Aquino's "honesty has not been matched by the political will to punish the corrupt" (Timberman 1991, 233–35). The *Tanodbayan* or Office of the Ombudsman was "reborn" in 1988, during Aquino's term of office. But the *Tanodbayan* was inefficient as it took a long time to process the complaints received. Consequently, it was not surprising that the *Tanodbayan* had accumulated a huge backlog of 14,652 cases or 65 percent of its total workload by December 1994. The *Sandiganbayan* had a higher profile than the *Tanodbayan*, but the former was less efficient, completing only 13 percent of its total caseload in 1996 (Coronel 1998, 247–51).

In 1994, two years after assuming office, President Fidel Ramos appointed Eufemio Domingo to head the Presidential Commission against Graft and Corruption (PCAGC). In June 1997, the Inter-Agency Anti-Graft Coordinating Council (IACC) was formed to control graft in government through the sharing of information and resources among the Commission on Audit, the Civil Service Commission, the National Bureau of Investigation, and the PCAGC. The Philippines' rank of 54, along with Turkey, among the 99 countries covered in TI's 1999 CPI reflects the ineffectiveness of the PCAGC, IACC, *Sandiganbayan,* and *Tanodbayan* to minimize corruption. The major reason for the failure of these agencies was provided in 1997 by Domingo, the head of the PCAGC:

The system [of fighting corruption] is not working. We are not making it work. We have all the laws, rules and regulations and especially institutions not only to curb, but to eliminate, corruption. The problem is that these laws, rules and regulations are not being faithfully implemented. . . . I am afraid that many people are accepting [corruption] as another part of our way of life. Big-time grafters are lionized in society, they are invited to all sorts of social events, elected and re-elected to government offices. It is considered an honor—in fact a social distinction—to have them as guests in family and community affairs. (Coronel 1998, 267–28)

In 2000, accusations against President Joseph Estrada and successful calls for his replacement by a new head of state with cleaner hands seem to confirm popular opinion that whoever heads the state, the system does not seem to change much.

China

After overthrowing the corrupt Kuomintang government in October 1949, the Chinese Communist Party (CCP) was concerned about curbing corruption in the new People's Republic of China (PRC). Accordingly, the Act of the PRC for the Punishment of Corruption, which defined corruption and stipulated its punishment, was adopted in 1952. As corruption became endemic in China during the post-1978 reform period, Deng Xiaoping's regime relied on the Criminal Law of 1979 as the major legal measure for fighting corruption. This law was amended in 1982 to impose stiffer punishment for corruption. It was further amended in 1997 to include a chapter on corruption, which specified the penalty for corruption, depending on the amount involved. For example, a person found guilty of corruption involving more than 100,000 yuan, or US$12,000, was to be punished by ten years imprisonment or the death penalty (Chan 1999, 300–301).

Unlike India and the Philippines, which are democracies, China has a Communist political system. Accordingly, the anticorruption agencies are organized along three sectors. First, the Supreme People's Procuratorate (SPP) was reestablished in 1978 to combat corruption in the judicial sector. The SPP formed the Procuratorial Division of Graft and Bribery in 1989 after the Tiananmen anticorruption and democracy movement. Below the SPP, the Bureau for Embezzlement and Bribery of the People's Procuratorate is responsible for handling and preventing cases of embezzlement and bribery. As China has a land area of 9,560,900 square kilometers, it is not surprising that there are 3,563 agencies for embezzlement and bribery.

Second, for the administrative sector, the Ministry of Supervision (MOS) was reestablished in December 1986 "in part to curb corruption and maladministration within the civil service." For the third sector involving the CCP, the Central Disciplinary Inspection Committee (CDIC) was formed in 1978 to check corruption among its members. Even though the MOS had received more than 700,000 reports in 1993, both the CDIC and MOS failed to reduce corruption because the "authorities appear[ed] to lack the political will to handle corruption cases among more senior party members" (Burns 1994, 57–58).

Until recently, few senior party officials have been convicted of corruption because they can "short-circuit corruption investigations by appealing to their protectors in the party hierarchy" (Root 1999, 58). In 1994, Li Yiaoshi, former Vice-Minister of the State Science and Technology Commission, was sentenced to twenty years' imprisonment for corruption (Burns 1994, 58). In July 1998, the former Beijing party chief Chen Xitong was the highest ranking party member to be jailed for corruption, when he was sentenced to 16 years for corruption and dereliction of duty (*Straits Time* 1 August 1998, 14).

More recently, Premier Zhu Rongji has been waging a crusade against corrupt officials (*Straits Time* 14 January 2000, 24). In March 2000, he informed party delegates at the National People's Congress (NPC) that "All major cases, no matter which department or who is involved, must be thoroughly investigated, and corrupt officials must be brought to justice" (*Straits Time* 6 March 2000, 23). To reinforce Zhu's message and to demonstrate his commitment to curbing corruption, three days later on March 8 Hu Changqing, deputy governor of Jiangxi province, became the highest ranking public official to be executed for corruption involving 5.44 million yuan between May 1995 and April 1999 (*Straits Time* 9 March 2000, 30). Similarly, Li Chenglong, deputy mayor of Guigang city, was executed on April 23, 2000 for taking US$478,500 worth of bribes (24 April 2000, 2). On July 31, 2000, Cheng Kejie, a former vice chairman of the influential Standing Committee of the NPC, was convicted in a Beijing court of accepting 41 million yuan in bribes while he was provincial governor of

Guangxi Zhuang Autonomous Region. He was then the highest-ranking CCP official to be executed for corruption since the PRC's inception in October 1949 (1 August 2000, 1). An intensified anticorruption campaign promises to catch more big fish and has increased the number of executions of senior officials found guilty of major corruption.

Pattern 3: Anticorruption Laws with an Independent Agency (Singapore, Hong Kong, and Malaysia)

The third pattern of fighting corruption is the combination of comprehensive anticorruption laws that are impartially implemented by an independent anticorruption agency. Singapore and Hong Kong employ this pattern effectively and this is reflected in the perception that they are the least corrupt countries in Asia. Malaysia is the third Asian country adopting this pattern of corruption control.

Singapore

In December 1937, the Prevention of Corruption Ordinance (POCO) was the first anticorruption law introduced in Singapore. It was implemented by the Anti-Corruption Branch (ACB) of the Criminal Investigation Department (CID) within the police. The ACB failed to curb corruption for two reasons: it was inadequately staffed and had limited resources; and it could not deal impartially with police corruption. The last straw was the discovery by the British colonial government that the police were involved in the theft of S$400,000 of opium in October 1951. The opium hijacking case demonstrated the ACB's ineffectiveness in fighting corruption and made the British authorities realize the importance of establishing an independent anticorruption agency that was separate from the police. Consequently, the ACB was dissolved and replaced by the Corrupt Practices Investigation Bureau in October 1952 (Qhah 1995, 393–94).

When the People's Action Party (PAP) government assumed office in June 1959, corruption was rampant in Singapore, perceived by many to be a low-risk, high-reward activity. To minimize corruption and change the public perception of corruption to a high-risk, low-reward activity, the PAP leaders introduced a comprehensive anticorruption strategy in 1960 by enacting the Prevention of Corruption Act (POCA) and strengthening the CPIB. In 1960 Singapore was a poor country with a gross national product (GNP) per capita of S$1,330 or US$443; thus the PAP government could not afford to raise the salaries of civil servants. The PAP government was left with the alternative of strengthening the existing anticorruption laws to reduce the opportunities for corruption and to increase the penalty for corrupt behavior. The POCA of 1960 removed the POCO's weaknesses, enhanced the penalty for corruption to five years' imprisonment and/or a fine of S$10,000 (increased tenfold in 1989), and gave the CPIB more powers to perform its duties.

The CPIB is the anticorruption agency responsible for enforcing the POCA's provisions. It has grown by nine times from eight persons in 1960 to its current seventy-one persons, comprising forty-nine investigators and twenty-two clerical and support staff. The CPIB performs three functions. First, it receives and investigates complaints on corruption in the public and private sectors. Second, the CPIB investigates malpractices and misconduct by public officials. Third, the CPIB examines the practices and procedures in the civil service to minimize opportunities for corrupt practices. Unlike Hong Kong's ICAC, which has 1,400 personnel, the CPIB can perform its duties efficiently without a large staff. Its location within the Prime Minister's Office and its legal powers enable it to obtain the required cooperation from both public and private organizations.

Hong Kong

In Hong Kong, the Prevention of Corruption Ordinance (POCO) was introduced in 1948 and implemented by the Anti-Corruption Branch (ACB), which was formed in the same year as a special unit within the Criminal Investigation Department (CID) of the Royal Hong Kong Police Force (RHKPF) to handle the investigation and prosecution of corruption cases (Lee 1981, 24). In 1952, the ACB was separated from the CID but kept its title and remained within the RHKPF (Lethbridge 1985, 87). The ACB reviewed the POCO in 1968 and recommended scrutiny of the anticorruption laws of Singapore and Ceylon (now Sri Lanka). A study team visited the two countries in 1968 to examine how their anticorruption laws worked in practice. The study team was impressed with the independence of the anticorruption agencies in these countries and attributed Singapore's success in minimizing corruption to the CPIB's independence from the police (Lee 1981, 47). The knowledge gained from the study tour contributed to the enactment of the Prevention of Bribery Ordinance (POBO) on May 15, 1971.

The enactment of the POBO led to the upgrading of the ACB into an Anti-Corruption Office (ACO). The June 1973 escape to England of corruption suspect Chief Superintendent P. F. Godber angered the public and undermined the ACO's credibility. Sir Alastair Blair-Kerr, Chairman of the Commission of Inquiry, concluded that the arguments for keeping the ACO within the RHKPF were largely organizational and the arguments for removing it were "largely political and psychological." The Governor, Sir Murray MacLehose, accepted Sir Alastair's advice of considering public opinion and decided to form a new anticorruption agency that was independent of the RHKPF (Qhah 1995, 402).

The Independent Commission Against Corruption (ICAC) was created in February 1974 with the enactment of the ICAC Ordinance and was entrusted with two tasks: "to root out corruption and to restore public confidence in the Government" (Lee 1981, 45). The ICAC is independent in terms of structure, personnel, finance, and power. Before the handover of Hong Kong to the PRC in July 1997, the ICAC was directly responsible to the governor, and its commissioner reported directly to the governor and had easy access to him. After July 1997, the ICAC reported directly to the chief executive of Hong Kong Special Administrative Region and is directly responsible to him.

Malaysia

In Malaysia, the first anticorruption law was the Prevention of Corruption Ordinance (POCO), 1937, which covered the Straits Settlements of Malacca, Penang, and Singapore. In 1938, the Prevention of Corruption Enactment extended the coverage to the Malay States. Both laws were replaced by the POCO 1950, which was in turn replaced by the Prevention of Corruption Act, 1961. The latter was amended in 1967 and 1971 to enhance its effectiveness (Quah 1982).

The Anti-Corruption Agency (ACA) was created in October 1967 through the merger of the Special Crime Division of the police and the Anti-Corruption Section in the Prime Minister's Department. The ACA's three functions were: the investigation and prosecution of offenses under POCA, 1961; the introduction of preventive measures against corruption in the civil service and statutory boards; and the investigation of conduct of those civil servants violating the Public Officers (Conduct and Discipline) Regulations (Marican 1979). But the ACA was ineffective for two reasons. First, its personnel were seconded police officers who lacked training for anticorruption work. Second, its officers were reluctant to investigate corruption in those departments where they might be posted in the future (Qhah 1982, 170).

The ACA's ineffectiveness led to its reorganization in 1968, and in 1973 it was renamed the National Bureau of Investigation (NBI), to reflect its wider scope—not only the investigation of corruption cases but also syndicated gambling, smuggling, serious criminal breach of trust, and organized fraud. In May 1982, the NBI's name was changed again to ACA to indicate that its main function was the prevention of corruption.

The Anti-Corruption Act of 1997 combined the POCA, 1961, the ACA Act of 1982, and the Emergency (Essential Powers) Ordinance No. 22 of 1970, and provided for new offenses, and additional powers for the public prosecutor and the ACA. Section 8 of the ACA of 1997 identified the ACA's three-pronged strategy to fight corruption: (1) detection and investigation of corrupt offenses by the Intelligence and Investigation Divisions; (2) communication and education of the population to support the fight against corruption; and (3) monitoring and consultative services to public agencies and population to reduce corruption.

Even though Malaysia has adopted the third pattern of corruption control, it is perceived to be less effective than Singapore and Hong Kong in curbing corruption. There are two reasons for Malaysia's lower ranking on the 1999 Transparency CPI. First, "Mahathir's greatest weakness in policy has been that he has failed to stem the growth of corruption, especially in the form of 'money politics' in UMNO" (Milne and Mauzy 1999, 171). Second, the ACA has been criticized for not impartially investigating corruption cases involving "big fish." The recent corruption trial of former Deputy Prime Minister Anwar Ibrahim appears to be largely politically motivated as other "big fish" have not been similarly targeted.

Minimizing Corruption in Asian Countries

Having compared how the governments of seven Asian countries have combated corruption according to the three patterns of corruption control, what can be said about corruption and governance in these countries? As corruption is only one factor determining the governance of these countries, minimizing corruption is a necessary but insufficient precondition for good governance. More specifically, the extent of corruption in these countries is inversely related to the quality of their governance. In other words, rampant corruption is usually associated with poor governance. In short, minimizing corruption in these countries will also help them improve their governance.

The question that arises now is: Is minimizing corruption in Asian countries an impossible dream or an attainable reality? The preceding analysis of how seven Asian countries have combated corruption shows that those countries that adopted the third pattern of corruption control are more effective than the other four countries that employed the first and second patterns. In other words, Singapore, Hong Kong, and Malaysia (pattern 3) are more effective than Mongolia (pattern 1) and India, Philippines, and China (pattern 2).

The experiences of Singapore and Hong Kong in minimizing corruption show that it is possible to minimize corruption when political leaders are sincerely committed to this task by impartially implementing comprehensive anticorruption measures. On the other hand, Malaysia's experience in fighting corruption demonstrates that adoption of the third pattern of corruption control does not necessarily guarantee success if the anticorruption agency is not fully independent, as it can be used for political purposes. When anticorruption laws are not implemented by an independent agency as in Mongolia, the anticorruption strategy employed is not effective. Similarly, when the anticorruption laws are implemented by many agencies in India, Philippines, and China, the results are equally unimpressive as these countries continue to be plagued by rampant corruption. In short, minimizing corruption to improve governance in Asian countries is not an impossible dream but an attainable reality if they adopt the third pattern of using an independent anticorruption agency to implement the anticorruption laws impartially. Never has there been a better time to take heed as people take to the streets in protest at kleptocracy, nepotism, cronyism, backroom deals, and kickbacks. They blame the late 1990s economic crisis on elite collusion, business malpractices, non- or selective implementation of the rule of law and official payoffs. They demand relief and they refer to the successful anticorruption measures in other parts of the continent as illustrated here. Above all, they are increasingly effective in ousting corrupt officials throughout Asia from Pakistan to South Korea and from Thailand to Indonesia in a "wave of anti-corruption sentiment" sweeping through the region (International Herald Tribune, 22 January 2001, 6).

References

Alfiler, Concepcion P. 1979. Administrative measures against bureaucratic corruption: The Philippine experience. *The Philippines Journal of Public Administration* 23 (3/4).

Anti-Corruption Agency, Malaysia. n.d. Strengthening integrity by promoting good governance in the Malaysian public administration—issues and challenges. Kuala Lumpur.

Burns, John. 1994. Civil service reform in China. *Asian Journal of Political Science* 2 (2).

Carino, Ledivina V., ed. 1986. *Bureaucratic corruption in Asia: Causes, consequences and control.* Quezon City: JMC Press.

Chan, Kin-Man. 1999. Corruption in China: A Principal-Agent Perspective. In *Handbook of Public Administration in the Asia-Pacific Basin*, edited by Hoi-Kwok Wong and Hon S. Chan. New York: Marcel Dekker Inc.

Chua, Yvonne T. 1999. *Robbed: An investigation of corruption in Philippine education.* Metro Manila: Philippine Center for Investigative Journalism.

Coronel, Sheila S., ed. 1998. *Pork and other perks: Corruption and governance in the Philippines.* Metro Manila: Center for Investigative Journalism.

Gill, S. S. 1998. *The pathology of corruption.* New Delhi: HarperCollins Publishers.

Gong, Ting. 1994. *The politics of corruption in contemporary China: An analysis of policy outcomes.* Westport, Conn.: Praeger.

Guhan, S. and Samuel Paul., eds. 1997. *Corruption in India: Agenda for action.* New Delhi: Vision Books.

Kim, Young Jong. 1994. *Bureaucratic Corruption: The case of Korea.* 4th ed. Seoul: Chomyung Press.

Kwong, Julia. 1997. *The political economy of corruption in China.* Armonk: M. E. Sharpe.

Lee, Rance P.L., ed. 1981. *Corruption and its control in Hong Kong.* Hong Kong: The Chinese University Press.

Lethbridge, H. J. 1985. *Hard graft in Hong Kong.* Hong Kong: Oxford University Press.

Liu, Alan. 1983. The politics of corruption in the People's Republic of China. *American Political Science Review* 77 (3): 602–23.

Marican, Y. Mansoor. 1979. Combating corruption: The Malaysian experience. *Asian Survey* 19 (6): 597–610.

McPhail, Stephanie. *Developing Mongolia's legal framework: A needs analysis.* Manila: Asian Development Bank.

Milne, R. S. and Diane K Mauzy. 1999. *Malaysian politics under Mahathir.* London: Routledge.

Mitchell, Richard H. 1996. *Political bribery in Japan.* Honolulu: University of Hawaii Press.

Mitra, Chandran. 1998. *The corrupt society: The criminalization of India from independence to the 1990s.* New Delhi: Penguin Books India.

Narasimhan, C. V. 1997. Prevention of corruption: Towards effective enforcement. In *Corruption in India: Agenda for Action,* edited by Guhan and Paul. New Delhi: Vision Books.

Palmier, Leslie. 1985. *The control of bureaucratic corruption: Case studies in Asia* (New Delhi: Allied Publishers).

Pasuk Phongpaichit and Sungsidh Piriyarangsan. 1996. *Corruption and democracy in Thailand* 2nd ed. Bangkok: Silkworm Books.

Quah, Jon S.T. 1982. Bureaucratic corruption in the ASEAN countries: A comparative analysis of their anti-corruption strategies. *Journal of Southeast Asian Studies* 13 (1): 153–77.

———. 1989. Singapore's Experience in Curbing Corruption. In *Political corruption: A handbook,* edited by Arnold J. Heidenheimer, Michael Johnston, and Victor T. LeVine. New Brunswick: Transaction Publishers.

———. 1995. "Controlling corruption in city-states: A comparative study of Hong Kong and Singapore." *Crime, Law and Social Change* 22: 391–414.

———.1999a. *Combating corruption in Mongolia: Problems and prospects.* Working Paper No. 22. Department of Political Science, National University of Singapore.

———.1999b. Corruption in Asian countries: Can it be minimized?" *Public Administration Review* 59 (6): 483–94.

Robertson-Snape, Fiona. 1999. Corruption, collusion and nepotism in Indonesia." *Third World Quarterly* 20 (3): 589–602.

Root, Hilton. 1999. Corruption in China: Has it become systemic?" *Asian Survey* 36 (8): 741–57.

Timberman, David G. 1991. *A changeless land—Continuity and change in Philippine politics.* Singapore: Institute of Southeast Asian Studies.

United Nations Development Programme. 1997. *Re-conceptualizing governance.* New York: United Nations Development Programme.

United Nations Development Programme. 1999. *Fighting corruption to improve governance.* New York: United Nations Development Programme.

Brian Woodall. 1996. *Japan under construction: Corruption, politics, and public works.* Berkeley: University of California Press.

11

The Culture of Corruption in Post-Mao China

Stephen K. Ma

THE WORLD'S MOST POPULOUS COUNTRY has slipped into place as the world's second largest economy behind the United States. Its share of the world's GNP has doubled in the past twenty or so years to 10 percent, a remarkable achievement for what has been an economically backward and isolated part of the globe. But the cost in corruption has been so high as to raise serious questions whether the Chinese Communist Party (CCP) has become kleptomaniac, whether the country's leadership is really serious about tackling endemic corruption and a virulent underground economy, whether age-old corruption practices can be reversed without fundamental changes in Chinese culture, and whether the diversion of investments from official to unofficial projects has been of greater benefit to the Chinese people as a whole by widening the distribution of wealth from a narrow privileged elite in a favored part of the country.

Take for instance, the evidence that has leaked out of China just in the past few years. Official pronouncements have revealed that the country's largest state companies, security forces, power utilities, and insurance and securities firms misappropriated or lost more than $10 billion in 1998 alone. Managers of the Three Gorges Dam project embezzled some $28 million meant for the relocation of residents whose habitats were to be flooded, and one senior official absconded with over $100 million from the project. Government officials in the coal, rail and oil industries misappropriated over $700 million, and utility companies collected nearly $1.4 billion in illegal fees (*Wall Street Journal* 26 January 1999). Because of shoddy work and corruption, bridges, roads, dikes, buildings, and dams all over the country have collapsed. The dikes were filled with mud instead of concrete. Buildings were constructed with no or very weak foundations. Roads were built on swamps. Even Beijing's Western Train Station was already crumbling just one year after its completion in late 1998. All of these are called "bean curd" projects because they fall apart so easily. Without a financial system in which borrowers are conscious of the cost of capital, billions are wasted, misused, and stolen. There is no real process for tendering contracts and little accountability once projects are started. Contracts are usually handed to relatives and friends of local Communist Party bosses, then subcontracted to inefficient state firms. Much is diverted to private self-serving projects and invested in unneeded, empty, and unsold buildings, while safety regulations are ignored (*Washington Post Weekly* 8 April 1999, 10).

Indeed, it is calculated that some $25 billion, about 3 percent of China's GNP, has been siphoned off the nation's grain storage program, which has encouraged graft and squandering among local officials. Corruption has deeply penetrated China's network of 20,000 state grain purchasing stations, which lost $1.8 billion a month and which no one claimed to know about. The state bought grain from local farmers at guaranteed prices, stored it, and then sold it at a loss. Between 1992 and 1998, China's Agricultural Development Bank loaned some $66 billion to the state granaries to buy grain although stocks were worth only about $40 billion. The gap was due to embezzlement and diversion to sideline investments and bureaucratic siphoning. Disgruntled farmers and employees who had not been paid furnished state auditors with ledgers of phony members.

To understand the extent of official involvement, one can look at a smuggling ring exposed in 1999 in Xiamen, formerly Amoy, a major port in Fujian. The case involved top-level city government officials, customs officers, bankers, and military and police officials, all connected with the now defunct Farewell Group into which thousands of allegedly fraudulent invoices were poured, estimated at more than $5 billion. Such smuggling is only one of the many channels for government officials to extort bribes or engage in illicit activities that have accounted for the surge in Communist Party graft in recent years. The Xiamen ring smuggled cars, crude and diesel oil, firearms, and electronic goods estimated at $10 billion, and possibly emigrants willing to pay huge fees to escape China. At times, diesel oil smuggled into China accounted for one-fifth of all diesel oil distributed nationwide, cutting deeply into the reserves of state-run oil companies, but this figure also includes estimates of other ports including Hong Kong (*Wall Street Journal* 9 December 1999).

To illustrate the depth of involvement of local party officials, one need only refer to the 40,000 residents of sprawling, smoggy Chongqing, China's largest city of some 31 million residents, who lost their life savings in one of the most audacious banking scandals in the post-Mao reform era. They lost their money in an illegal bank organized and run by city officials in collusion with officials of the People's Bank of China, the central bank that regulates the nation's banking system. The Chongqing New Hand High-Tech Development Company, one of 162 illegal banks set up since 1993, squandered nearly $20 million (about one-third of its deposits) and revealed how China's banks are mired in a mountain of bad debts that made them technically bankrupt. To attract depositors, the bank rented billboards all over the city, set up offices in government buildings, and guaranteed an annual return of 30 percent. It spent money bribing bank regulators and investing in projects but soon went bankrupt after paying its staff very handsome compensation. The government in Beijing had to issue emergency loans to the city to repay the poorest depositors but in so doing it saddled the local government with the debt. Similar banking scandals previously occurred in the Zhanjiang branch (Guangdong province) of the state-run China Construction Bank in 1996 and its Shiyang branch (Hubei province) in 1997 (*Wall Street Journal* 1 June 2000).

Hence, few were surprised when Jiang Zemin, the General Secretary of the Chinese Communist Party (CCP), admitted at the fifteenth National Congress held in September 1997 that bureaucratic corruption has continued to spread and grow. From October 1992 to June 1997 the CCP had to discipline a large number of its corrupted cadres. Bureaucratic immorality was caused "by the surge of . . . opportunities and the failure of internal and external controls" (Chan 2000). One wonders whether there could be a correlation between rapid economic development and the inevitable emergence of a new culture of corruption in a modernizing nation, as demonstrated by the Chinese case.

Modernization and a New Culture

Rapid and radical economic development in the last two decades has greatly transformed China's culture, which in turn has considerably influenced the nation's public administration. Prior to Deng Xiaoping's ambitious modernization campaign launched in the late 1970s, China's political culture could be characterized as moralistic (Elazar 1984, 114–22), closely guided by the CCP's ideology. The relationship between political and bureaucratic elites was basically not an issue. The bureaucratic machinery in Mao's China could be set in motion easily according to the orders given by the CCP leadership. "[T]he Chinese Communists have made serious efforts to restrain the exercise of bureaucratic power" and "have tried to ensure bureaucracy's responsiveness to political controls" (Townsend and Womack 1986, 352). Consequently, government officials "have had to learn to uphold ideals of loyalty and obedience . . . [and] to worry about the sin of bureaucratism" (Pye 1994, 179). Overall, bureaucratic behavior was commendable, or at least satisfactory and acceptable.

Several factors accounted for this relatively smooth party-state relationship. Hong Yung Lee attributed this to the CCP personnel policy. Cadres were recruited from the lower classes. "Positions within the bureaucracy rather than economic interests largely dictated the political behavior of the cadres. As a result, the cadres were more responsive to their superiors in the party state than to the particular class from which they were recruited" (Lee 1991, 69). In addition, for decades, China's administrative apparatus was under the CCP's close supervision. Organization and ideology were instrumental for the CCP in achieving this goal (Schurmann, 1968).

At the level of administrative culture, which has much to do with authority and motivation (Peters 1989, 63–68), organization and ideology also played an important role. Indeed, it was with their help that the CCP managed to produce a relatively compliant administrative culture, as transgressions of law and neglect of duty among government officials were largely uncommon. Although all four motivational techniques available in management practice—namely coercion, ideology, money, and involvement of rank and file—were employed at different times and for different purpose in Mao's China, financial incentive was seldom emphasized and rarely used. The state bureaucrats were accustomed to nonmaterial motivation.

The founding of the People's Republic of China in 1949 also brought about a new society. The "very general value orientations" (Peters 1989, 40) were such that it would be safe to claim that the societal culture in Mao's China favored a simple life and hard work." *Jianku Pusu, Qinjian Jieyue*" (hard work, plain living, and thrift) were household words during that period. Examining the postrevolutionary phases in China and Russia, Richard Lowenthal has pointed out the dilemma between institutionalized revolution and economic modernization. He argued that "both the tendency to institutionalize revolution as a recurrent phenomenon due to the utopian impulses of communist ideology, and the necessity for the revolutionary process to exhaust itself due to the requirements of economic modernization, are inherent in communist party regimes," but that "to combine the struggle for equality with the struggle for economic modernization" is "to reconcile the irreconcilable" because economic modernization "necessarily requires social differentiation and material incentives" (Lowenthal 1983, 191–201). Modernization and emphasis on economic development have greatly changed post-Mao China's culture. The two tools indispensable for the CCP's control over state bureaucracy were undermined by Deng's reformist policies. While the Cultural Revolution yielded such unintended consequences as emasculated political control, de-Maoization has been designed to depoliticize part of the system. Deng's pragmatism, which has replaced Mao's belief in ideology and politics in post-Mao China, undisguisedly depreciated the role of ideological indoctrination and political organization. Meanwhile, his efforts to catch up with richer countries have led to, among other things, elite transformation from revolutionary cadres to party technocrats. Deng "changed the criteria for personnel management from political loyalty to the ability to further economic development" (Lee 1991, 228).

The relationship between political and bureaucratic elites was no longer that of control and compliance. The demise of political domination over state bureaucracy and a new recruitment policy for government officials posed a serious challenge for the post-Mao China leadership. On the one hand, political education and party discipline were de-emphasized. Lax political supervision tended to make it more difficult to restrain bureaucratic behavior. On the other hand, more and more state cadres were hired on professional merit rather than political criteria. These newly recruited bureaucrats' respect for their political superiors was conceivably less than their predecessors', whose life experience was to obey the CCP. They did not feel that they owed their position to the Party. Recruitment through competition has made them more confident in their abilities and less obedient to their political bosses. Naturally, these technocrats demonstrate less interest in political education, which preaches allegiance to the state and compliance with CCP policies. They are likely to show more concern about their own interest, professional or personal. In the process, the political culture was being transformed rapidly, becoming increasingly individualistic and materialistic. Deng's bold reform has created a new environment where many government officials found themselves "in the position of enjoying access to decision-makers, as well as to the resources, capital, and information necessary to get ahead in the market." When official policy called them to lead the society in becoming rich, they were "more interested in enriching themselves" (Lee 1991, 323).

"To get rich" has greatly changed administrative and societal culture in post-Mao China. Management and authority in public organizations quickly became coveted sources of personal wealth. A new, recalcitrant administrative culture emerged as obedience to the CCP was being supplanted by pursuit of personal profit through public office, which began to corrode many bureaucrats. The Chinese state can no longer be ruled by fiat from above. Bureaucrats at the lower levels "are increasingly ignoring their leaders in Beijing, flouting policy and often frustrating some of the central government's best-laid plans." Post-Mao China "has in many respects become an unruly behemoth, difficult to govern from the center as market reforms and the clamor for a stake in the new economy take root" in almost every corner of the country (*Los Angeles Times* 30 September 1999).

"To get rich" has also transformed the societal culture, which no longer appreciates plain and thrifty living. Increasingly hedonistic, the societal culture in post-Mao China advocates and admires money making and pleasure seeking. Everyone looks up to fortune and wealth, first dreaming of possessing ten thousand yuan and soon aspiring to become a millionaire at all costs. To summarize the societal culture in the 1980s and 1990s, He Qinglian used several folk rhymes. These include, for example, "Money may not be omnipotent, but with no money one can only be impotent," and "It is worth risking imprisonment for ten-odd years to reap a profit of several hundred thousand yuan" (He 1998, 205). Thus, with these cultural changes, the level of bureaucratic corruption has grown alarmingly high. China has become one of the three most corrupt countries in Asia, according to a survey of expatriate managers (mainly from Europe and America) carried out by the Hong Kong–based Political and Economic Risk Consultancy (*Economist* 27 May 1995, 61).

Respect for the nation's once uncorrupt administrative apparatus has been replaced by disdain and dislike. A major theme in the Tiananmen student demonstrations during the spring of 1989 was to eliminate official corruption. Their profiteering through public office became so widespread that a new term *guandao*—the activities of the CCP and government cadres in reselling goods at a profit—has been added to the Chinese vocabulary.

As China's state bureaucracy has grown rampantly corrupt in the process of modernization, the CCP has had to learn to deal with this new problem of bureaucratic behavior. Since revolutionary means no longer function, can the CCP find other ways by which bureaucratic behavior may be kept from becoming corrupt? To paraphrase Deng's renowned quotation on a white or black cat (that it doesn't matter whether it is a white cat or black cat as long as it catches mice): it does not matter whether supervision is political or professional as long as it bridles bureaucratic behavior. In order to keep tight rein on China's huge administrative apparatus and to ensure that the nation's army of bureaucrats will be supervised properly, the post-Mao China leadership turned to the enactment of codes of ethics for government officials.

Codes of Ethics

New codes of public ethics could help to inculcate a sense of obligation into the minds of government officials. Deng's modernization has de-Maoization as a component of the program. Mao is no longer treated as a god and his thoughts as golden rules. Contrary to Mao's egalitarian ideas, Deng has been urging people to pursue self-interest by getting rich first. The ideological confusion has led to a crisis of confidence. A lack of confidence in the system and the uncertainty about life goals haunt hundreds of millions of Chinese, including those who serve in the state bureaucracy. Many state cadres, who are supposedly public servants, do not feel obligated to serve the state and the public interest.

As early as 1928, a board of inquiry in the United Kingdom stated, "The first duty of a civil servant is to give his undivided allegiance to the state at all times and on all occasions when the state has a claim on his service" (Waldo 1994). The Chinese authorities in post-Mao China certainly would very much like to see the nation's civil servants fulfill this duty faithfully. Actually, government officials in any country in the world are expected to recognize and observe their obligation to the state, although the degree of their response may vary. China's civil servants are no exception. Codes of professional ethics could assist in guiding them toward that goal in an environment of ideological confusion and crisis of confidence.

In addition, other situations prompted the post-Mao China leadership to establish codes of ethics for the nation's state bureaucracy. The Chinese authorities obviously intended to regain legitimacy for the regime by establishing guidelines for administrative behavior. Many cadre-related groups "hoped to assure the Party's revolutionary legitimacy for the future" through purging corruption (White 1989, 13). One demand raised during the student prodemocracy demonstrations in 1989 was that corruption had to be curbed or otherwise it would bankrupt the regime. A statement made by Xu Simin, a delegate from Hong Kong to the Seventh Chinese People's Political Consultative Conference, exemplified many people's feelings. He pointed out that the situation of unchecked corruption was "extremely dangerous" and that unless the Chinese authorities took the problem seriously "then it will be very difficult to keep the Chinese Communist Party, which I have supported, from continuing to sink further and further into corruption, even to the point of final self-destruction" (Cheng 1990, 34). The Chinese authorities have had to learn lessons the hard way. With the regime's survival at stake, they have had to deal with the problem of bureaucratic corruption effectively.

Moreover, an anticorruption campaign serves as a weapon in the power struggle against political adversaries. "In a totalitarian state, fighting 'corruption' is a convenient way to eliminate political rivals" (*US News and World Report* 15 May 1995, 50–51). In an attempt to consolidate his position in the behind-the-scenes struggle to succeed the dying Deng, CCP Chief and President Jiang Zemin has managed to oust one of the principal power contenders, Beijing's CCP secretary and the CCP Politburo member Chen Xitong, through purging corruption. Soon after one of Chen's deputies, Beijing's Executive Vice Mayor Wang Baosen, committed suicide amid allegations of blatant corruption, Chen was put under house arrest. Grudging Jiang his rapid ascent to the top position in China's power hierarchy after 1989, Chen had seldom showed respect for the newly anointed Party Chief. The anticorruption campaign has helped Jiang to remove a major obstacle on his way to achieving indisputable authority in the post-Deng era.

What merits attention is that the current anticorruption campaign differs from previous political movements against bureaucratic abuse of power in that in the process it has enacted codes of ethics for millions of government officials. These new rules not only contribute to an honest administration but also blur the picture of fierce struggle among power contenders. In this sense, codes of ethics serve as useful instruments in the power struggle.

Two types of corruption exist. One helps enhance the wealth of officeholders. The other helps maintain or expand their personal power (Bollens and Schmandt 1979, 17). The codes of ethics in post-Mao China deal basically with the first type of corruption, which is an inevitable although not intentional consequence of the call to "get rich first." Beginning in 1993, when the Chinese authorities decided to launch the anticorruption campaign, a series of codes of ethics designed to set guidelines for Party and state bureaucracy were established. They include the first and second "five rules" on anticorruption and self-restraint by leading cadres, developed by the Party's Central Commission for Discipline Inspection in August 1993 and March 1994, respectively. Both codes prohibit cadres at or above the county level from getting involved in commercial activities, accepting such benefits as gifts or bonds, credit cards, and club memberships, using luxury cars, buying houses at special prices, squandering public money, and defaulting on state loans. Later, four additions were made to the two "five rules." The added codes forbid state cadres from building private houses, using vehicle license plates designated for police or foreigners, reimbursing entertainment, and attending banquets that may influence official business.

Obviously, unhealthy bureaucratic behavior has not been deterred by these codes. The authorities decided to come up with more specific codes targeting certain aspects of corruption. In September 1994, the General Office of the Party's Central Committee and the General Office of the State Council issued "The Rules on the Use and Administration of Vehicles in Party and Government Institutions." Vehicles appropriated to ministers, governors, and officials at that level were not to be equipped with engines over 3.0 liters. Lower-ranked vice-ministers or vice-governors, could use only vehicles with engines of under 2.5 liters and gradually had to switch to domestic vehicles.

In December 1994 the State Council issued specific rules in regard to gifts. No government officials could accept gifts worth more than two hundred yuan in their official dealings with foreign nationals or organizations. Months later, the General Office of the Party's Central Committee and the General Office of the State Council also issued "The Rules on Registration of Gifts in Domestic Activities among Party and Government Personnel."

Like millions of average Chinese, many state cadres consider the newly opened stock market a shortcut to quick money and want to make a profit there with the help of their networks. To bar them from playing in the stock market, the Party's Central Commission for Discipline Inspection decided in August 1993 to ban Party and government officials from stock trading and other market pursuits. To keep track of bureaucrats' personal financial situations, the General Office of the Party's Central Committee and the General Office of the State Council issued in April 1995 "The Rules on Filing an Income Disclosure by Leading Party and Government Cadres at the County/Division Level." Although a semiannual disclosure is now required of those covered by the codes, the information remains confidential, which raises doubts about the effectiveness of the measure. There are also codes on travel abroad. Late in 1993, the authorities issued a notice attempting to slow the flow of state-funded delegations of cadres going abroad. Still, groups of tourists, often dressed Western style, can be seen regularly sightseeing abroad.

How to curb the bureaucratic addiction of eating and drinking wantonly at public expense is a perennial problem in China. The central government issued thirty-two directives in this regard in 1992. They were of no avail. The cost of state-funded banquets reached 100 billion yuan in 1993. "The Rules on Barring Industrial and Commercial Administrators From Attending Banquets Which May Influence the Proper Conducting of Official Business" issued in early 1995 were just an additional attempt to tackle the vexing bureaucratic pathology. The codes cover only cadres at bureaus of industry and commerce. But many CCP and government agencies at the central level soon followed suit and established their own rules on accepting invitations to banquets.

In early 1997, the Office of Law and Regulations under the CCP's Central Commission for Inspection published a booklet entitled *Codes of Conduct and Related Rules and Regulations for Honest Government* with a first printing of 300,000 copies. Included in the volume is a 1997 circular issued by the General Offices of the CCP and the Central Government stipulating that all leading cadres at or above the level of deputy county head had to report to their superiors on important matters in their personal lives. Apparently, the authorities felt that more measures were required to keep state bureaucracy in line, no matter how intrusive they might be. In sum, designed to promote a positive image of public administration in an era of reform, all these codes of ethics have illustrated the efforts by the post-Mao leadership to deal with a new, recalcitrant administrative culture.

Addressing the Culture of Corruption

Have the newly promulgated codes of ethics successfully resolved the issue of a recalcitrant administrative culture in post-Mao China? Obviously not yet. Despite the fact that these codes have been widely publicized, the situation continues to deteriorate steadily. In his speech at the Fourth Plenum of the CCP's Central Commission for Discipline Inspection in January 2000, Wei Jianxing, the Commission's Secretary and a member of the Standing Committee of the CCP's Politburo, disclosed that in 1999 alone the authorities had taken disciplinary actions against more than 132,000 corrupted CCP and state cadres, of whom more than four thousand served at the county level, over three hundred at the bureau level, and seventeen at the provincial/ministerial level (*Chinese Daily News* 13 January 2000). The data for 1999 disclose little progress from the 1992–1997 period. Meanwhile, the number of corrupt bureaucrats who manage to escape from investigation and prosecution is anyone's guess. The anticorruption campaign has still much work to do.

As for China's law enforcement, the picture looks even more dismal. The key tool in the battle to control bureaucratic misconduct ought to be law enforcement. Only when the law is upheld, when everybody has equal access to it, when the public trusts and identifies with enforcement agencies, these achievements "will do much to clean up the rest of government and keep all other public officials honest" (Caiden 1990). Unfortunately, agencies of China's law enforcement which constitute a major force in the struggle against bureaucratic corruption, have become no less corrupt. In comparison with 1994, officers in law enforcement that were involved in criminal cases increased by almost 40 percent in 1995. In the Xiamen smuggling case, which has so far implicated more than two hundred officials of the municipal government, including almost the entire Party and government leadership of the city, the Director of the Municipal Bureau of State Security has had the audacity to assist in a deputy mayor's escape (*Chinese Daily News* 12 January 2000).

Why have the codes of ethics not yielded the expected results? Bureaucratic behavior is influenced by a combination of political, administrative, and social factors. The newly promulgated codes of ethics focused only on administrative culture. Efforts will also be needed to address political culture and societal culture that have played an important part in bringing about a culture of corruption in post-Mao China. A new political culture must be fostered. Daniel Elazar has suggested that there are three types of political culture: individualistic, moralistic, and traditionalistic (Elazar 1984). In the case of post-Mao China, the tendency to move from moralistic to individualistic culture must be stopped and reversed. The so-called "socialist market economy" has forced millions of

Chinese to take responsibility for their own success and failure. Values such as the public good, selflessness, and commitment to serve the people are giving way to endeavors to pursue personal gains. Without halting individualistic values, few state cadres will show interest in observing the new codes of ethics.

There must be a switch from subject culture to citizen culture. Three roles played by average people have been identified: subjects, participants, and parochials. China is still largely a subject culture. The average Chinese are expected to obey and follow as subjects rather than to participate as citizens who have the right to monitor their government. A transition to a citizen culture cannot take place peacefully. To disclose bureaucratic misbehavior often entails a price. Hence the warning "if you are going to sin, sin against God, but not against the bureaucracy—God will forgive you, but bureaucracy never will" (Cody and Lynn 1992, 76). Incomplete statistics for 1991 have shown that about ten thousand whistleblowers were persecuted in China, including three who were killed. Nonetheless, a transition is taking place. For example, in 1997, more than two thousand peasant households in the Sichuan Province defied threats from local officials, sued them, and won the case. In 1998 about one hundred thousand lawsuits were filed by Chinese citizens against government bodies. Even the *People's Daily*, the CCP's official newspaper, could not escape rebuke in a libel lawsuit by an ordinary worker. On the other hand, to establish the citizen culture in post-Mao China is likely to take a while. To quote a China watcher, "The officials ensnared by the law have all been rather small fry" (*Los Angeles Times* 1 October 1999).

Bureaucratic resistance to the citizen culture is formidable. Many government agencies have refused to be interviewed by news reporters, who have been treated as troublemakers. They have been followed. Their investigations of administrative abuse of power have been disturbed and obstructed. A CCP's municipal Department of Propaganda in Jiangsu Province even issued an official document, forbidding any interview with reporters from outside the city unless approved by the department. In addition to the political culture, more needs to be done to rehabilitate the administrative culture and revive professional ethics in the state bureaucracy. Chinese government officers have gone through an evolution of professional ethics, from "listening to the Party" in Mao's China to "listening to the purse" in Deng's China. The codes of ethics are urging them not to use public office for personal gains. State cadres are expected to serve the state properly. How can the need to serve the state be justified while the majority are busy enriching themselves? On the other hand, will emphasizing the need to serve the state dampen individuals' enthusiasm to get rich, which is the primary force advancing China's economic prosperity? Officially, China is a regime that has the know-how about political ideology. But it seems to be experiencing difficulty dealing with the ideology of improving bureaucratic professional ethics.

Finally, the issue of societal culture must be addressed. Deng's modernization program has transformed China's platonic societal culture into a hedonistic one. The former largely resulted from Mao's discouragement of people's craving for material good. Reform and its emphasis on economic prosperity have opened the Pandora's box of human desire, which, with its built-up momentum, would be hard to hold back. "Thirst for dividends," the term coined by a Chinese scholar (Zhuang 1998, 103), swept like a fast-spreading epidemic across the nation, throwing people into the market scrambling for the most benefits. For the post-Mao China leadership, how to keep modernization moving while at the same time restoring a culture of plain living might prove to be a fight to reconcile the irreconcilable.

Conclusion

Deng Xiaoping's modernization program has produced conspicuous economic achievements. His efforts to catch up with other countries also led to an individualistic political culture, a recalcitrant administrative culture, and a hedonistic societal culture. Combined, they have led to a new culture of corruption. To deal with the rampant corruption among Party and government officers, the authorities in post-Mao China have enacted a series of ethical codes. Unfortunately, these codes have addressed only part of the cause: administrative culture. Even in this regard, the job has not been well done. Without bringing about appropriate political and societal cultures that would contribute to an honest government, anticorruption campaigns can hardly be effective. The problem is that further cultural rehabilitation may go against the driving force of modernization—stress on material prosperity. Can the leadership of post-Mao China prove that it is not mission impossible?

Possibly not. Corruption has toppled the party in other Communist regimes, and China is unlikely to avoid this fate. Indeed, corrupt officials are probably already adopting the traditional practice of "liu hou lu" or leaving an escape route for their anticipated collapse of the regime and the transformation of the CCP. They emigrate the country when they get official permission to leave on business or to study abroad. They move assets and relatives overseas. They launder money through foreign banks. They refer to some of those executed for corruption had planned ahead to evacuate their relatives and assets before they were tried. Others are plotting to amass power to benefit in a post-Communist regime by weaving networks of connections, secret circles, and double identities. These have abandoned communism, studied what to do from other post-

Communist countries of the ex-Soviet Union, and kept their corrupt activities away from investigation and public exposure so as to emerge later as the new elite. They may well succeed unless the CCP purges them first and restores public morality, clearly a major task ahead.

References

Bollens, John C., and Henry J. Schmandt. 1979. *Political corruption: Power, money, and sex.* Pacific Palisades, Calif.: Palisades Publishers.

Caiden, Gerald. 1990. Abuse of public trust: Fact or way of life? *USA Today Magazine* (July), 58–60.

Chan, Kin-man. 2000. Toward an integrated model of corruption: Opportunities and control in China. *International Journal of Public Administration* 23 (4), 507–51.

Cheng, Chu-yuan. 1990. *Behind the Tiananmen massacre: Social, political, and economic ferment in China.* Boulder, Colo.: Westview Press.

Cody, W. J. Michael, and Richardson R. Lynn . 1992. *Honest government: An ethics guide for public service.* Westport, Conn.: Praeger Publishers.

Daohe, Zhuang. 1998. *Shilun Fubai de shehui Lishi Yuanyin. On the social and historical causes for corruption, Dianda Jiaoxue* (Hangzhou). In *Fuyin Baokan Ziliao (Zhongguo Zhengzhi)* July, 103.

Elazar, Daniel J. 1984. *American federalism: A view from the states.* 3rd ed. New York: Harper & Row.

He, Qinglian. 1998. *The pitfalls of modernization.* Beijing: Jinri Zhongguo Chubanshe.

Lee, Hong Yung. 1991. *From revolutionary cadres to party technocrats in socialist China.* Berkeley: University of California Press.

Lowenthal, Richard. 1983. The post-revolutionary phase in China and Russia. *Studies in Comparative Communism* (Autumn), 191–201.

Peters, B. Guy. 1989. *The politics of bureaucracy.* 3rd ed. New York: Longman.

Pye, Lucian W. 1984. *China: An introduction.* 3rd ed. Boston, Mass.: Little, Brown and Co.

Schurmann, Franz. 1968. *Ideology and organization in Communist China.* 2nd ed. Berkeley, Calif.: University of California Press.

Townsend, James R., and Brantly Womack. 1986. *Politics in China.* 3rd ed. Boston, Mass.: Little, Brown and Co.

Waldo, Dwight. 1994. Public administration and ethics. In *Current Issues in Public Administration,* edited by Frederick S. Lane, ed, 5th ed.,. New York: St. Martin's Press.

White, Lynn T. III. 1989. *Politics of chaos: The organizational causes of violence in China's cultural revolution.* Princeton, N.J.: Princeton University Press.

12

Government Corruption in Latin America

Jorge Nef

FOR MANY SCHOOLED in the prevailing acritical Western mold, corruption largely appears as a characteristic of the politics of developing areas. From a conventional wisdom perspective, the discrepancy between norm and behavior (formality and reality), generating ethical double standards, is a direct consequence of the prevalence of structural and cultural dualism. While modernity breeds ethical congruities, the process of modernization exacerbates contradictions and discontinuities. Corruption could be seen as a dysfunction or social pathology emerging out of the discontinuities brought about by socioeconomic change. A number of common beliefs are derived from this conceptualization. One is that corruption is largely a function of underdevelopment. Another assertion is that higher ethical standards in government and administrative behavior are more likely to be found among cultures where amoral familism has been displaced by achievement-oriented and work-ethic values. A third belief is that democracy and corruption are inversely related. Finally, there is the belief that the greater the degree of privatization of the economy or, conversely, the smaller the public sector, the greater the likelihood that corruption would diminish. In all these propositions, Latin America appears to contrast sharply with North America: it is distinctively Third World; it is outside the axiological realm of the Protestant ethic; it exhibits a less than healthy democratic record; and it has a tradition of statism.

But corruption does not occur in a vacuum. It is a system of behavior that straddles public and private spheres, that is, the corrupted is always faced with a corruptor, often originating with those able to buy influence. As for the differential levels of corruption between developed and underdeveloped countries, it could be argued that, more than an inverse association, there are different forms of corruption that relate to different levels of development. In this sense, underdeveloped societies may exhibit highly manifest, annoying, and ubiquitous forms of retail corruption: bribery, tips, nepotism, and particularistic transactions. Developed societies have more developed manifestations of corruption. These are less ostensible, and more institutional, legal, and selective wholesale corruption. Unlike its retail counterpart—expressed in monetary bribes at the administrative level of the petty clerk, the police officer on the street, or the customs official—developed forms of corruption take part in the rarified atmosphere of intra-elite exchanges at the political level. There, under the veneer of legality and formality, the currency is mainly political and the economic stakes extremely high.

A word of warning about cultural determinism and other ethnocentric biases is in order here. Though cultural explanations are always more attractive than macroanalysis at the aggregate level, the danger exists of imposing biased criteria. This is particularly the case when methodologies are uncritically applied to non-Anglo Saxon contexts. The same applies to the relationship between transparency and democracy, which is heavily tilted toward Western notions of procedural democracy, and more so to the neoliberal belief that corruption diminishes in direct proportion to the shrinkage of government functions.

It has been commonplace to associate Latin America and the Caribbean region with government corruption, especially by invidious and intentional contrast with North America. Stories about drug trafficking, influence peddling, fraud, plain theft of public funds, and persistent abuses of human rights are abundant. Colorful terms such as *coima* or *mordida* are frequently used to describe varieties of bribes. Anecdotal as they can be, these stereotypes often reveal the surface of a persistent—and for many, growing—trend. Of a list of ninety-nine countries, measuring the degree of *absence of* corruption prepared by Transparency International (TI), Latin America and the Caribbean as a whole appears to be corruption-prone (Transparency International 1999). Empirically then, the Latin American countries appear characterized by high incidence of corruption although they also exhibit wide variations among them. Most Latin American countries are closer to Eastern European or African states. History and culture largely explain this.

The Patrimonial Legacy

Before Independence

Since the 1500s, European colonialism laid the foundations of Latin America's socioeconomic structure, and the dominant administrative mode, uprooting and driving underground Amerindian practices. The institutional superstructure of the New World was born as a dependency of Madrid and Lisbon (Jaguaribe 1964). In this hierarchical order, the absolute power of the king was at the center of legitimacy and wisdom. Authority emanated, in theory at least, directly from the Crown. But geographical and operational reality made this power distant, aloof, and often merely symbolic. Under legalistic trappings, formality and reality were worlds apart as functionaries enjoyed a great deal of discretion in interpreting and applying norms to concrete situations. An imitative and ritualistic administrative culture emerged. Even the cosmopolitan appearance of today's modern administrative culture can be traced back to the colonial tradition of obedience with avoidance (Moreno 1969).

Three centuries of peninsular government entrenched a pattern of exogenous modernization. European social and political events, more than internal needs, determined the life cycle of colonial officials. Semifeudal and patrimonial forms inherited from the Hapsburg dynasty, with their emphasis on town councils, sinecures, patrimonialism, the selling of government offices, and limited home rule, were displaced in the middle of the eighteenth century by the enlightened despotism of the Bourbon reforms. The latter pursued greater fiscal responsibility and accountability, enhanced efficiency, and probity in public office. But above all they aimed at more effective administrative and political centralization and control. They also set the stage for the transition from mercantilism to early capitalism.

Independence

Latin American independence in the early 1800s was more the consequence of European conflicts and big-power politics, such as Napoleon's invasion of the Iberian Peninsula, than widespread nationalism among New World aristocrats (Keen 1992). The disintegration of Spanish and Portuguese colonialism was also a manifestation of a legitimacy crisis inside the monarchies, which until then had been the apex of the carefully crafted system of imperial domain. Emancipation was not a bourgeois revolution based upon ideas of liberty, equality, civil rights, or effective citizenship. Political liberation, though violent, left almost intact the property and privilege of the same landed oligarchy who profited from colonialism. In the midst of growing disintegration, the key issues of governance in the early nineteenth century were state and nation building (Burns 1986). Centralization, order, and the preservation of property relations constituted the primary tasks of the new governments. So was the reinsertion of the recently independent nations, with their structurally dependent economies, into the international division of labor. National unity meant the curbing of local loyalties and chieftains and the foundation of a credible pact among various national oligarchies. The very viability and legitimation of the state became paramount, overriding questions of accountability and good government.

Constitutional experiments throughout the region ranged from utopian attempts at grafting Benthamite utilitarian principles into constitutions to drives to reinstitute monarchies under republican guise, all under the spell of a home-grown variety of Bonapartist authoritarianism.

Most countries remained in the throes of civil strife; the public treasury and the state became the spoils of the victor, until unifying dictatorships under triumphant warlords managed to bring about a semblance of order. By the middle of the nineteenth century, with expanding demand for Latin American raw materials and greater surplus to split among the elites, more stable and institutionalized forms of power sharing began to take shape (Burns 1986). Republican structures, formally resembling either the French or American models, increasingly replaced warlordism. But deeply ingrained practices, such as sinecures, nepotism, particularism, and clientelism, went hand in hand with universalistic discourse. The patrimonial tradition of the state was largely untouched (Keen 1992). As the states developed, civil society remained weak: families, clients, and subjects, rather than citizens with rights. The growing discrepancy between norm and behavior, discourse and reality, presented a widening double-standard. Corruption, paternalism, and violence filled the gap.

The political systems that evolved in the region, even in the most institutionalized and stable countries, were at best autocratic republics, not popular democracies by any standard of definition (Burns 1998). Responsible and constitutional government meant in this context abeyance to the formal rules of the game, not an entrenched view of rights and accountability. Constitutional and legal forms transplanted from the North were often a measuring rod of modernity by imitation, not a substantial rendering of a public service. Government jobs were mostly recognition of loyalty to the powers that be, not the presence of a neutral representative and responsible bureaucracy (Gouldner 1954). Even when efforts at the professionalization of the civilian and military cadres of the state began in the 1880s, this seemingly neutral body of state employees was an elitist stratum to which ordinary people had little access. Bureaucratic and authoritarian traditions intersected in a political and social order that was patrimonial at its core and only superficially legal-rational.

Waves of migration, foreign and internal, pouring into the expanding cities, combined by the transformation of peasants into blue-collar labor in the first decades of the twentieth century, brought about a simultaneous process of state expansion and professionalization of government functions. The export-driven growth mentioned earlier (1880s to the 1920s) undermined the old patterns of paternalistic social relations. Acute polarization pitched an ever more alienated labor force against a socioeconomic order based upon land ownership, money, and privilege. Further insertion into the world economy, accompanied by rapid urbanization, incipient industrialization, and the upsurge of the middle strata, made white-collar employment, especially public service, the venue of choice to attain limited social mobility (Burns 1998). A broad social alliance of non-elites posed a threat to oligarchic interests. The professionalization of the civil service, the expansion of public education, and budding social security reforms were aimed by the ruling elites at diffusing a volatile social environment. It was also a way to build a coalition between the aristocracy and the middle sectors. It configured a butler class of sorts: objectively proletarian while subjectively oligarchic and dependent upon the patronage of the aristocracy. In this sense, the expansion of the state sector was a way to prevent further mobilization and threats to social peace. Patronage politics under the guise of educational merit were entrenched.

The administrative culture to emerge from this alliance reflected distinctively aristocratic values. Secondary, technical, normal, military, and postsecondary/professional education were geared not only to develop managerial, technical, and clerical skills, but to socialize the new middle classes into gentlemanly values. As the state was becoming the single largest employer, it also prepared them for roles in an expanding public sector. Since industrial development lagged far behind the export-driven economy and with the dramatic expansion of urbanization, the nascent white-collar ideology, nurtured by the public education system, was more clearly nested among public employees than in the nonstate components of the service sector. Middle-class respectability, a growing corporate identity, and rhetorical nationalism remained at the core of this emerging professional bureaucratic mentality. Yet equally imbedded and seemingly contradictory attitudes toward authoritarianism, formalism, patrimonialism, and venality coexisted as distinct cultural layers in this incipient state class (Graf 1988; 1995). This ideological amalgam was particularly noticeable among one of the most typical fractions of the Latin American middle classes: the officer corps (Nun 1968).

Since the 1930s

The social order resting upon the export economy collapsed with the 1930s Depression. The consequence of the catastrophe on bureaucratic culture was twofold. On the one hand, the role of the military as conflict managers and enforcers of last resort (and as ultimate protectors of elite privilege) was enhanced. On the other, it expanded the mediatory function of a now middle-class–controlled and relatively autonomous state to arbitrate social conflict by means of economic management. Thus, to the early law and order, educational, and social tasks of the state, a new mission was added: economic development. A rational-productivity techno-bureaucracy grew side by side with the more traditional patrimonial and legal-rational central administration. This meant the creation of a myriad of vertically departmentalized parastatals with broad functions in planning, financing, energy, industry, and marketing. It also meant a Keynesian policy orientation known as Import Substitution Industrialization (ISI) (Furtado 1976).

The specific effects of ISI varied with time and place, but on the whole it meant a corporatist arrangement: an enlarged state apparatus, with the white-collar classes playing broker between business and labor, while maintaining the status quo. In the more developed countries (Argentina, Brazil, Uruguay, Chile, Costa Rica, and Mexico) a combination of ISI policies and populism helped reduce social tensions by means of tactical alliances between the urban blue-collar unions and the state classes. Populism meant significant fiscal largesse in the use of the public purse to dispense favors to various social groups. It also meant the provision of public employment subsidies, transfer payments, huge contracts, and large-scale demagoguery. The cases of Brazil under Vargas (1930–1945), Argentina under Peron (1946–1955) and Mexico under the rule of the Institutional Revolutionary Party (PRI, 1923–2000) are examples of populism, a provider state, and government corruption going hand in hand.

In the less developed countries—comprising most of Central America, the Caribbean, and the Andean region—the initial social and economic conditions for a Keynesian project were absent and military rule ended up prevailing over economic management. Of course, military rule came at a price: besides the cost of repression, the officers developed a voracious tendency to plunder the national treasury without external constraints. In contrast, in the more developed economies, and for as long as fiscal resources (depending on export surpluses) were available, autonomous development extended well into the 1950s, and further professionalization of some of the leading sectors of the bureaucracy took place. It also gave rise to an embryonic administrative state and a public service ethos. This institutional proclivity remained in place until these regimes entered into crisis in the late 1960s.

In the poorer countries, the civil service remained ineffectual and patrimonial, while the commanding heights of the state continued in the hands of military rulers. As chronic deficit financing, inflation, and paralysis signaled the exhaustion of ISI policies, tensions between labor and business increased, this time in the context of the Cold War. Lower-class defiance grew in intensity. Populism of the kind espoused by ISI was simultaneously under attack by both ends of the social spectrum. Political and administrative immobilism, deadlock, and hyperinflation fed on each other. Legitimation crises affected the relatively more institutionalized administrative states in Brazil, Argentina, Uruguay, and Chile, while those under protracted military rule faced crises of domination:

the inability of the repressive apparatus to control by force.

The American-sponsored Alliance for Progress (1961), a reaction to the Cuban revolution, was a belated attempt to stabilize the region by means of development assistance. Development administration and administrative development were part of a strategy using development as counterinsurgency (Nef and Dwivedi 1981). Foreign aid, training, and development planning played an important role in a broad effort to refurbish the administrative cadres of Latin America. Under USAID sponsorship, increasing numbers of Latin American students and trainees were exposed to American ways. Money was also pouring in to carry on domestic programs on educational, agrarian, and tax reforms, and also for the training and modernization of the civil service under the spell of scientific management, program budgeting, and the like. But more important were the modernization and retooling of the security apparatus along national security and counterinsurgency lines (Barber and Ronning 1966). While the reforms of the civil service, though extensive, remained largely unfocused and piecemeal, the transformation of the security apparatus had an enormous and long-term systemic impact.

The Alliance came in too late, and subsequent American administrations saw it as ineffectual. As the Keynesian postulates of the program—the same ones underpinning ISI—were profoundly questioned by business and intellectual elites in the center, the very substance of the administrative reforms became objectionable. Dreams of a Marshall Plan for Latin America were finally scuttled by the Nixon administration in 1969. With the failure of the reformist project, the Latin American middle-class–controlled states were once again in crisis. The military bureaucracies became the pivot of a new alliance of panicking oligarchs, United States military and business elites, and disgruntled segments of the professional sectors. These "reactionary coalitions" (Moore 1966; North 1978) managed to bring down more than a leftist threat; populism and constitutional democracy went down too, ushering in military rule instead.

In their beginnings, some national security regimes were associated with the so-called bureaucratic authoritarian state (O'Donnell 1977). But the main function of these regimes was to effect a transition between Keynesian structuralism to monetarist neoliberalism and from nationalism to transnational control. Even in the rare cases when the military regimes pursued protectionist industrial policies, their net effect was to reduce the role of the civilian technobureaucracy to that of a tool of the military. The early neoliberal "shock treatments" (Garreton 1993) of structural adjustment, privatization, denationalization, deregulation, and downsizing started by the military regimes deflated the status of the public sector. They also deepened corruption, as groups within and outside the state positioned themselves to appropriate segments of the public sector. As military rule became ever more associated with corruption, gross human rights violations, and sheer terror, the public service function as a whole lost prestige and sank to even lower levels of performance and probity. Despite nationalist rhetoric, the military regimes of the 1970s were parasitic and instrumental in undermining the limited sovereignty of the Latin American nations. The "managers of violence" also had proved to be incompetent conflict and development managers (Burns 1986). Yet they succeeded in radically restructuring the nature of the Latin American state as well as its relations with both civil society and the international system. The U.S.-sponsored transitions to democracy in the 1980s occurred in the context of these profound alterations (Black 1998).

While military rule floundered in the midst of a staggering debt burden and Western mismanagement critics began to perceive such regimes as a liability for the survival of their economic and strategic interests, carefully orchestrated transition to restricted democracy, superintended by the regional superpower, ensued (Nef 1998). This return had strict limits and conditions. On the whole, it maintained the socioeconomic and political forces that had benefited by decades of military rule, while excluding radical and popular alternatives. The exiting security establishments were to be both the warrantor of the transition process and the central authoritarian enclave of the new institutional arrangement. This "low-intensity" democracy (Gil, Rocamora, and Wilson 1993) also preserved the basic neoliberal economic agendas of the authoritarian era. Chief among these legacies was a receiver state, whose prime goal was to manage the self-inflicted fiscal bankruptcies and facilitate the implementation of International Monetary Fund–inspired structural adjustment packages (Vilas 1995). Incomplete transition, restricted democracy, and the receiver state have had profound effects upon administrative values and attitudes. Privatization, budget cuts, downsizing, deregulation, and denationalization—especially in the social and developmental areas—have radically minimized the scope and function of government. As profit and personal gain on the one hand, and the national interest on the other, become blurred, the notion of public service appears increasingly redundant. Furthermore, as the status and income levels of civil servants sink, and with a thriving illegal economy such as the drug trade (Lee 1988), systemic corruption has been on the rise, reaching to the highest levels of government and administration.

The Culture of Corruption

These historical continuities and discontinuities have resulted in a complex cultural matrix in which there is not so much a synthesis as the coexistence of numerous and often incongruous elements, or layers. They include foreign and domestic influences, attempted reform, and persistent crises. The above-mentioned administrative mentality reflects deep contradictions affecting Latin American societies and is generally defined by three main parameters. The first is the opposition between growing social expectations and limited economic capabilities. The second tension is that between the haves and the have-nots. The third tension is that between the formality of sovereignty and the reality of dependence. The outcome of such contradictions is a zero-sum game, where politics and administration oscillate between stalemate and repression (Nef 1982). To systematize, the content of these layers can be sketched into an ideotypical cultural construct with five characteristics.

Particularism

In its outer layer, the administrative cultural mix of Latin America presents significant universal and achievement-oriented traits. Yet the core component of Latin America's administrative culture is defined by the persistence of amoral familism. Primary groups, especially extended families, and friends play a fundamental role in social life, even in the allegedly modern confines of urban life. The endurance of patrimonialism, *amiguismo* and *compadrazgo* are manifestations of this built-in particularism. So is the overall level of inwardness, ascription, lack of transparency, and distrust of strangers surrounding the performance of public functions.

Formalism

The Latin American state classes have been since their origins a status officialdom (Morstein-Marx 1963, 63), derived from their possessing official titles. These official titles serve in turn as a mechanism to access private consultancies and alternative (and not always transparent) sources of income. A bureaucrat (even a white-collar employee in a private corporation) or an officer, irrespective of the discredit in which the service may find itself, is a somebody. In a hierarchical social order, being middle class confers a degree of respectability and an aura of modernity. Ritualism, hyperlegalism, and the profound incidence of law makes the behavior and expectations of officials depend upon deductive and detailed interpretations of norms. There is a fundamental double standard: a public facade for outsiders and a private zone of exceptionality for insiders (Riggs 1967). The same applies to the use of time: delays, waiting, and slowness are selectively used to define the importance of the relationship and delineate power and hierarchy.

Discretionality

Under the mantle of formalism as described above, there is a perceived role expectation on the part of functionaries as having a surprisingly great degree of operational autonomy. Formalism and particularism ostensibly clash, with the former becoming a mechanism for avoiding responsibility, or for justifying dynamic immobilism and aloofness. The flip side of this contradiction is that it transforms the role of the civil servant into one of dispensing—and at times trading—personal favors as well as facilitating exceptions from existing norms. This exceptionalism gives rise to recurrent nepotism, corruption, patronage, and abuse.

Corporatism and Authoritarianism

The official's understanding of the relations between state and society is influenced by the weak brokerage and associational representation for most of the public vis-à-vis the government. In turn, elite interests are grossly overrepresented, with wide access to all levels of decision making. Moreover, the recognition of an entrenched elitist socioeconomic structure enhances a self-perception of autocracy, where the government and the bureaucracy act as mediators and arbiters of social conflict (Heady 1984). This reinforces the profound schism between insiders and outsiders. Clientelism, patrimonialism, the ubiquitous use of "pull," and the persistence of episodes of military intervention, reinforce the aforementioned traits. Though the white-collar military and civilian state classes cannot be equated with the landed and commercial oligarchy, public officials are in the domain of the elites and a few of them are able to make their way into the upper crust. Their connection with essentially undemocratic practices and governments makes the functionaries prone to assume an attitude of arbitrariness and disregard for the public at large. This demeanor toward outsiders, especially the lower strata, is pervasive not only in government but also in the private sector.

Centralism

Most administrative structures and processes are heavily centralized at the top. The administrator's values, behaviors, and expectations reflect a view of the public characterized by high levels of territorial and operational concentration. Decisions normally flow up to the top; so does responsibility. Although operational autonomy is not uncommon in practice, propensity to delegate is rather infrequent. In many instances, influence peddling flows upstream, at times creating a system of pyramidal corruption.

Corruption and the Administrative Process

The ideological "software" of the Latin American public sector is the result of an ongoing process of immersion, acculturation, and socialization, whose structural drivers are both implicit and induced. The primary vehicles for reproducing the administrative culture are the family, the educational system, peer groups, and direct experience with government and the public service. As indicated earlier, the fundamental class identification of civil servants is with the middle strata. There is a sort of circular causation here: the middle strata produces employees, while becoming a white-collar worker confers the attribute of middle-classness.

Class distinctions are paramount in Latin America, social identity being a function of ancestry, neighborhood, education, tastes, gender, ethnicity, and language. This by itself creates a double standard. The educational system, especially its secondary and tertiary levels, are exclusive and discriminating. High school and university education are in general the points of entry for employee roles. More specific training may occur at the postsecondary levels, either in public service schools or in university careers geared to administrative postings. These are connected to law, business, and economics but also the study of public administration. Few countries have developed an administrative class (Heady 1984), and many point to Costa Rica, Uruguay, and Chile as possible examples approaching the model of a neutral, effective, and relatively more transparent bureaucracy. At least two of these (Chile and Costa Rica) are also relatively free of corruption according to Transparency International, but even these cases appear problematic when closely examined.

In the case of the military, officers' academies at the secondary and postsecondary levels give specificity to a distinct body of doctrine and esprit de corps. National security and counterinsurgency doctrines define a predominantly antidemocratic and ultraconservative view of the world, heavily dependent upon ideological and material support from the United States. In fact, beyond a veneer of nationalism, most military establishments behave as occupying forces of their own countries. Civilian and military roles are sharply divided, with military professionalism being largely defined by the control over the instruments of force, institutional autonomy, verticality, rigidity, secrecy, high transnational integration, hubris, isolation, and corporate identity (Nef 1974). All these traits are enhanced by lack of accountability, creating conditions that facilitate endemic corruption. In many countries strong ties have developed between the security forces and organized crime, especially narco-traffickers. With the shrinkage of the developmental function of the state, by design and by default, security management has evolved into the most ostensible

function of the state (Nef and Bensabat 1992). With the Cold War over, the role
of national security has been redefined to encompass wars on drugs, terrorism,
or whatever justifies the paramountcy of the institutional interests of the security forces. The key latent function of armed force in the region remains that of
being a high-premium insurance policy for elite interests.

Conclusion

This tentative exploration into the structural, historical, and cultural roots
of government corruption in Latin America advances some tentative propositions and observations on the relationships among the phenomenon of corruption, the modal pattern of administrative culture sketched above, and the
larger social and political context. The persistence of government and administrative corruption in the region has to be seen within this broad contextual and
cultural matrix. Far from an irrational pathology, it constitutes a learned rational adaptation to circumstances in the politico-administrative milieu in which
officials operate. Stereotypes notwithstanding, Latin Americans are not more
inherently corrupt than their Western European or North American counterparts; nor do they exhibit a built-in predisposition to deviant behavior. It is
precisely the "normality" of corruption in the Latin American context that needs
to be understood. Explanatory theories, such as those centered upon the association between modernization and transparency, are of limited heuristic value
unless used in conjunction with other more interpretative approaches. Conversely, cultural and historical factors seem to render a more nuanced grasp of
the subject at hand. Yet they are not sufficient by themselves. This suggests that
a systemic and configurative approach, shifting between explanation and understanding, the micro and the macro, could provide keys to grasp the phenomenon under study. As a general conclusion, six historical and cultural propositions can be derived.

First, the administrative culture (or more properly, cultures) of Latin
America reflect the distinctiveness and complexity of the various national realities. These include persistent dependence, the perpetuation of rigid and particularistic social structures, chronic economic vulnerability, weak and unstable
growth, marginalization, low institutionalization, and acute social polarization.
The above translates into high levels of ambiguity, uncertainty, and widespread
systemic corruption.

Second, historically, the administrative culture of Latin America has been
molded by numerous failed attempts at modernization and cyclical crises. The
end result of crises and failed modernizations is a continuing condition of
underdevelopment. It has also contributed to perpetuating a self-fulfilling

prophecy of immobility (Adie and Poitras 1974), goal displacement, and venality.

Third, the outer layers of the region's administrative culture are directly affected by current circumstances and challenges. The incomplete transition to democracy of the 1980s, the debt crises, and structural adjustment policies are altering the very essence of public policy (Nef 1997). There is also a revolution of rising frustrations resulting from demographic pressures, urbanization, and the demonstration effect. The paradox is that while demands on the public sector to provide more services are growing, the state apparatus is shrinking. Competition for scarce resources, special favors, and influence in the context of an ever-shrinking and incompetent state creates conditions for the private appropriation of public interests.

Fourth, Latin America's administrative ideology is part of a larger ideological domain, containing values, practices, and orientations toward the physical environment, the economy, the social system, the polity, and culture itself. A predatory attitude toward resource extraction (often fueled by foreign debt), possessive individualism, amoral familism, a weak civic consciousness and a tendency to imitate "the modern," configures a conservative mind-set lacking the capacity and the will to anticipate and make strategic policy shifts. Most importantly, this mind-set is geared to avoiding moral responsibility for one's actions and their consequences.

Fifth, the administrative culture of Latin America has been distinctively derivative. As a reflection of an entrenched center-periphery regional and global order, it has tended to follow vogues in the developed societies. In this sense, it has been exogenous in its motivations, definition of problems, and prescriptions, which makes it hard to internalize, as far as ethical prescriptions are concerned.

Last, any profound administrative reform entails significant attitudinal and value changes. Thus, efforts at administrative restructuring, modernization, and the like must first address either directly or indirectly the question of administrative culture and ethics. This culture is heterogeneous and dynamic: syncretism, continuities, and discontinuities are part and parcel of its fabric and texture. In the last analysis, the socialization and training of the administrative cadres remain the crucial link for attitudinal and axiological change. In this, the mobilization of the civic culture is beginning to achieve some success. Freer mass media are having a benign effect likely to be heightened by the recently established Journalists Against Corruption or PFC (Periodistas Frente a la Corrupcion) use of the Internet (pfc@cipe.org) to support watchdog journalists who investigate or report corruption and to rally civic support behind anti-corruption measures.

References

Adie, Robert, and Guy Poitras. 1974. *Latin America: The politics of immobility.* Englewood Cliffs, N.J.: Prentice-Hall.

Barber, William, and Neale Ronning. 1966. *Internal security and military power: Counterinsurgency and civic action in Latin America.* Columbus, Ohio: Ohio State University Press.

Black, Jan. 1998. Participation and the political process: The collapsible pyramid. In *Latin America. Its problems and its promise. A multidisciplinary introduction,* edited by Jan Black. Boulder, Colo.: Westview Press.

Burns, E. Bradford. 1986. *Latin America. A concise interpretative history.* 4th ed. Englewood Cliffs, N.J.: Prentice-Hall.

Furtado, Celso. 1976. *Economic Development of Latin America.* 2d ed. Cambridge: Cambridge University Press.

Garreton, Manuel Antonio. 1993. The political evolution of the Chilean military regime. In *Transitions from authoritarian rule in Latin America,* edited by Guillermo O'Donnell, Philippe Schmitter, and Laurence Whitehead. Baltimore, Md.: The Johns Hopkins University Press.

Gil, Barry, Joel Rocamora, and Richard Wilson. 1993. *Low intensity democracy: Political power in the new world order.* London: Pluto Press.

Graf, William D. 1988. *The Nigerian State: Political economy, state class and political system in the post colonial era.* London: James Currey.

———. 1995. The state in the third world. In *The Socialist Register 1995,* edited by Leo Panitch. London: Merlin Press.

Heady, Ferrel. 1984. *Public administration: A comparative perspective.* 3d ed. New York: Marcel Dekker.

Jaguaribe, Helio. 1964. *Desarrollo economico y desarrollo politico.* Buenos Aires: EUDEBA.

Keen, Benjamin. 1992. *A history of Latin America.* 4th ed. Boston, Mass.: Houghton-Mifflin.

Lee, Rensselaer W. 1988. Dimensions of the South American cocaine industry. *Journal of Interamerican Studies* 30 (3/4): 87–104.

Mills, C. Wright. 1957. *The power elite.* New York: Oxford University Press.

Moore, Barrington. 1966. *Social origins of dictatorship and democracy. Lord and peasant in the making of the modern world.* Boston, Mass.: Beacon Press, 1966.

Moreno, Francisco Jose. 1969. *Legitimacy and stability in Latin America. A study of Chilean political culture.* New York: New York University Press.

Morstein-Marx, Fritz. 1963. The higher civil service as an action group in western political development. In *Bureaucracy and Political Development,* edited by Joseph LaPalombara. Princeton, N.J.: Princeton University Press.

Nef, Jorge. 1982. Empate politico, inmobilismo e inflacion: Algunas notas preliminares. *Revisita Centroamericana de Administracion Publica* 2 (3): 141–55.

————. 1974. The politics of repression: The social pathology of the Chilean military. *Latin American Perspectives* 1 (2): 58–77.

————. 1997. Estado, poder y politicas sociales: una vision critical. In *Cambios sociales y politica publicas en America Latina*, edited by Raul Urzuia. Santiago: Andros.

————. 1998. Administrative culture in Latin America: Historical and structural outline. *Africanus. Journal of Development Administration* 28 (2): 19–32.

Nef, Jorge and R. Bensabat. 1992. Governability and the Receiver State in Latin America: Analysis and Prospects. In *Latin America to the year 2000. Reactivating growth, improving equity, sustaining democracy*, edited by Archibald Ritter, Maxwell Cameron and David Pollock. New York: Praeger, 171–75.

Nef, Jorge and O. P. Dwivedi. 1981. Development theory and administration: A fence around an empty lot? *The Indian Journal of Public Administration* 28 (1): 42–66.

North, Lisa. 1978. Development and underdevelopment in Latin America. In *Canada and the Latin American Challenge*, edited by J. Nef. Toronto: OCPLACS.

Nun, Jose. 1968. A middle-class phenomenon: The middle-class military coup. In *Latin America: Reform or Revolution? A Reader*, edited by James Petras and Maurice Zeitlin. Greenwich: Fawcett.

O'Donnell, Guillermo. 1977. Corporatism and the question of the state. In *Authoritarianism and corporatism in Latin America*, edited by James Malloy. Pittsburgh, Pa.: Pittsburgh University Press, 47–84.

Riggs, Fred. 1967. The Sala model: An ecological approach to the study of comparative administration. In *Readings in Comparative Public Administration*, edited by Nimrod Raphaeli. Boston, Mass.: Allyn and Bacon.

Smucker, J. 1988. La culture de l'organisation comme ideologie de gestion: une analyse critique. In *La culture des organizations*, edited by Gladys Symmons. Quebec: Institut Quebecois de recherche sur la culture.

Transparency International. 1999. Bribe Payers Index and 1999 Corruption Perceptions Index. Internet document: www.transparency.de/documents/cpi/index.html. 20 January 2000.

Vilas, Carlos. 1995. Economic restructuring, neoliberal reforms, and the working class in Latin America. In *Capital, power, and inequality in Latin America*, edited by Sandor Halebsky and Richard Harris. Boulder, Colo.: Westview Press.

13

Corruption in Australia: Its Prevention and Control

Peter Larmour and Peter Grabosky

AUSTRALIA'S REPUTATION FOR INTEGRITY in government is now among the world's highest. It scores well on Transparency International's comparisons, which give the top ranking to those countries perceived to be least corrupt. Australia is twelve out of ninety-nine on the 2000 Corruption Perception Index and second on the new index of bribe-paying by major exporters. But these benign external perceptions mask the fact that corruption has afflicted some sectors of Australian public life for a long time. The military unit that policed the first penal settlement in New South Wales was called the Rum Corps after the trade it monopolized (Evatt 1938). In a settler colony, the government's role in disposing of land provided many opportunities for corruption. In 1906 a Royal Commission found the New South Wales Minister for Lands had accepted bribes, but no jury would convict him (Clune 1957). Since then a variety of public officials have been implicated in numerous scandals, from corruption in the conduct of local government, to irregularities in government purchasing of everything from land to defense equipment (Grabosky 1989). In the last two decades, a New South Wales prisons minister, a Queensland police commissioner, and two former premiers and a deputy premier of Western Australia have all been jailed for different corruption offenses (Brown 1998, 84).

Standing Commissions Against Corruption

While some corruption in Australia has come to light as a result of sudden and dramatic disclosure, most instances have been the subject of widespread speculation or tacit acknowledgment. Official attention is triggered only when denial is no longer sustainable. The conventional response has been the appointment of a formal inquiry, the most substantial of which is a Royal

Commission. Where corruption is found to be systemic, the inquiries have usually recommended some degree of reform, often the creation of new institutions or systems to reduce opportunity or enhance guardianship (Rozenes 1995). The conclusion of the inquiry is usually accompanied by criminal prosecution of the most egregious offenders. The federal Crimes Act of 1914 deals with the corruption and bribery of Members of Parliament:

A member of either House of Parliament who asks for or receives or obtains, or offers or agrees to ask for or receive or obtain, any property or benefit of any kind for himself or any other person, on an understanding that the exercise by him of his duty or authority as such a member will, in any manner, be influenced or affected, is guilty of an offence (Section 73A (1)).

Otherwise, criminal justice in Australia is largely a state rather than federal responsibility, and corruption is defined and dealt with differently in different states. Most service delivery and infrastructure development is a state responsibility. State ombudsman offices, government auditors, police, and public service commissions have related and sometimes overlapping interests in uncovering and preventing corruption.

There is no federal agency specifically tasked with anticorruption activity. Corruption is not a federal offense and Australia has no counterpart to the American Operation Greylord in which the judicial system of Cook County became the target of an undercover FBI investigation. Nevertheless, there is national level machinery that can be brought to bear on some forms of corrupt practice at the state level. The National Crime Authority (NCA), an investigative body established to investigate organized crime in Australia, does work jointly with state and territory law enforcement agencies. One such investigation resulted in the imprisonment of the head of the South Australian Police Drug Squad, who had been engaged in selling drugs. In March 2000, following a lengthy NCA investigation, a member of the Federal Parliament was charged with receiving payments in relation to immigration matters. The Commonwealth (federal) government has also developed systems to assist its own agencies in controlling fraud and corruption within their own areas of responsibility.

Long-running scandals in three states have led to the creation of more permanent anticorruption bodies, sometimes called as standing Royal Commissions. Their specialization and institutionalization has allowed them to build up their own distinctive doctrines. Besides their roles in investigating corruption they perform an important educative function for both public servants and for the general public. They help raise awareness of corruption and its consequences, foster a climate of intolerance for corruption, suggest ways it may be prevented, and promote the principle that it is not an acceptable way to conduct the public's business (Williams 1999).

Western Australia

During the 1980s a series of government-private business projects resulted in massive financial losses to both private investors and the state's treasury. A Royal Commission was appointed, and a number of senior public officials and business leaders were prosecuted and imprisoned. An Anti-Corruption Commission was subsequently established (Peachment 1995).

Queensland

The Fitzgerald Inquiry, provoked by a television documentary entitled "The Moonlight State" aired in 1987, identified a systemically corrupt police service, the use of ministerial privileges for personal gain, special deals for party supporters, pork barrel legislation, and a politicized public service. It was followed by a number of prosecutions of public officials and the establishment of the Criminal Justice Commission (CJC) and the Electoral and Administrative Review Commission (EARC).

New South Wales

Scandals in the police force and the judiciary in the 1980s, some of which seemed to involve senior government figures, led the new Liberal government to set up the Independent Commission Against Corruption (ICAC) in 1988. Its scope was the whole of the public sector, including the police. Some of its early work included a report on police-informer relationships. In 1994 an Independent member of the New South Parliament, John Hatton, forced the government to appoint a Royal Commission into police corruption in New South Wales. After a number of public hearings, and some very sophisticated undercover investigation, the Commission found evidence of an

identifiable pattern of police providing protection, receiving bribes and benefits from the criminal milieu, failing to exercise their office to bring to justice those criminals with whom they have formed an illicit association, and engaging directly in criminality and extortion themselves (New South Wales 1996, 45).

This led to numerous prosecutions and to the establishment of a Police Integrity Commission (New South Wales 1997) separate from the ICAC.

What Counts as Corruption?

The word corruption has connotations of decay from a more pristine earlier condition, but Australia's history suggests there was no golden age of good government. In the national vernacular the term rorting, which means trick, lurk, or scheme, is often used interchangeably with corruption. A book about rorting (Brown 1998) traces the term back to antiauthoritarian attitudes and the misuse of state power in the early convict history of Australia.

Research carried out by the Independent Commission Against Corruption (ICAC) in New South Wales finds there is no single popular, universal view of what counts as corruption in Australia. Angela Gorta presented a sample of public servants with a series of situations, such as officials using their position to get a friend a job, and asked whether they thought the behavior was corrupt. While there was agreement about the corruptness of some situations (for example an official accepting money from a company for a tender, and spending it on a stereo), there was no unanimity across all of them. People tended to agree that situations of direct financial gain and illegality were corrupt. But there was much less agreement over the effect of mitigating circumstances and bending the rules to achieve a reasonable outcome (ICAC 1994). Different background characteristics (gender, salary, level) were associated with different perceptions of some but not all situations.

The ICAC's own legislation defines corrupt conduct very widely, including action by nonofficials that might affect the "honest or impartial exercise of official functions," breach of public trust, and misuse of official information (Section 8.1). It lists sample activities that might adversely affect the carrying out of official functions, including bribery, tax evasion, and election fraud (Section 8.2). Finally, it qualifies its scope to more serious conduct, defined as that which would constitute a criminal offense, a disciplinary offense, or provide grounds for dismissal (Section 9). An ICAC report summarizes its definition as "the dishonest or partial (that is, biased) exercise of official functions by a public official" (ICAC 1998, 5). There is no clear line between what constitutes corruption and what does not. What the public and the law define as corruption is not immutable. Behavior that, in a previous generation, may have been dismissed as a fact of political or commercial life may now be regarded as unacceptable. It is often said that the public may be becoming more cynical about politicians and suspicious of the motives of public servants. This may be a result of scandals as much as the occasion for them.

ICAC's regular research on public opinion about corruption sheds some light on changing attitudes. Surveys in 1999 found that a majority (55 percent) of people felt that corruption—however defined—was a "major problem" for the community. But the figure had not been constant: It was higher in 1995 and lower in 1996. So there seems no clear trend in attitudes, nor does the research suggest that attitudes are linked to political sentiments of cynicism or distrust. Rather, financial effects were most cited among the ways corruption was believed to affect people, while its effect on the legitimacy of government was mentioned by only 7 percent of the people sampled (ICAC 1999).

The courts may be taking a more stringent view. A review of the evolution of the idea of corruption in Australia describes how Australian courts introduced ideas about public trust into decisions about allegations of bribery against politicians (Sturgess 1990). This trend is likely to continue.

How Much Corruption?

If it is difficult to find agreement on what constitutes corruption, it is even more difficult to assess whether the amount is increasing or decreasing. Corruption does not lend itself to objective measurement, because it is a low visibility phenomenon, and one whose boundaries are not always clearly defined. Statistics are rare, and in those unusual cases where they are compiled, tend to raise more questions than answers. A given number of prosecutions may represent all of the corrupt practices within a jurisdiction or just the tip of an iceberg.

The most common means of assessing the prevalence of corruption is through subjective judgment and expert opinion, which form the basis of Transparency International's cited indices. There are as yet no similar indices comparing Australia's states, and the absence of anticorruption agencies in, for example, Victoria is no reason to think that corruption may be any less in that state. Indeed, high levels of infrastructure spending, close connections between politicians and businessmen, secrecy over government-commercial dealings, and reductions in the powers of the auditor general suggest the conditions have been right for corruption. The New South Wales Auditor General recently warned that Victoria had not learned the lessons about corruption from other states, and a royal commission there was "inevitable." He was denounced by the then-premier in the usual way as "absolutely irresponsible" (*Australian* 20 August, 1999). A new state government has since promised to restrengthen the powers of the auditor general in Victoria.

What can be seen is what is uncovered, or at least glimpsed through newspaper reports and the findings of Royal Commissions. Difficulties of getting evidence mean that the glimpses are partial and intermittent, leaving to the imagination construction of the bigger picture they might reveal.

The Role of the Media

Newspapers and television played a decisive role in the scandals that led to the creation of commissions in the three states. There is a kind of symbiotic relationship between the media and anticorruption campaigns. Exposure may discourage corruption, while newspapers thrive on scandal. So the amount of corruption reported may be more a function of journalistic attention and editorial policy than any underlying rate of corruption. Competition between media is thus an important driver of revelations about corruption. Not all of this media interest can be dignified as investigative journalism. A study of scandals, the media, and corruption in Australia (Tiffen 1999) found reporting generally reactive, erratic, and reliant on information provided through routine channels: "Limited resources, the press of deadlines, limited commercial incentives, all tell against the practice of investigative reporting on a large scale" (*Canberra Times* 21 August 1999). Libel laws continue to discourage open and robust discussion of official, and particularly private sector, misconduct.

The media themselves are also vulnerable to conflicts of interest. The Australian Broadcasting Authority recently criticized radio talk show personalities who failed to disclose to their listeners that they had received substantial fees for favorable mention of their clients. Reportage by travel journalists and financial journalists is also vulnerable to "spin" in a manner that serves their private interests. *News Limited* and *The Sydney Morning Herald* recently announced new codes of practice, with the Herald refusing subsidized travel and gifts (*Australian* 4 October 1999). Political journalists, that is, those members of the profession who cover Parliament, may receive implicit or explicit access to public officials in return for continued favorable coverage.

More broadly, the concentration of ownership and intervention by newspaper proprietors may allow public interests to be undermined by private financial or political purposes. Australian media ownership is highly concentrated. It is notable that it was the federal public broadcaster, the Australian Broadcasting Commission, which led the uncovering of corruption in Queensland.

Police Corruption

The prohibition of certain kinds of drugs and gambling has provided opportunities for criminals who in turn have subverted the police and judiciary. Gambling on horse races in bars and on street corners—called in Australia SP bookmaking—was once widespread and popular although illegal. In the 1970s it was centralized and brought under the control of organized crime that used the proceeds to fund other crimes and pay off police, politicians, and local party branches (Hickie 1985, 330–36). By the 1990s, police were alleged to be extorting money from drug dealers as part of a wider pattern of franchising criminals, and taking commissions from crime (Brown 1998, 25–64). Police orchestrated, falsified, or suppressed evidence. Police corruption spread into the judiciary. A chief magistrate in New South Wales was convicted and imprisoned for attempting to influence another magistrate in a committal hearing. A justice of the High Court of Australia was also prosecuted for allegedly seeking to influence proceedings in a lower court case. The conviction was later overturned on appeal. Ironically, allegations against the judge arose from the disclosure of telephone conversations that had been illegally intercepted by police officers (Grabosky 1989).

The particular vulnerability of police to corrupt practices is generally related to the significant powers that they possess, the wide discretion that they exercise, their day-to-day contacts with criminals, and the low public visibility of many of their activities. The Australian inquiries in the 1990s show the corruption to have been embedded in a wider pattern of weak management, poor record keeping, denial, and an informal culture that dealt harshly with anyone who criticized their colleagues. Compounding these factors is the system of industrial relations in Australia, which vests considerable power in police unions and has significantly impeded disciplinary action against police officers who might otherwise be subject to dismissal for corrupt practices. These managerial weaknesses are being addressed in New South Wales by a new commissioner appointed from outside the country, with a salary higher than the premier's and new powers to dismiss suspected officers.

Investigation and Prevention

Investigative responses to corruption allegations have traditionally entailed prevailing upon a coconspirator to give evidence against a target. Recent years have seen the introduction of more aggressive investigative practices to combat police corruption. Most prominent among these have been the undercover investigations undertaken in the mid-1990s on behalf of the Wood Royal Commission into the New South Wales Police Service. Extensive use was made of surveillance cameras and sound recording devices. In one instance, a camera mounted in the dashboard of a motor vehicle recorded a corrupt police officer receiving an illicit payment.

Probably only a small amount of the corruption that happens is tunneled into detection, prosecution, and conviction. Corruption is almost by definition secret and with no obvious or immediate victims. Enormous pressures are brought to bear against whistle-blowers—insiders who expose corruption in their own organization. A study of whistle-blowing in Australia finds the usual organizational response is to harass or vilify the complainant, rather than address the problem (Demaria 1999). Potentially corrupt officials presumably make these calculations, and one of the surprising findings of ICAC investigations is how people are prepared to risk their careers for quite small sums (several thousand dollars and a used car, in the case of an investigation to the NSW Police Air Wing).

Similar official resources devoted upstream, in other words, to means of prevention, might therefore have greater impact on resources devoted downstream, on investigation. New South Wales's ICAC has developed particular expertise in prevention, which it ties to its investigatory work. It has emphasized the role of leaders in determining the organizational culture, which in turn determined whether or not people behaved corruptly, and whether incidents were dealt with. ICAC learned this through its dealings with the State Rail Authority (SRA) when it carried out investigations into the SRA in the early 1990s when it discovered corruption "ingrained, serious, and widespread." But the limited corruption prevention programs that the SRA installed soon faltered. The ICAC found

it appeared incapable of dealing in any effective manner with the widespread corruption that was evident within its ranks. The prevailing culture tolerated corruption and this was exacerbated by fundamental systemic flaws. Management and control arrangements were not effective and were themselves prone to corruption (ICAC 1998, 4).

The ICAC turned its attention to leadership and the ethical climate that leaders set in their organizations. Restructuring provided an opportunity to secure commitment from the top. The SRA was to be divided into four new corporations, and the Minister insisted that the new CEOs take responsibility for eliminating corruption. The ICAC used its powers to hold public hearings to ask the new CEOs to make "public presentations and submissions on the steps they had taken to reduce opportunities for corrupt behavior" (ICAC 1995, 5) ICAC's review of the research suggested that "the tendency to behave ethically in the workplace may be related more to aspects of the organization than to attributes of the individual" (ICAC 1995, 10). In turn, managers were particularly important in establishing, by example, an ethical culture in the organization. Rather than relying on detailed procedures, which are often not followed or might be subverted, ICAC looked for ways to encourage officials to apply broadly defined values to their day-to-day decisions.

Corruption and Privatization

The definition of corruption used by Transparency International—the use of public office for private gain—points to the importance of the boundary between public and private, and the way it is being redrawn in many countries, including Australia. The Australian economy has been rapidly liberalized since its dollar was floated in 1983. Public enterprises formerly run as departments of state governments are being turned into self-managing corporations or privatized. Work formerly carried out by public servants is being carried out by the private or voluntary sectors, on contract. Work once done by full-time tenured officials is now often carried out by consultants.

There are many examples from Australia where selective and inept government intervention in the economy has created opportunities for corruption. The scandals in Western Australia, referred to above, were related to government business dealings, including cronyism and reckless lending. In Victoria in the 1970s the Housing Commission spent just under A$11 million in purchasing semirural land less than 50 km from Melbourne. Nearly half of this sum was given to speculators and developers who had purchased the land at low prices and then sold it to the Housing Commission at a profit. The amount spent on the purchase of land restricted the money available to develop the low-cost housing and the land remained undeveloped for years afterward. The land also had not been surveyed thoroughly; some was flood prone and other land had zoning restrictions (Grabosky 1989).

The administrative apparatus of the welfare state has also created opportunities for corruption. Australia's national health system involves massive public expenditure and detailed regulation of private health providers. Doctors are regularly accused of overservicing patients, and in 1999 it became apparent that a large number of practicing radiologists in Australia may have profited from access to confidential information about impending changes to regulations relating to the purchase of imaging technology.

Australia's experience also shows that privatization can create new opportunities for corruption as well as closing others off. On the one hand, the process of privatization is vulnerable to favoritism, and the results may put the activity of large corporations outside the scrutiny of ombudsman offices or audit commissions. Public servants on short-term contracts or consultancies may be more tempted to place their private interests before those of the public. The auditor general offices have warned of the way governments have hidden behind arguments that their contracts are "commercial in confidence." On the other hand, competition can act as a form of discipline on an organization and force it to face up to the costs of corruption. The corporatization of the State

Rail Authority, for example, allowed the ICAC to insist on stronger prevention strategies.

Redrawing the boundary between public and private is one issue. ICAC's legislation allows it to continue to take an interest in public functions that have become privatized. The existence—even the possibility—of corruption within the private sector is another. ICAC has regularly surveyed popular opinion about the different standards that might apply in the private sector. Thirty-nine percent of people agreed that standards differed: "corruption in the public sector is seen as good business in the private sector" (ICAC 1999, 9). Australia has had its share of "Corporate Cowboys" who have exploited public companies and their shareholders for private gain (Sykes 1988; 1994). There have been many investigations but fewer prosecutions, the most prominent of which involved the entrepreneur Alan Bond, whose corporate empire collapsed and who was sentenced to prison on fraud-related charges in 1996. New requirements for corporate disclosure were introduced in the 1990s to make it more difficult for the directors of publicly held companies to exploit their corporate offices for private gain. It may be that the distinction between public and private responsibilities is easier to make for large bureaucratic corporations than for small family businesses, but both kinds are becoming more important as the state withdraws.

Parliamentary Corruption

Australia's parliamentary systems provide in principle for measures of public accountability. Ministers may be called to account by the parliamentary opposition, and the activities of departments of state are subject to the scrutiny of parliamentary committees composed of representatives of all parties. Upper houses provide a check in some states, while the federal Senate has become a strong check on the use of executive power.

The style of politics in Australia is combative and partisan. Labor governments typically alternate with coalitions of the Liberal and National parties at the state and federal level. Incoming governments accuse their predecessors of corruption and promise reform. Single party dominance of a legislature can muffle criticism, as in the long period of National Party rule in Queensland that ended with the uncovering of corruption by the Fitzgerald inquiry. The Kennett government in Victoria used its majority to limit the powers of the auditor general during a controversial period of government sponsorship of privately financed construction projects.

The Australian Electoral Commission requires parties to report donations, but the published figures do not distinguish donations from other kinds of payments, such as dividends. Donations can be made to associated entities which then pass it on to the party, without having to publicize its source. A report on the top twenty corporate donors found them mostly cagey in explaining why they did so. A party official explained, "The minimum is access and the maximum is outcomes that favor them and their shareholders" (*The Eye* 23 February 2000). Yet strong parties are not all bad. Where party discipline is weak, or coalitions have to be stitched together, governments may turn to handouts and slush funds to retain their majorities in Parliament. Minor parties and independents are becoming important, particularly at the state level where most explicit anticorruption activity takes place. The Australian Democrats are the largest of the minor parties and were founded on a promise to "keep the bastards honest." Two recent corruption scandals have turned on major party attempts to reduce the influence of Independents.

In Tasmania in 1989 an attempt was made to bribe a Member of Parliament to cross the floor and vote against an anticipated no-confidence motion in the Liberal government of Premier Robin Gray. A Royal Commission was appointed in November 1990 to try to identify others who may have been involved in the attempted bribery. A prominent businessman was convicted of the offense. He was motivated by a desire to keep the Labor party out of power, as it had promised to govern in an accord with the minor Green party (Larmour and Haward 1993).

In New South Wales, the Premier who had set up the ICAC was then brought down by it. He offered a public service job to an Independent Member of Parliament who had threatened to obstruct legislation. The conduct was deemed to be technically corrupt by the ICAC. Although the finding was later challenged successfully in court, the premier retired from political life. The challenge succeeded on the basis that there was no objective standard against which to judge the premier's conduct, and led eventually to a code of conduct for NSW Members of Parliament.

Conflicts of interest and misuse of travel allowances are perennial issues in federal and state politics. On coming to power in 1996, the federal Liberal prime minister publicized a set of guidelines for ministerial conduct that included avoidance of conflicts of interest. They would, he claimed, set higher standards than his predecessors. They have since been much watered down as a series of members of the government were caught by them and forced to resign or step aside. In early 2000 the prime minister himself became the subject of accusations over a government intervention to protect the workers of a collapsed textile firm. His brother was a director of the firm. The prime minister replied that he had offered to leave cabinet when the issue was discussed, but his colleagues prevailed upon him to stay as his motives were not political. But without any higher level of oversight, parliaments themselves are particularly prone to bending the rules they themselves make. A steady trickle of members of federal and state parliaments has been the subject of investigations and successful prosecutions, and others have resigned, over abuses of travel entitlements (Brown 1998, 353–82). At the end of 2000, the Queensland branch of the Australian Labor Party was being investigated for possible voter fraud.

The Transnational Dimension

During the period in which the specialized anticorruption agencies became established, the Australian economy has become increasingly internationalized. The ICAC has publicly justified its activities in terms of increasing New South Wales's relative attractiveness to foreign investment, comparing itself to states like Victoria without such commissions. Corruption abroad can subtly shift the terms upon which Australian exports compete. Where neighboring governments are corrupt or corruptible, they are vulnerable to exploitation by organized criminals whose activities, whether they entail traffic in drugs, illegal migrants, or firearms, may impact Australian society. To the extent that the political systems of Australia's near neighbors such as Indonesia, Papua New Guinea, and the Pacific Islands are threatened with decay, the risk of state collapse can impact on Australia's national security (McFarlane 1996).

But Australians have also been acting corruptly overseas. In 1992, a federal minister was forced to resign after he phoned the president of the Marshall Islands to seek the release on bail of an Australian businessman who had been arrested for suspected fraud involving an immigration scheme (Richardson 1994, 340–47). Australian consultants were involved with local officials in the corruption of a World Bank education project in the Solomon Islands (Larmour 1997). To counter corruption by its citizens abroad, Australia ratified the OECD Convention to criminalize bribery of foreign public officials on 18 October 1999, and legislation to end tax deductions for bribes of foreign public officials is being considered by the Commonwealth Parliament. Corruption in Australia's international aid programs is also difficult to monitor and audit, as expenditure takes place through another country's systems of government. But corruption prevention is becoming an explicit part of Australia's aid program. ICAC is also involved in international training and technical assistance in Papua New Guinea.

Australia's international reputation may also be at risk from its participation in high profile international activities like the Olympic games. The corruption of the process of bidding to host the Olympics was well documented before it erupted into a global scandal in 1999 (Jennings 1996). There has been detailed but inconclusive press scrutiny of the gift giving and travel involved in Australia's successful bid to hold the 2000 games in Sydney. An Australian sporting official was also found to have improperly accepted gifts in the earlier Salt Lake City bid. More worrying than small gifts and expenses, perhaps, was the lack of external oversight or investigative reporting into the massive and rapid public expenditure on Olympic facilities in Sydney. The outgoing Auditor General expressed concern about the secrecy of the contracts being made, which he compared unfavorably with the practice at the Atlanta games (*Sydney Morning Herald* 21 August 1999).

Conclusion

Australia's performance in corruption control is of a relatively high standard and has improved significantly since the late 1980s. Parliamentary scrutiny in the context of a vibrant Westminster-style democratic system, a framework of institutions devoted to public sector integrity, transparency borne of freedom of information, judicial review of administrative decisions, a relatively free and independent press, and increasing expectations among the citizenry and their representatives of a high standard of behavior on the part of public officials, have combined to deliver a degree of integrity in Australian public life. No one of these alone can be regarded as the magic remedy. Much as a web is stronger than its component strands, the strength of these various institutions lies in their combination and their mutual reinforcement.

References

Brown, M. ed. 1998. *Rorting: The great Australian crime.* Sydney: Lansdowne.

Clune, F. 1957. *Scandals of Sydney town.* Sydney: Angus and Robertson.

De Maria, W. 1999. *Deadly disclosures: Whistleblowing and the ethical meltdown in Australia.* Adelaide: Wakefield Press.

Evatt, H. V. 1938. *Rum rebellion.* Sydney: Angus and Robertson.

Gorta, A. 1994. Unravelling corruption: A public sector perspective. A survey of NSW public sector employees' understanding of corruption and their willingness to take action. Research Report No 1. Sydney: Independent Commission Against Corruption.

Grabosky, P. N. 1989. *Wayward governance: Illegality and its control in the public sector.* Canberra: Australian Institute of Criminology.

Hickie, D. 1985. *The prince and the premier.* North Ryde, NSW: Angus and Robertson.

Independent Commission Against Corruption. 1998. A major investigation into corruption in the former state rail authority of New South Wales. Sydney: ICAC.

Jennings, A. 1996. *The new lords of the rings.* London: Simon and Schuster.

Larmour, P. 1997. Corruption and governance in the South Pacific. *Pacific Studies* 20 (3): 1–17.

Larmour, P., and M. Haward, eds. 1993. *The Tasmanian parliamentary accord and public policy 1989–92: Accommodating the new politics.* Canberra: Federalism Research Centre.

McFarlane, John. 1996. Transnational Organised Crime and National Security. In *Transnational Crime: A New Security Threat?*, edited by J. Ciccarelli. Canberra: Australian Defence Studies Centre.

New South Wales. 1996. Interim report (of the Royal Commission into the New South Wales Police Service). Sydney: Royal Commission into the New South Wales Police Service.

———. 1997. Final report (of the Royal Commission into the New South Wales Police Service). Sydney: Royal Commission into the New South Wales Police Service.

Newton, Stephen. 1997. Integrity testing as an anti-corruption strategy. *Australian Police Journal* 51 (4): 222–25.

Peachment, A. 1995. The Royal Commission into WA Inc. In *Westminster Inc.*, edited by A. Peachment. Sydney: Federation Press.

Rozenes, M. 1995. Crime commissions and the criminal trial. *Criminal Law Journal* 19 (2): 65–73.

Sturgess, G. 1990. Corruption: The evolution of an idea 1788–1988. In *Corruption and reform: The Fitzgerald vision*, edited by S. Prasser, R. Wear, and J. Nethercote. St Lucia: University of Queensland Press.

Sykes, Trevor. 1988. *Two centuries of panic: A history of corporate collapses in Australia.* Sydney: Unwin Hyman.

———. 1994. *The bold riders: Behind Australia's corporate collapses.* Sydney: Allen and Unwin.

Tasmania. 1991. Report of the Royal Commission into an attempt to bribe a member of the House of Assembly; and other matters. 3 Vols. Hobart: Government Printer.

Tiffen, R. 1999. *Scandals, media politics and corruption in contemporary Australia.* Sydney: University of New South Wales Press.

Williams, R. 1999. Democracy, development, and anti-corruption strategies: Learning from the Australian experience. *Journal of Commonwealth and Comparative Politics* 37: 135–49.

14

Transparency International's Network to Curb Global Corruption

Fredrik Galtung

THIS CHAPTER EXPLORES THE GENESIS, evolution, and effectiveness of Transparency International (TI), a transnational nongovernmental organization founded in 1993 to curb corruption worldwide. TI began as a small initiative among like-minded individuals, but today leads a fast-growing number of more than 80 national chapters worldwide. It is realizing its aims of bringing about international agreements, curbing corruption, and leading public opinion toward a worldwide rejection of corrupt practices. One of TI's main challenges today is that its services are almost too much in demand in relation to its existing resources, as its rate of growth has exceeded all expectations.

The Changing International Context

The international community is, of course, prone to faddism—and the fight against corruption is one of the hottest fads right now. Systemic corruption has long been known as a moral, economic, and even cultural problem, but by the mid-1990s it had clearly become an institutional and political one as well. Now suddenly there are few newly elected governments in Latin America, Africa, and Asia that do not promise sweeping legal and administrative reforms to reduce corruption. International financial organizations and bilateral development agencies are supporting this trend and have recently even begun to link corruption control to the disbursement of aid and loans.

Until recent shifts in global politics, such policy changes by governments and international organizations would have been impossible. Before the fall of the Berlin Wall, for instance, corrupt tyrants on every continent were shored up by Western governments anxious to secure and retain support for their own anti-Communist agendas. Much of this mutual support between Western governments and foreign regimes was channeled through international organizations. But with the Cold War imperative gone, the scope and willingness for action against corrupt governments, wherever they may be, has suddenly opened up. Previously excused (supposedly in favor of a so-called trickle-down theory), systemic corruption has at last come to be understood and named as a major impediment to development, to governance, and to the legitimacy of democratic institutions.

TI has worked to bring about globally the realization that in the long-term corruption causes everybody to lose. Those losses accumulate, affecting multinational corporations, the legitimacy of states, and the grassroots in developing countries. Thus the fight against corruption may in some sense have much in common with networks campaigning against environmental damage (another damage that will, at least in the long-term, affect everyone), rather than with networks against world poverty or the abuse of human rights—issues by which certain powerful sectors of society may consider themselves untouched. This understanding that it is everyone's interest to curb corruption is very new and is the product of a recent process of public education and attitude-changing, which was part of the task that TI set for itself back in 1993.

Behind these issues still stands a range of deeper questions. In a global sense, what are the real agendas behind anticorruption work? Whose interests does the work really serve most, or can it serve the interests of very different, and perhaps even opposed, protagonists simultaneously? Even if TI makes very clear mission statements about the coalition of interests that it serves and the strategies that it employs, there is still the background question for all organizations of how they stand in relation to overreaching world realities like the inequities of capitalism and the deeply rooted privileges of the North in world affairs.

TI subsequently took on the even more delicate challenge of cementing the "natural coalitions of interests" against corruption—coalitions between parties who in the past have tended to be pitted against each other. Hence, TI's present reality of functioning as a bridge between unlikely parties like the World Bank and women's groups in Ugandan villages, and the OECD countries and investigative journalists in Russia. But of course, these alliances are also symptomatic of the general effects of globalization which, as well as exporting and accelerating corruption, also export and accelerate potentials for dialogue and cooperation, in ways that can be fertile for public policy networks.

Unfortunately work against corruption, like the efforts of so many campaigning networks, is itself rife with dilemmas. Should membership and leadership be grassroots, from below upward, or more professionalized and elitist from the top down? Should the strategy be one of investigation, pursuit, exposure, and condemnation, or of diplomacy and tact? Corruption, after all, has come to be a media-friendly subject with high press value for the juicy scandals and exposés produced by the investigative approach. Nonetheless and perhaps unpredictably, TI decided to launch its worldwide assault on corruption employing a policy of noninvestigation and nonexposure, limiting all its members' activities instead to cooperation, encouragement, advice giving, education, and personal influence. Surely this was a recipe for total failure, in a world scene that was fraught with almost criminally self-interested corruption, and with age-old cynicism about limiting what it considered anyway to be the merely human vice of corruption. Apparently not. With this surprisingly noncoercive policy, TI has outstripped all expectations. TI's initial little office in Berlin now caters to national chapters worldwide. TI contributes to the monitoring process of an international anticorruption treaty between thirty-five countries and is a consultant to international organizations now keen to institutionalize their own fights against corruption.

Initiating the Network

This section explores both the obvious and the hidden challenges behind TI's two initial tasks of raising awareness about corruption and of bringing together the actors needed to successfully combat it. We look first at the complexities of raising awareness and securing partners, while the ensuing section looks at the actual policies that TI evolved as responses to the complexities of those areas.

Raising Awareness

Although corruption had, of course, long been implicit in all societies, a number of factors combined in the 1990s to induce what commentators have described as a veritable eruption of corruption across the world. Naturally, even without help from TI, this eruption could to some extent have spontaneously helped bring corruption to international awareness and concern. Thus TI argues in its mission statement that "corruption is one of the greatest challenges of the contemporary world. It undermines good government, fundamentally distorts public policy, leads to the misallocation of resources, harms the public sector and private sector development, and particularly hurts the poor." One estimate from the World Bank sets the average cost of bribery among transnational corporations alone at $80 billion per year. Until recently only one country—the United States—legally prohibited bribe paying by its citizens in its Foreign Corrupt Practices Act of 1977.

According to sources from the U.S. Department of Commerce, American companies lost more than 100 international contracts, valued at $45 billion, in 1994 and 1995 as a result of their inability to bribe. The U.S. Treasury estimates that American corporations lose $30 billion in contracts every year because of their nonparticipation in bribery (Wang and Rosenau 1999, 15). Of course, their competitors retort that the 1977 Act did not prevent American corporations from bribing but rather taught them to bribe more covertly and artfully, learning to pay bribes through middlemen. Indeed, the U.S. government has not been at all tough; rather, it has been a powerful promoter of American business interests and has smoothed their way abroad (*Los Angeles Times* 31 October 2000, B9). More recent data from the U.S. Department of Commerce reported allegations of foreign bribery in 55 contracts estimated at $37 billion in the first four months of 2000 alone. Over a five-year period, bribery is believed to have influenced decisions on 294 commercial contracts worth some $145 billion. These reports are characterized as merely the tip of the iceberg. About half the corruption complaints concern international defense procurement.

The scale of bribery worldwide seems to have escalated fast in recent years. Factors nourishing this boom in corruption have included the deregulation and privatization of markets in former Soviet Bloc countries, the mushrooming of opportunities for international economic transactions between innumerable actors all over the world, and the acceleration and relative democratization of information technologies that can move information and monies instantaneously and discreetly around the planet. Together, conditions like these seem to have created a hothouse for the flourishing of an unprecedented "corruption without frontiers." Three factors in particular must be competently addressed if a network is to succeed in its intended work around a problem, namely, the shared, public or international awareness of a problem, actors' willingness and ability to use and share terms to name the problem as a problem, and their willingness and ability to respond to and resolve the problem.

It seems that global policy networks need to clarify whether the main difficulties lie in a lack of awareness about their problem area or in a lack of open acknowledgement about an awareness that is tacitly there. (In TI's case, the public and private sectors were aware, but silent, while the public was unaware.) A lack of discussion, in turn, may be due either to an unwillingness or to a sense of powerlessness and futility, or to a lack of language and concepts with which to communicate the problem. With corruption, the universal silence was due to a sense of powerlessness and the inability to imagine methods and concepts by which corruption could ever be halted. Within that wider paralysis, more specific islands of a different sort of silence were, of course, resolutely protecting actual corrupt deals. So awareness about bribery is complex: by its very nature corruption benefits the immediate parties to such a transaction. The negative consequences are borne by others. So while awareness among the immediate parties is, strictly speaking, not lacking here, excuses proliferate, as corporations protest that they must keep bribing for contracts as long as their competitors do, while corrupt officials in the public sectors of poorer countries may feel justified in topping up often paltry salaries, or they may do so simply out of greed.

So one of TI's first goals in terms of awareness-raising became the breaking of the taboo surrounding open discussion of corruption in the media. This taboo generated in the business world and the public sector was rooted in fears of exposure, scandal, prosecution, bad public relations, loss of contracts, and income (both legitimate and illicit), and loss of jobs. But it was more subtly rooted, too, in old distortions caused by the Cold War, which had discouraged transparency, and the sort of transnational accountabilities that are now becoming more current. Finally, the taboo had even finer roots in the uneasy feeling that the North (which, after all, produced TI) could not discuss corruption without seeming morally superior (as indeed many Northerners initially thought they were, until they found out more about the North/South dynamics of corruption) and without the South and East feeling they were under attack.

TI, as well as bringing the public a new awareness of bribery, also needed to help the media and the public understand how Northern countries actively, but legally, export corruption, by giving tax deductions for bribery, by refusing to criminalize corrupt conduct in their citizens' dealings abroad, and by providing their citizens with advice and support in corruption matters through the good offices of diplomats stationed abroad. At the same time, public opinion in the North had to be alerted to the fact that their taxes were going not only to pay for programs of official overseas aid, but also to subsidize the bribery elements in corruptly obtained contracts. This, too, was potentially difficult territory for TI, as it would have been all too easy for efforts in this field to have fuelled the antiaid lobby and to be used as a weapon against the provision of any aid at all to the developing world—which was precisely the opposite of what TI was trying to achieve.

But in fact, the media's activities vital to explaining TI's agenda have been remarkable from the beginning, with the TI *Corruption Perceptions Index*, which rates countries' levels of corruption, ensuring that hardly a day passes without references to the organization somewhere in the media. Of course, corruption is in many ways a media-friendly topic, with its atmospheres of subterfuge and scandal and its colorful exposés. And clearly, such friendly relations with and cooperation from the media are invaluable to a campaigning network. On the other hand, media attention for TI has been so prolific that at times the organization has been concerned that its appearances in the media (and thus high-profile expectations of TI in the public eye) have sometimes seemed to be running ahead of TI's actual capacities in terms of funding, human resources, and practical abilities.

Bringing Actors Together

From the outset, TI saw that awareness of the damage arising out of corrupt practices (an awareness suppressed, of course, by those interested in continuing corruption) and an ability to communicate sensitively and openly about such damage could draw in all the very diverse parties. TI learned that these parties actually do care passionately about the particular effects that corruption is having on them, and that they would like to do something about it if they could. In the private sector, for instance, the business community had long lamented that corruption added huge margins to the costs of their businesses, but they didn't know what to do about it. More recently they have also become concerned that in an increasingly interdependent global economy, corruption constantly threatens to undermine global economic stability.

Meanwhile, the World Bank has now gone so far as to name corruption as the single biggest obstacles to economic development in the Third World. In the donor community, large proportions of donor aid have been found to have been fraudulently diverted for personal profit. Developing countries then lose out all over again on foreign investment, due to this reputation for fiscal mismanagement and corrupt bureaucracy. On yet another front, those committed to improving governance and strengthening the potentials of civil society worldwide recognize corruption to be a key enemy of good governance. And on still another front, environmental campaigners know that the relatively new regulations set in place to protect the environment are particularly attracting corruption, with companies bribing officials to overlook the regulations and grant environmentally harmful contracts. It is no wonder that TI's mission statement unequivocally draws attention to the damage that corruption inflicts on—and on relationships between—the public sector, the private sector, and civil society, as well as on all their combined efforts to improve governance.

From its discussions with sympathetic business leaders, TI knew that a significant business lobby was ready to start evolving corporate conduct toward an anticorruption culture that upholds sharp distinctions between public duty and private gain. Crucially, this collective culture would be supported only if corruption could be controlled without conceding competitive advantages to business rivals. It was a classic case of the *prisoner's dilemma*: businesses did not trust their competitors, who were imprisoned with them by the snares of corruption. Yet unless they all cooperated, none of them would escape the corruption scenario. The rules, TI saw clearly, must change for everyone.

Meanwhile, international organizations were also beginning to stir. In 1990 World Bank representatives stationed in Africa met in Swaziland to discuss its *Long Term Perspective Study* on improving governance as a condition for economic development. Doubts quickly emerged about the possibility of taking on this agenda. Representatives felt that to tackle corruption would clearly interfere with the Bank charter's requirement to abstain from political considerations in lending decisions, and was therefore not an option. Frustrated by the Bank's unwillingness to change from within, Peter Eigen, then regional director for East Africa, took early retirement and set out on an odyssey to concretize the anticorruption concepts proposed in Swaziland. With support from the German technical assistance agency (GTZ), which had encountered corruption in its own development assistance projects and was eager to confront what seemed to be a growing menace, Eigen and his supporters launched TI in 1993 with a small secretariat in Berlin.

TI's first international triumph was when a number of TI national chapters lobbied to place the issue of corruption on the agenda for the Summit of the Americas, held in Miami in 1994. It was important that the voice of the South was heard as being behind such a move. In an official communiqué, over thirty elected heads of state and government from countries as diverse as Colombia and Canada unanimously agreed that corruption was a problem in all of their countries and required concerted action, both at the national and international levels, to remedy the position. This was a landmark declaration, representing the first time that leaders from both South and North had so clearly laid the groundwork for a regional convention. Furthermore, their declaration specifically addressed the need to incorporate civil society into any anticorruption effort. Thus the taboo around the "c" word was finally shattered.

The next task of TI was to lobby the Paris-based Organization for Economic Cooperation and Development (OECD). TI knew that mechanisms emerging from the OECD had the potential to curb the export of international corruption, and that these mechanisms could also be extended to include non-OECD countries once the process was ratified. Meanwhile, TI was also convincing the World Bank and the International Monetary Fund (IMF) to adopt more assertive postures against corruption. TI was creating a partnership out in the field with the Economic Development Institute (EDI) of the World Bank. EDI argued that it was possible to engage in anticorruption work without courting controversy, provided the work was implemented with a careful partner-NGO like TI. While EDI was carrying out experimental work in the field, incoming World Bank President James Wolfensohn was determined to mainstream anti-corruption values into the core of the Bank's activities. He invited a TI group to conduct a half-day seminar on corruption. As a result, TI was engaged on a consultancy basis to assist the World Bank internally to develop its own strategy against corruption. Several TI national chapters now work actively with the World Bank in its member countries, and there is a relatively free flow of information between the international financial institutions and TI.

TI's institutional strategy has always been to build "natural coalitions of interests." In fact, one independent academic study has observed that "a profoundly co-operative approach . . . constitutes a kind of hallmark of TI" (Van Ham 1998, 18). This emphasis on coalitions reflects TI's conviction that anti-corruption programs will succeed only if they have broad-based support, and if a wide cross-section of civil society recognizes specific reasons (beyond the general public good) for curbing corruption. Thus, rather than pursuing or defaming "wrongdoers," TI sees one of its tasks as being to educate about the hidden ways in which corruption stunts and corrodes the protection of human rights, the enforcement of property rights essential for business, the development of professional standards (for instance in law, accounting, and engineering), the protection of children against exploitation, and environmental protection. Global transparency and openness about such effects means that the anticorruption movement can bring together actors who are normally strangers to one another.

This international coalition of interests against corruption would never have been possible without individual leadership and commitment, as well as TI's large network of voluntary supporters. TI's Chairman, Peter Eigen, has worked as a full-time volunteer from the beginning, alongside an active board of ten to fifteen people from all continents, a number of them contributing a substantial part of their working day to TI's ongoing activities, again on a pro bono basis. They are assisted by an elected advisory council—a range of international experts from different geographic and professional areas, and TI also uses the volunteer services of two support groups, one based in Washington, D.C. and the other in London. The involvement of these high level professionals and the access that they, in turn, provide to key decision makers, undoubtedly makes TI more powerful. To this end, in many countries TI has formed small, expert working parties of lawyers and accountants who are dedicated to developing approaches that abolish the tax deductibility of bribes and that criminalize foreign bribery. Academics also contribute actively to TI's work in research and dissemination. TI consults a steering committee of leading academics and professionals for its work on the annual corruption indices. This international network of skilled specialized volunteers helps explain how TI was able to operate initially with only minimal professional capacity in its Berlin office.

TI's early policy of coalition building remains unchanged. Peter Eigen can still describe TI as "looking for partners everywhere." TI "brings relevant actors together under one umbrella from government and business, from organized labor and the churches, from academia and the professions, and from the diversity of non-governmental associations" (Eigen 1999, 8). This highlights the potential for a new kind of devolution—not from central to local government, but from government to civil society. This "growing strength of global society" points to the possibility of a "highly democratic, albeit non-electoral, system of transnational governance" (Eigen 1999, 8).

Policy Formulation and Decision Making

A Northern or Southern Focus?

In terms of funding, the early TI thought that to safeguard the independence of the organization, care should be taken to avoid becoming overly dependent on funding from the public sector. TI receives significant grants from several governmental and institutional sources. Its fund-raising in the private sector has been slower than had been hoped but stands presently at about 10 percent of its budget. Funding now comes from more than a dozen countries. Reflecting a considerable growth in activities and institutional support, TI's budget has recently increased substantially.

In campaigning terms, it was decided from the beginning that TI would be a one-issue nonprofit organization aimed at curbing corruption both in the South and in the post-Communist countries. Corruption is of course found everywhere, but while "countries of the North may be able to afford the luxury of corruption, those elsewhere cannot" (Pope 1998, 1). TI decided to focus at first on the countries in the North whose business communities were fueling corruption as they bribed to obtain export orders. It was felt that this sort of international "grand corruption" had the most devastating impact on the economic and social development of countries in the South and in transition. In those early days, TI considered that the petty corruption within countries, in culturally specific contexts, remained an issue that was at that time best left to local institutions. Therefore TI's motto in the first few years described the organization as "the coalition against corruption in international business transactions." This policy of particular focus on bribery produced or offered by the North also avoided the risk of TI supporting any Northern condescension against a supposedly more corrupt South.

The early TI, with its very limited initial means also decided against lobbying right away for a global convention against international bribery (although six years later, TI would see this long-term goal fulfilled in the 1997 OECD treaty against corruption). The risks of going straight for that goal would have been too high. Past experience suggested that such a convention would take years of consultation to draft and longer to implement. Reluctant countries would find it easy to set the threshold at a higher level, limiting the number of countries accepting the convention. And even if that were not the case, there would be a continuing need for monitoring (which is not a feature of most international conventions), because without determined monitoring, compliance would no doubt be minimal.

Confrontation or Cooperation?

Initially, some supporters advocated an organization devoted to exposing cases of corruption throughout the world, much like Amnesty International does for human rights abuses. But Ian Martin, Amnesty's former secretary general, was among those who convincingly argued that this model would not suit TI: an exposing role would be incompatible with TI's coalition-building resolve to reform corrupt systems. The two approaches were determined to be mutually exclusive. One could not seek to work with the government and the private sector in strengthening a country's procurement system, for example, while at the same time exposing the corrupt practices of those very same companies and public officials. Nor could TI claim any obvious competitive advantage in this area of exposure, which was more the legitimate concern of the investigative journalists. Curiously, it was the journalists who from the outset criticized TI for adopting its noninvestigative approach. But these critics generally came to understand the legitimacy of the approach, and a number have since joined the TI movement. Membership of TI does not, of course, impose fetters on individual actions. But an investigative and exposing role would entail considerable personal risk, as well as the threat of ongoing libel actions.

Over and above all these objections, it was clear that governments most amenable to the TI approach were likely to be those least implicated in corruption. Therefore, resources would have greater impact when directed at those countries where structural anticorruption measures would be more readily accepted, rather than wasting resources on pursuing governments at the top of the corruption league that showed no inclination to mend their ways. The TI approach would need to be evolutionary and focused on reforming systems, and to this end the name *Transparency International* was chosen. Indeed, a key element in TI's success has been its choice of "changing underlying structures— legal and institutional frameworks—instead of exposing single cases" (Van Ham

1998, 30). This policy is uniquely adapted to aspects of the corruption scene. It is not the tool itself, but its finely tuned adaptability to the given context that makes it so effective. Interestingly, cooperative policies are a hallmark of Anglo-Saxon thinking on anticorruption strategies, whereas grassroots movements in the South tend to take a more rebellious, confrontational approach (presumably because they have fewer spheres of influence and are experiencing more direct suffering).

A final cornerstone of TI's working policy has been that while corruption is undoubtedly a moral issue, a sufficiently broad coalition of interests could only be built around the social, political, and economic *costs* and drawbacks of corruption. The issue simply could not be convincingly sold to a sufficiently wide range of interests on moral grounds alone. So while TI's own primary commitment—openly stated in its mission statement and brochures—is a humanitarian one, its strategic policy is to generate and diffuse the varying messages of self-interest that will reach diverse potential partners.

TI Enlarges

In May 1993, TI held its launching conference in Berlin with over 70 participants from all continents. They included people from the three core sectors of international stakeholders in this anticorruption process: national governments in the South, the international development community, and transnational corporations. In the years since its establishment, TI has been widely recognized as meeting its own aim of setting the agenda for corruption reform among international stakeholders such as the World Bank, the EU, and the OECD. But in addition to influencing intergovernmental organizations and drafting conventions, TI has also found itself armed with a global reach of national chapters that were not foreseen by TI's initial, more narrow policy of focusing on Northern multinational corruption. In fact, TI national chapters have been formed in over 70 countries, and programs have been undertaken by chapters in more than two dozen of those countries.

So by the time of its 1997 *Mission Statement,* the core policy of TI had significantly broadened from its relatively narrow initial focus on international bribery. Impressed by the spontaneous proliferation of the national chapters and inspired by their demands for practical help in curbing corruption in their own countries, TI now had ready a second phase to let its policy broaden into a resolve "to curb corruption by mobilizing a global coalition to promote and strengthen international and national integrity systems." The Berlin secretariat now includes a growing team of paid management and staff who support the work of the national chapters and coordinate the mass of anticorruption information that TI processes and produces. This includes maintenance of an electronic database, an intensive Web site carrying a wealth of anticorruption information as well as links to national chapters, the publication of the TI *Guidelines, Source Book, Corruption Perception Index* and forthcoming *Bribe Payers Index*, as well as other documents and newsletters that convey TI's philosophy, policy, goals, strategies, and challenges.

Implementation: Methods and Actions

Providing Services

The service that TI offers all its prospective users or partners has two phases. TI's first phase of interaction with a prospective partner—whether an individual or an organization from any of the three sectors—tends to involve mutual contact and communication, both formal and informal, until it is clear that the partner understands and is willing to engage in or support the anticorruption perspective. The second phase is then to deliver to the partner an extensive menu of applied resources for counteracting and reforming corruption in specific scenarios, relationships, deals, contracts, and organizations. These resources (workshops, guidelines, source books, reusable pacts and agreements, best practice examples, codes of conduct, support groups, and so on) are very much designed for ease of transfer and use. Any individual or group "of integrity" can become a willing presence against corruption and an active educator, organizer, motivator, trainer, and negotiator against corruption in their own milieu and on behalf of integrity. TI is not an organization that campaigns only to attract a critical mass of passive sympathy from the public.

TI's most focused interest today is on empowering, equipping, and rapidly training a global web of trisectoral partners to actively regain control of and responsibility for all their interactions. Thus actors learn to use and share with others certain simple techniques that can regulate the interaction in a zone of integrity, making it a safer exchange—a win/win encounter—for all involved. This strategy of implementation is an important horizontal process. When TI hands over resources such as its Integrity Workshops and the Integrity Pacts guaranteeing all parties that a given deal will be corruption-free, it is offering people a new arena, model, and experience within which they can train and equip themselves with strategies to combat corruption in their own milieu. So rather than remaining the expert, TI much prefers to train others, who, under TI's supervision and guidance, bring anticorruption strategies into their own communities.

A democratizing feature of the whole TI education package is that it is delivered from village groups in the poorest developing countries to the heads of the world's largest international organizations and multinationals. Although TI is known for its diplomacy and insider knowledge about adapting its message to the ears of powerful Northern institutions, ironically it finds that it has often adapted versions of the same generic tools like the Integrity Pact or the mutually agreed-upon code of conduct that are equally needed in local deals such as those conducted in the field in a rural Argentinean province or global ones signed across the mahogany tables of the IMF. In terms of promoting better governance all over the globe, TI does much more than simply supply the communities of developing countries with checks against corruption. In fact, the TI governance models are also, in wider ways, enormously empowering to citizens and groups who may never before (either because of corrupt, autocratic regimes or simply through the absence of any local infrastructure for governance) have had the experience of taking democratic control over the destinies of their communities. While speaking from a single-issue platform against corruption, TI is at the same time a clarion call to civil society in developing countries, encouraging people to see themselves as responsible, potent actors who can shape their society for the better.

Negotiating Agreements

A telling expression of TI's leadership internationally in the anticorruption sphere has been its recent role as the secretariat for the International Anti-Corruption Conference (IACC). Originally the main international meeting for public officials engaged in corruption and fraud control, it has expanded to embrace multilateral organizations, the private sector, academia, and NGOs. At the 1995 7th IACC in Beijing, TI was invited to act as facilitator, with responsibility for ensuring that future conferences were not held in a vacuum but were instead contextualized into a sense of international continuity and follow-up. At the 1997 meeting for which TI played this facilitating role, the Lima Declaration was issued, setting out the actions and responsibilities that needed to be undertaken in the coming years. The 9th IACC was held in Durban, South Africa in 1999, with contributions for the first time from the heads of the United Nations, World Bank, OECD, Interpol, numerous heads of state, CEOs, and more than 1,300 participants from some 100 countries.

In 1997, an even more significant step toward achieving TI's goals issued from a process that TI had nurtured since its inception. An American diplomatic initiative that envisaged an international anticorruption treaty began to take shape back in 1993, coinciding with the launching of the TI movement. Leading U.S. corporations wanted to pressure the International Chamber of Commerce (ICC) to revise and strengthen its own 1997 "Rules of Conduct to Combat Extortion and Bribery." Understandably, American corporate interests were seeking a level playing field for the conduct of export business and the removal of the perceived competitive disadvantage that the Foreign Corrupt Practices Act of 1977 imposed on its members. TI decided to lobby support for the proposed initiative toward an international agreement, so TI chapters in OECD countries maintained a continuing dialogue with their own governments and with missions at the OECD. The result was that in November 1997, the twenty-nine industrialized member countries of the OECD, along with five additional non-OECD countries, completed a treaty requiring all signatories to ban overseas bribery, thus going well beyond the original objective of ending the tax-deductibility of bribes paid abroad.

The National Chapters

National chapters have become the backbone of TI's activities and are its highest priority. They embed TI's agenda clearly and coherently into the civil society of over seventy countries worldwide. They are the ones who will ensure the sustainability of TI over the medium to long term. TI's national chapters unite trisectoral individuals from all segments of professional society and tend not to be grassroots organizations. In essence, they aim to be "non-governmental institutions which [are] strong enough to counterbalance the state [without] preventing the state from fulfilling its role of keeper of the peace and arbitrator between major interests" (Gellner 1994, 5).

The diversity of people worldwide who are engaged in or calling for the formation of national chapters indicates that TI has been largely demand-driven. So TI has not followed a blueprint for the formation of local chapters but has preferred to await local expressions of interest. A review of the literature on development case studies corroborates this choice, finding that to be effective, NGOs must have local roots and cannot simply be implanted from the outside (Esman and Uphoff 1984, 90). Nonetheless, TI does insist that the nonpartisan and noninvestigative policies be respected by all national chapters. And in fact, this balance of firm guidelines and of decentralized autonomy has empowered national chapters to improvise a wide range of strategies that are effective within their own specific cultures.

Some commentators have pointed out that the national chapters of TI are primarily a lobbying force not of the grassroots, but of elites (Wang and Rosenau 1998, 16)—that is, of professional, specialized, and highly placed "insider" individuals. Because of its emphasis on institutional change rather than scandalous exposures, TI did initially prioritize top-down leadership over grassroots mobilization. TI's chairman is quick to point out that TI happily adapts to the needs of the field, either "playing supplementary and complimentary roles relative to other civil society organizations," or offering clearer leadership, as the need arises (Eigen 1999, 5). TI chapters in developed countries often assist new chapters in developing countries, which in turn form their own alliances with other NGOs, such as churches and human rights organizations whose goals overlap with theirs. National chapters also initiate their own regional alliances, as did the chapters of Latin America and the Caribbean, for instance, in 1996 when they formed a regional chapter together.

The Corruption Perception's Index

TI's most effective public awareness tool by far has been the TI *Corruption Perceptions Index* (CPI). The CPI is a poll of professional polls and surveys that captures the perception of thousands of international business leaders, risk analysts, and business journalists about the relative degree of corruption in almost 100 countries. Countries are included in the CPI if they are covered by at least four polls, and their score is averaged on a scale of zero to ten, where zero would be entirely corrupt and ten a perfectly "clean" state. In the 1999 CPI, for instance, Cameroon and Denmark ranked as the most and the least corrupt countries respectively. The CPI captures more than a single indicator as it combines several measures of political corruption for each country. It is perhaps the most useful indicator of corruption available, and there are few scholarly publications on corruption in recent years that do not cite it or use it in some manner.

Precisely because of the CPI's considerable impact, TI is under pressure to improve and expand on the CPI's original methodology. But at best this sort of survey can measure only two things: trends over time and relative positions vis-a-vis other countries. It does not capture the absolute amount of corruption in any one country, nor does it go much into detail. One of the first criticisms made of the CPI when it was first published in 1995 was it illustrated only one side of the international corruption equation: the receiving end. It said nothing at all about the bribe payers in international trade. The ranks of corruption-prone countries are overwhelmingly poor. The countries with low levels of corruption are all advanced, industrialized countries. Yet TI highlighted the international dimension of corruption, addressing it as a shared problem of both the bribe payer and the bribe taker.

A ranking of the propensity to pay bribes among leading exporting countries was therefore urgently needed. The problem TI faced was the lack of any empirical evidence for such a ranking. Whereas numerous companies regularly provide data on corruption among officials, no one has so far published a ranking along these lines. A "poll of polls" approach was therefore not an option for a new BPI, the Bribe Payers Index. The initial response from a few leading economists of corruption was that such a study could not be done or did not make sense. Conducting a new survey on this sensitive topic would have to be done from a clean slate by developing a sample questionnaire, focus groups and pilot testing—and the necessary funding for a major international survey. Only in 1999 was TI able to bring the necessary resources together. A first successful pilot was then conducted in Argentina in June 1999. Gallup International has been retained as the market research company responsible for conducting the study among business leaders in fourteen emerging markets in mostly non-OECD countries not largely dependent on foreign financial assistance. The publication of the BPI in 2000 coincided with the entry into force of the 1997 OECD convention against the bribery of foreign public officials, for which it will serve as a benchmark in the implementation and enforcement process.

Conclusion

So why, in essence, has TI been so unexpectedly successful, with its work mushrooming in the space of seven or so years to proportions that one might expect from an NGO of much longer standing? Three factors predominate. First, the time was ripe, and countries were crying out for such an initiative. Second, TI was from the outset a network of worldwide experts and highly placed insiders, as opposed to a grassroots protest movement. Third, there is no doubt that TI (perhaps *because* of being so professionalized) has been particularly careful and knowledgeable about handling the delicate dynamics involved in being a lobbying NGO.

And what about the future? In a sense the first phase of TI has been achieved beyond all expectations. But the very extent of this success, if not met with adequate second-phase resources, could become a problem in itself. The task of continuing to support its mushrooming worldwide network requires resources. The need for funding and for paid, stable human resources are, of course, constants for NGOs in general. TI, with its worldwide catchment area and its seventy national chapters calling daily for all sorts of expertise and advice, also has an equally great need for specialist knowledge and renewed theoretical insights. This can come from a deeper interaction between the anticorruption movement, other global public policy networks, and the academic experts and institutions that can theorize, educate, and inform about the complex dynamics that will face transnational NGOs in the twenty-first century.

To summarize, TI policies are: insider insight, adaptive and tailor-made strategies, carrots rather than sticks, diplomacy rather than confrontation, local/global bifocalism and, perhaps most important of all, civil power. One of TI's most distinctive features has been to assert the role of civil society as the missing factor in previous efforts to curb corruption. By challenging the monopoly previously claimed for governments and international agencies, TI is intent on training and developing the profound potential of civil society's authority, empowering it in a climate where the authority of nation-states is weakening and that of corporate multinationals alarmingly strong.

But civility in all its wider meaning is also fundamental to TI. Though it never relies on ethical slogans, and presents its partners instead with hardheaded, tailor-made solutions, TI's own ethos is actually built on a profound belief in the civil. At its root, the *civil* is the underlying insight that deep down, the vast majority of human beings—whether in government, business, or the wider society—have a natural desire to see human societies working well and fairly. TI is aware that this potential civility in most people means that they feel a chronic, collective shame and disappointment when social systems malfunction in serious, avoidable ways. So TI offers on the one hand, specialist legal and economic knowledge that assures citizens that our systems *could* be run more humanely, and on the other, an invitation to citizens to arrange for such systems to be put in place in their own businesses, organizations, and communities.

References

Eigen, Peter. 1996. Combating corruption around the world. *Journal of Democracy* 7: 158–68.

———. 1999. The central roles of civil society in combating corruption in the era of globalization. Address to the Carter Center *Transparency for Growth* Conference. Atlanta, Ga. January.

Esman, Milton J. and Norman T. Uphoff. 1984. *Local organizations: Intermediaries in rural development.* Ithaca, N.Y.: Cornell University Press.

Gellner, Ernest. 1994. *Conditions of liberty: Civil society and its rivals.* London: Penguin.

Gordencker, Leon and Thomas Weiss. 1995. NGO participation in the international policy process. *Third World Quarterly* 16: 543–55.

Homann, K. 1997. Unternehemensethik und Korruption. In *Schmalenbachs Zeitschrift fur Betriebswirtschafltliche,* Forschung 3. Frankfurt.

Kaufmann, Daniel. 1997. Corruption: The facts. *Foreign Policy* (Summer): 114–27.

Klitgaard, R. 1978. *Controlling corruption.* Los Angeles: University of California Press.

Naylor, R. T. 1994. *Hot money and the politics of debt.* Montreal: Black Rose Books.

Tarrow, Sidney. 1996. Making social science work across space and time: A critical reflection on Robert Putnam's *Making Democracy Work. American Political Science Review* 90: 389–97.

Van Ham, Werner, 1998. *Transparency International—The international NGO against corruption: Strategic positions achieved and challenges ahead (a case study).* MBA Thesis, Anglia University, England.

Wang, Hongying, and James Rosenau. 1999. Contesting corruption globally: Exploring a normative transformation. Paper presented at the *Conference on International Institutions—Global Processes—Domestic Consequences,* Duke University, Durham, N.C.

World Bank. 1989. *Sub-Saharan Africa: From crisis to sustainable growth.* Washington, D.C.: World Bank.

———. 1994. *Governance: The World Bank experience.* Washington, D.C.: World Bank.

15

The UNDP Integrity Improvement Initiatives

Pauline F. Tamesis

IN RESPONSE TO THE UNITED NATIONS General Assembly Resolution A/RES/51/59 adopted 28 January 1997 calling for action against corruption, the United Nations Development Programme (UNDP) immediately embarked on developing and implementing a program that addressed the issue as a problem of poor governance. Minimizing corruption is critical in achieving UNDP's overall goal of poverty alleviation and promoting social and people-centered sustainable development. UNDP's emphasis on long-term systemic changes and the human dimensions of development, coupled with its impartiality, underscore its unique contributions in promoting good governance and public accountability and transparency.

In the fight against corruption, UNDP has aimed to strengthen its role in facilitating the involvement of civil society and the private sector in policy development and in the management of development resources that enhances transparency and accountability of economic and financial management. In this endeavor, UNDP works with key partners and coalitions, facilitates policy dialogue that brings together stakeholders and beneficiaries, and introduces phased, systemic reform in the countries that it works with for capacity and institutional building. Furthermore, in its lead role in aid coordination, UNDP advocates its approaches, shapes policy, and helps mobilize resources for national programs that improve integrity in governance. UNDP's flexible approach carefully considers the different country needs and priorities and ensures that responsibilities are clearly defined.

Within UNDP, the responsibility for integrity improvement (or the fight against corruption) is at three levels. Leadership by country offices is crucial because most of UNDP's resources and capacity are at the national country level. Vital tasks for the country offices include identifying entry points and program partners, and designing and monitoring projects. Subregional resource facilities build capacity to support country operations. Regional programs related to accountability and transparency, among others, help share experiences, establish regional networks and centers of excellence, and undertake regional studies of trends. The International Development and Governance Division (IDGD) spearheads the efforts in collaboration with regional bureaus and country offices to translate into action the UNDP policy against corruption, under the Program for Accountability and Transparency.

The Program for Accountability and Transparency (PACT)

PACT aims to build and strengthen capacities to improve accountability and transparency through two main components: (1) financial management and accountability systems, and (2) integrity improvement (anticorruption) initiatives. The Integrity Improvement Initiative, under PACT, focuses on three critical areas: facilitating coordination and dialogue, building partnerships, and strengthening capacities at the national level to develop comprehensive anticorruption strategies.

PACT has also taken the lead in developing policies, tools, and methodologies; researching issues of priority to UNDP; and documenting good practices based on country experiences. These efforts include the review and analysis of UNDP's past and existing initiatives, and facilitating internal collaboration through the Inter-Bureau Task Force on Governance. To provide a solid information base to facilitate policy dialogue, coordination, networking, and capacity building, PACT is developing an inventory of anticorruption-related projects and programs within the UN system to identify who is doing what in anticorruption.

PACT's contributions in the fight against corruption include the following:

1. The production of information, resource, and advocacy materials to help broaden the policy debate and to facilitate international action against corruption, such as the *Corruption and Good Governance* Discussion Paper 3 (July 1997) and the joint UNDP/OECD report on *Corruption and Integrity Improvement Initiatives in Developing Countries* (June 1998) which reproduced the Lima Declaration formulated at the IACC meeting in September 1997 and spelled out a forty-point program to tackle corruption on a global basis.

2. Development of a UNDP corporate position paper, *Fighting Corruption to Improve Governance*, approved by the Executive Committee in July 1998 (see Appendix at the end of the chapter) which provides a cohesive policy

on corruption for UNDP staff use in program countries, and also suggests a framework to address the issue.

3. Conduct of research and development of innovative strategies, such as the joint UNDP/OECD Comparative Country Case Study on Anti-Corruption covering five countries: Benin, Bolivia, Morocco, Pakistan, and the Philippines.

4. Organization of and support to international and regional workshops.

5. Construction of partnerships with key international and regional stakeholders.

6. Facilitation of national capacity building in selected pilot countries, including ongoing and planned support for and development of national action plans to prevent and control corruption in Mongolia, Yemen, Jordan, Burundi, Nigeria, and Venezuela.

In terms of developing tools and assessment methodologies, PACT has also spearheaded the creation of CONTACT guidelines (or Country Assessments in Accountability and Transparency). CONTACT is a set of mission guidelines for undertaking assessments of a country's public financial systems. These guidelines are intended as a tool to review the effectiveness of public sector financial accountability. From this an assessment will be developed to accompany the recommendations of how public sector financial management and audit functions can be improved in the public sector. The current version of CONTACT also includes elements of political and administrative accountability, including a chapter on anticorruption assessment methodology developed under the joint UNDP/OECD comparative case study.

Country Initiatives

Numerous programs targeting the prevention and control of corruption have also been directly initiated from the country and regional levels. They include the following:

1. In Pakistan, the UNDP Asia Governance Resource Facility produced a learning guide and study course on corruption for UN and national staff in the Asia-Pacific region. The effort aims to help promote good governance by detailing anticorruption strategies and by training staff to prepare culturally sensitive projects that can help spot and deter corruption.

2. In Romania, UNDP and the UN Center for International Crime Prevention designed a program to strengthen the capacity of the criminal justice system to fight corruption and to establish a national anticorruption commission.

3. In the Philippines, UNDP is collaborating with the Center for Investigative Journalism to strengthen the effectiveness of journalism for deterring and exposing corruption and to strengthen the role of the media in public accountability.

4. In Georgia, UNDP supported the creation of the Anti-Corruption Group, an independent NGO that is researching and developing innovative ways to prevent corruption.

5. In Guyana, UNDP recently supported the introduction of the Ascyuda Customs program. The initiative, originally designed by the UN Conference of Trade and Development (UNCTAD), introduces methodologies and computerized processing mechanisms that reduce the possibility of corruption in customs.

6. In Bolivia, UNDP has financed the development, elaboration, and publication of the National Integrity Plan, also known as the Public Sector Institutional Reform Program. This ten-year project includes a large civil service reform component and other activities focusing on the fight against corruption, targeting the customs and tax departments, prevention mechanisms, and simplifying administrative procedures.

7. In Mongolia, UNDP began its first pilot initiative to develop national capacity to prevent and control corruption, focusing on the particular vulnerabilities of economies in transition.

There are other country level examples that touch upon anticorruption issues in a broader sense. The following lists the UNDP activities designed to strengthen accountability and transparency in governance.

1. Support Supreme Audit Institutions (SAIs) including review of institutional and legal framework to ensure independence and strengthen capability to pursue compliance, efficiency, and performance.

2. Improve accounting institutions, skills, and standards to meet international criteria.

3. Review and reform customs and tax procedures, including computerization and methodologies to reduce possibility of system corruption.

4. Ensure open, competitive procurement practices.

5. Promote professionalism and ethics in civil service, including development of codes of conduct.

6. Support investigative journalism and professionalization of media, including training and publication of manuals and guidelines.

7. Facilitate and organize civil society and private sector partnerships to promote public advocacy and improve oversight/watchdog functions.

8. Strengthen ombudsman offices and public advocate institutions.

9. Strengthen criminal justice systems to fight corruption through training and legislation.

10. Develop national anticorruption plans and support the creation of anticorruption agencies.

11. Conduct national surveys on public perception of corruption.

12. Organize awareness raising and skills-building workshops to prevent and control corruption.

Partnerships: UNDP and Transparency International

UNDP and Transparency International have worked together informally on various initiatives for the last four years. In December 1998, an official memorandum of understanding was signed by the organizations, with the mutual exchange of expertise and resources as the foundation for the formal agreement. Both are committed to work together and exploit possible sources of synergy created by joint initiatives. The Partnership for Transparency Fund, currently a joint collaboration of UNDP and TI supports an independent and effective role for civil society in the design, implementation, and monitoring of anticorruption programs in developing countries and also promotes South-South exchanges.

Appendix:
Fighting Corruption to Improve Governance[1]

Foreword

IN MOST COUNTRIES, corruption is a criminal offense. But the real crime is that everybody suffers, especially the poor and vulnerable, including women, who cannot afford to pay bribes even for the bare necessities and whose share in economic wealth is already scant. Corruption also damages economies, the environment and, in developing countries, can slow (even reverse) development because it diverts resources and discourages international aid and foreign and domestic investment. In extreme cases, law and order can fall apart as rules and regulations fail to be enforced. Crime, violence, and social unrest can follow.

In recent years, many governments, institutions, civil society, and the international community have become increasingly alarmed at the potentially devastating effects that corruption can have on growth, development, and most important, people and their quality of life. Thus, they are stepping up their efforts against corruption, wherever it may lurk—in government, among civil servants, or in the private sector.

UNDP is unwaveringly committed to the war against corruption. Minimizing corruption is critical if its mission to alleviate poverty and achieve social and people-centered development is to succeed. A multilateral development agency, UNDP support is not conditional. It does, however, have a mandate to create an enabling environment for sustainable human development. Since corruption clearly works against such an environment, UNDP does support projects that address the fundamental elements of the problem.

UNDP sees corruption as a problem of poor governance. Good governance is participatory, transparent, and accountable—its social, political, and economic priorities are reached by consensus and the poorest and most vulnerable have their say in matters affecting their well being and in the allocation of development resources. Bad governance, rife with bribery, corruption, and maladministration, has the opposite effect. So, how to get from here to there?

First, UNDP's priorities are institutional development and reform. Each strengthens governance and fosters an open and effective relationship between the state, the private sector, and civil society.

Second, a successful war against corruption requires efficient public and private sector management. Bad management is a fertile breeding ground for bribery and corruption.

Third, every citizen should have the right to participate in decision-making and governance. Decentralization of government will bring members of even the smallest community within reach of government. Transparency and accountability will stand guard against corruption. A strong independent media will help. So too will independent watchdogs with sharp teeth.

Fourth, as UNDP experience has shown, building partnerships and encouraging closer cooperation with international and local organizations can be critical in the fight against corruption. It should also stimulate more participation of the poorer and poorest in society.

This document explains the problem of corruption and poor governance, its roots, causes, and effects and what is being done and must be done to eliminate it. There must be genuine political will for change, without which government promises to improve transparency and accountability are unlikely to be more than political posturing. It must involve commitment, collaboration, cooperation, and ultimately consensus of all—government, the public sector and civil society. It also means strengthening many institutions, including legislative, the executive, and the judiciary. Easier said than done? Probably. It will certainly take time, perhaps a long time, but it can be done. It must be done.

James Gustave Speth
Administrator, UNDP

Part 2: UNDP's Approach to Fighting Corruption (WHAT?)

UNDP approaches the issue of corruption as a governance problem. Minimizing corruption is critical in achieving its overall purpose to alleviate poverty and promote social and people-centered sustainable development. UNDP's emphasis on long-term systemic changes and the human dimensions of development underscore the effectiveness of the unique qualities inherent in measures that promote good governance and public accountability. The UNDP's strength is impartiality in work toward improving capacity for governance and its comprehensive strategy to address governance.

Creating an Enabling Environment through Good Governance Interventions

Competent legislatures and judiciaries are critical in helping to eradicate poverty. Support for institutional development and reforms are UNDP priorities. UNDP assists in creating a framework for institutional change that fosters a relationship between state institutions, the private sector, and civil society. Corruption is one manifestation of institutional decay. Consequently, strengthening institutions is crucial to reform primarily because they are the vehicles for economic, political, and legal activities. Many poor countries have weaker institutions and therefore more corruption and weaker economic performance than wealthier ones. As a result, governance can be abused. UNDP's focus on strengthening institutions helps countries understand corruption as a failure of governance with corrosive political and economic effects. Accountability and transparency are essential elements of good governance, achieved through strong institutions.

Helping to create national capacities is one of UNDP's greatest strengths. Constructive change requires careful planning that encompasses a clear vision of goals and how to reach them; identifies politicians and leaders in civil society who can help reach those goals, and provides for the formation of accountable managerial capacities and institutional structures to effectively implement change.

Anticorruption programs require leadership skills and efficient management of the public and private sectors. Fraud and opportunities for abuse are directly linked to poor management. Poor service delivery indicates corruption and inordinately impacts the country's poorest. Reducing opportunities for fraud and instituting a work ethic that values efficiency and quality in the delivery of services grows out of improvements in management. Public and private sector management is crucial for effective reform.

Decentralizing government increases its accessibility both politically and physically. People in all of a country's regions, districts, towns, municipalities, rural areas, settlements, and communities can participate more directly in governance and decision making when government is more accessible. Transparency and accountability are the mainstays of anticorruption strategies. They ensure that expenditures are legitimate and that foreign aid and investment are used properly. Decentralization increases transparency and accountability because it removes layers of bureaucracy that present opportunities for dishonest civil servants and politicians.

Collaboration with local organizations to create reforms increases responsiveness and innovation. It establishes a direct relationship with the poor and creates the capacity to stimulate participation and articulate local views. These collaborative ventures are cost-effective, are accountable to local governments, and can independently assess programs and issues. UNDP's country experience has underscored the usefulness of partnerships with civil society to fight corruption. Because laws are not sufficient deterrents, UNDP has elicited the help of civil society where coalitions with different interests but similar goals can jointly fight corruption. UNDP attempts to forge a creative partnership between government and civil society. Civil society is essential to the anticorruption movement because it provides another avenue of pressure to improve governance, train professionals, and disseminate information critical for sustainable reform. Additionally it is influential in changing private-sector behavior. Public administrative corruption functions with the cooperation and full participation of dishonest businesspeople, who grease the slow wheels of bureaucracy with bribes and create an underground market that artificially sets prices. A civil society committed to reform is instrumental in developing an honest private sector that is a genuine partner in the fight against corruption.

UNDP's governance policy also incorporates plans to develop long-term needs that confront issues created during a crisis or political transition. That usually means rapid and coordinated responses, and UNDP's ability to work with and bring together government, civil society, and the private sector can be invaluable both during and after a crisis. Transitions are a particularly vulnerable time for governments and may actually present more opportunities for abusive behavior by civil servants. UNDP's intervention protects transitional governments from dishonest politicians and civil servants who may institute policies that facilitate a return to pre-reform ways.

UNDP's Value-Added Contribution to the Fight against Corruption

UNDP has a special responsibility to help poor countries tackle corruption. Malfeasance attacks the capabilities of governments, and the UNDP takes this into account when designating projects. Currently it supports numerous measures for change. These include programs on institutional and policy reform, methods for reducing the motivation and opportunities for bribery; reducing administrative regulation; and increasing transparency through improved financial management and a responsible, independent media.

Historically, UNDP has involved civil society and the private sector in policy development and resource management that enhance transparency and accountability. In many countries, it has elicited the help of politically strong organizations and coalitions, initiating policy dialogue that brings together stakeholders and beneficiaries. These organizations, with UNDP's assistance, have introduced phased, systematic reform measures to their governments and people. Spearheading the coordination of the reform process allows UNDP to advocate its approaches, influence policy, and help mobilize resources for national programs. Its value-added contribution lies not only in its humanitarian response and relief but also in its long-term development presence and ability to respond to complex and multifaceted development challenges. A successful fight against corruption is a lengthy process. It is most effective when it is inclusive, systematic, and structured—integrating all institutions and policies in the war against malfeasance.

Note:

1. Excerpted from UNDP document "Fighting Corruption to Improve Governance," February 1999, 3–4, 13–19.

16

The International Anticorruption Campaigns: Whose Ethics?

Demetrios Argyriades

ONLY TEN YEARS AGO, any mention of bribery and corruption at international meetings would have been brushed aside. It was viewed as too sensitive, too value laden, too culture bound, too vague to be the subject of international debate. Not any longer. The rapid proliferation of kleptocracies around the world has shed new light on the issue and on the perils of inaction. What is more, one of the outcomes of globalization has been to make apparent the need for international cooperation in fighting this pandemic.

Suddenly the trickle became a flood. Since 1996 a number of agreements, conventions, declarations, and resolutions of international agencies have focused attention on ethics, viewed mostly in the reverse, as in the lack of integrity in public life and the urgent need, accordingly, to do something about it. A few of these post-1996 international pronouncements and collective agreements follow.

The *Inter-American Convention Against Corruption*, adopted and signed in Caracas, Venezuela, in March 1996, by members of the Organization of American States (OAS) whose purposes, outlined in Article 11, are "to promote and strengthen the development . . . of the mechanisms needed to prevent, detect, punish and eradicate corruption"; and to "promote, facilitate and regulate cooperation among the States Parties to ensure the effectiveness of measures and actions to prevent, detect, punish and eradicate corruption in the performance of public functions and acts of corruption specifically related to such performance."

The *United Nations Declaration Against Corruption and Bribery in International Commercial Transactions* was passed less than one year later by the UN General

Assembly, resolution 51/191 of 21 February 1997, prompted by a report of the Second Committee (A/51/601), which had been asked to consider a draft international agreement on illicit payments in general. The declaration welcomed the steps that had been taken at the national, regional, and interregional levels to fight corruption and bribery, as well as recent developments that promoted international cooperation in the fight against corruption in commercial transactions. It noted in particular the OAS convention and "the continuing work of the Council of Europe and the European Union to combat international bribery, as well as the commitment by the members of the Organization for Economic Cooperation and Development (OECD) to criminalize bribery of foreign public officials and further examine modalities and international instruments to facilitate criminalization and to re-examine the tax deductibility of such bribes, with the intention of denying such tax deductibility in the Member States that do not already do so."

A 1997 *OECD Convention on International Bribery* similarly seeks to criminalize the bribery of public officials in interstate transactions and European Union (EU) measures also point in the same direction.

A signal manifestation of this international drive to combat corruption is the elaboration of codes of ethics for public officials. Of singular importance in this regard is the one adopted by the General Assembly during its fifty-first session in Resolution 51/57, *Action Against Corruption*, taken on 2 December 1996. The resolution requested the secretary-general to intensify his efforts in this domain and to provide increased advisory services to member states in elaborating legislative measures and other national strategies designed to invigorate the fight against corruption and to enhance capacities in this domain. The resolution encompassed an *International Code for Public Officials*, which contains provisions on issues of conflict of interests, disclosure of assets, acceptance of favors and gifts, political activity, and use of confidential information that might be in the possession of public servants.

A regional initiative in this direction was taken by the Second Pan-African Conference of Ministers of the Civil Service. A ministerial task force, broadly representative of the main groups and traditions on that continent, was set up to design a code of ethics for African public servants. It reported its findings to a meeting of experts convened at the UN Headquarters, New York, on 24–26 November 1999. The meeting approved a draft for submission to a meeting of ministers in Rabat, Morocco (17–19 January 2000), and is expected to serve as a model for similar regional codes of ethics.

The international conferences on corruption and bribery are legion. What follows is a sample of the broad range of meetings sponsored or organized by the UN and the OECD. The need to build partnerships among the member states and international players—governmental and nongovernmental—was emphasized at the October 1997 Paris Conference on Corruption and Integrity Improvement Initiatives in Developing Countries jointly organized by the OECD Development Center and the UNDP Program for Accountability and Transparency (PACT). These followed the International Anti-Corruption Conference (IACC) in Lima; its final declaration has set the tone of all subsequent international meetings:

Fighting corruption is the business of everyone throughout society; the fight involves the defence and strengthening of the ethical values in all societies; it is essential that coalitions be formed between government, civil society and the private sector; a willingness to enter into such a coalition is a true test of an individual government's commitment to the elimination of corruption: the role of civil society is of special importance to overcome the resistance of those with a stake in the status quo and to mobilize people generally behind meaningful reforms; there must be a sustained campaign against corruption within the private sector as with greater privatization and deregulation, it assumes a greater role in activities traditionally performed by the state; and that top leadership sets the tone in all societies, as "you clean a staircase by starting at the top."

All other related conferences organized around this theme during the same period are too numerous to list. A sample includes the International Seminar on Ethics and Public Administration in Latin American countries, cosponsored by the United Nations Department of Economic and Social Affairs (UNDESA), at Isla Margarita, Venezuela, in October 1997; and a Symposium on Ethics in the Public Service: Challenges and Opportunities for OECD countries, by the Public Management Service (PUMA) of the OECD in November 1997.

This was immediately followed by a Multi-Country Seminar on Normative and Institutional Structures supporting Public Service Ethics, organized by Support for Improvement in Governance and Management (SIGMA) in Central and Eastern European Countries, at the OECD headquarters in Paris. Their findings were fed into the proceedings of yet another conference organized that same November in Thessaloniki, Greece, sponsored jointly by UNDESA and the United Nations Development Programme (UNDP). The title of the conference was *Public Service in Transition: Enhancing Its Role, Professionalism, Ethical Values and Standards.* Other subsequent events included the following:

1. The Colloquium on Promoting Ethics in the Public Service, coorganized by UNDESA, held in Brasilia in December 1997;

2. The United Nations Conference on Governance in Africa: Consolidating the Institutional Foundation; coorganized by UNDESA and the Economic

Commission for Africa, held in Addis Ababa, Ethiopia, in March 1998;

3. The XIVth Meeting of Experts on the United Nations Program in Public Administration and Finance, held in New York, May 1998;

4. The Second Pan-African Conference of Ministers of the Civil Service: co-organized by UNDESA, CAFRAD, and the government of Morocco, held in Rabat, Morocco, in December 1998; and

5. The grassroots 9th International Conference organized by the IACC, held in Durban, South Africa, in November 1999, where Transparency International provided the secretariat support.

Research and publications on bribery and corruption flourish. They have produced an army of specialists on ethics and ethics infrastructures. On the international level, of topical importance is the ongoing project jointly sponsored and conducted by the UNDP and the UNDESA. It involves the comparative study of measures undertaken in several African countries to bolster the public sector infrastructure against corruption and bribery. Especially noteworthy have been the anticorruption programs instigated by the OECD, the World Bank, and the UNDP's Program for Accountability and Transparency (PACT) and its Integrity Improvement Initiative.

This spotlight on corruption is certainly understandable. But there is a downside. This focus on corruption obscures the broader issues of public service ethics and frequently introduces a certain distortion in the very concept of public service professionalism, in the name of which corruption has been attacked. Far from promoting the image, prestige, performance, and role of the public service, attacks against corruption have become a plank in the familiar platform of neoliberal invectives against the administrative state. The argument is simple. Bureaucrats are corrupt. They are also inefficient and ineffective. Big government, accordingly, is not only ineffective, but is also prone to corruption. The logical conclusion that follows from this premise is also disarmingly simple: downsize the government further and punish offenders severely.

This reductionist approach rests on a two-fold assumption regarding the role of the state and the goals of state intervention. The state must "steer, not row." Its mission, first and foremost, is to enforce law and order. It is also supposed to establish and maintain a business-friendly environment. In sharp contrast to the past, when corruption was lightly dismissed as "speed money," or the grease that kept the wheels of business turning smoothly, the new climate might aptly be described as one of zero tolerance. Corruption is now viewed as inimical to business. The OECD Convention on International Bribery of 1997 reflects this change of climate and approach. In its preamble, the convention recalls that corruption is indeed a widespread phenomenon in international business transactions, including trade and investment. It raises serious concerns, undermines economic development and distorts international competitive conditions. The convention, which purports to criminalize the bribery of foreign public officials and to foster international cooperation in preventing money laundering, was prompted by the United States, which had complained that its European competitors either looked the other way, or even tacitly encouraged the practice of bribery by granting tax exemptions for what were reported as costs of doing business.

Most recently, some European countries have returned the compliment, charging that the United States was using its facilities on British soil in order to conduct industrial espionage on its allies and friends in Europe. Industrial espionage is not exactly comparable to bribery and corruption. Still, few would consider it ethical, or would dispute the fact that it "distorts international competitive conditions," in the words of the OECD Convention. True, the charge has been denied. But this only goes to show the breadth and the complexity of current ethical issues, while also demonstrating the somewhat narrow scope and limitations of ongoing antibribery campaigns.

The focus on the economy and business concerns might suggest that what is involved, as the basis of ethical conduct, is a purely utilitarian principle; applying, in other words, a calculus of benefits and costs. It would appear, accordingly, as if corrective action had been decided mostly because, in the light of experience, the imponderables and vagaries of bribery and corruption demonstrably outweigh any potential benefits in efficiency and effectiveness. While not intending to question the utility of utilitarian principles, let alone dispute the merits of the OECD Convention, it must be pointed out that far more is at stake.

The Lima Declaration, issued at the conclusion of the Eighth International Conference Against Corruption in Lima, Peru, in September 1997, put the problem of corruption in a much broader perspective. Corruption, it declared "[E]rodes the moral fabric of society; violates the social and economic rights of the poor and vulnerable; undermines democracy and subverts the rule of law, which is the basis of every civilized society; retards development, and denies society, and particularly the poor, the benefits of free and open competition." Viewed in this broader perspective, the bribery of officials in business transactions is merely incidental to a much bigger problem, with wider ramifications, both national and international: the problem of corruption of public life. The question that must be asked is whether directing the spotlight almost exclusively on various shady deals may not obscure the core of the problem itself, which in truth may lie elsewhere. Are we addressing the symptoms rather than the cause? If so, what is the cause for this unprecedented pandemic of corruption of public life, nationally and internationally? And how can we restore ethics to the core of democratic governance?

It is hardly accidental that concerns with ethical issues loom large on the horizon as the United Nations and other major actors on the international scene are trying to cope with the legacy of forty years of the Cold War and mounting global problems, so far with limited success. During those four decades of Cold War, neither side spared any means, fair or foul, in pursuit of strategic objectives. Both, in this process, produced a generation of kleptocrats and oligarchs who made their mark by plundering. They disappeared long after their antics had become a global embarrassment. Yet their legacy endures in a climate where the quest for short-term gains and recourse to various expedients are routinely justified and rationalized as pragmatism where efficiency and effectiveness hold sway in the scale of values.

In spite of the flag waving that accompanied the end of the Cold War, removal of the specter of a nuclear holocaust does not seem to have brought about any substantial uplift in global solidarity and ethical behavior on the international level. If anything, the triumph of global markets may have compounded some of the problems that represent the legacy of the Cold War. Governments' propensity to cooperate in addressing global issues is severely constrained by short-term domestic considerations, or what some like to call national and security interests.

In the meantime, global problems continue to grow beyond the capabilities of any single player to address them and resolve them. The United Nations, the UNDP, and the World Bank in several recent reports highlight some of those problems. They can be summed up as a dramatic rise in worldwide poverty tied to the deterioration of social capital; a widening gap between the rich and the poor, the powerful and the weak, the skilled and the unskilled, the networked and the isolated; a continued rise in corruption, violence, and organized crime; and the deterioration of the global physical environment.

The increasing polarization between the extremes of poverty and wealth, power and powerlessness, know-how and lack thereof is particularly alarming. If present trends continue, it is legitimate to ask whether freedom and democracy are sustainable worldwide, in the long run. This is not a rhetorical question. In spite of piecemeal gains in pockets of prosperity, mostly in the North and West (17 percent of the world's population), we seem to be regressing—in the mode of a replay of the film *Back to the Future*—not to the 1950s as in the film, but rather to *A Tale of Two Cities*, the world described by Dickens more than a century ago. The distinctive mark of that world is the growth of a large underclass living in dismal poverty and excluded from any of the amenities or benefits that knowledge, opportunity, and wealth bestow to the few. It took the administrative state the best part of half a century to build a caring society that gave democracy meaning. It took the retreat of the state barely two decades to undo much of this constructive work, leading to the disparities between the haves and the have-nots.

The increasing polarization between the extremes of poverty and wealth, power and powerlessness does not create conditions in which *convergence of values* becomes a possibility. The growth and consolidation of a shared and broadly based values system, and a veritable ethics infrastructure underpinning the process of governance and administration, nationally and internationally, also become problematic. In the absence of such underpinnings, extremes may drift apart, a process of reification of the other side preempts all meaningful dialogue and, gradually but surely, coercion and repression become the rulers' responses to what they perceive and define as lawlessness. This may already be happening in a number of countries, a trend described by Loic Wacquant in *Le Monde* (7 December 1999) as the passage from the welfare state to the penitentiary state.

Sanctions and punitive measures are absolutely necessary, but not enough. Given the global ramifications of organized crime and corruption, the closest cooperation among national governments as well as civil society and intergovernmental organizations will be required. But this is predicated on ownership and trust based on the firm foundation of ethical principles. The fight against corruption must be conducted fully within the rule of law, due process, and respect for human rights. The cure must not be worse than the disease. It must not lead to lawlessness, the oppression of marginal groups, and arbitrariness. Most importantly, either ethical principles are viewed as universal or else they are devoid of substance. To be credible and respected, they must be both applied and seen to be applied consistently.

The fight against corruption would stand to gain immensely if it could draw support from a reservoir of goodwill in society at large and a widely shared system of values that highlights and rewards the pursuit of the general interest and active participation in the affairs of the *res publica*. Conversely, it has been shown that anticorruption campaigns often remain dead letter, in a climate of generalized indifference, crass materialism, and cynicism. The values of society, national and international, are ultimately those that have a formative influence on public service ethics, that is to say in shaping the government official's daily actions, attitudes, and behaviors. Therefore, these are the values and attitudes to nurture, develop, and support through public education, as well as special training, pre-entry and in-service. Here are some of these values.

By far the most important is belief in public service as an end in itself, that is, devotion to the common good and service to society over that of one's personal interest. This must be tempered by deference to the rights of minorities and individual freedom, for such are the foundations of democratic government. In turn, belief in democracy and a democratic ethos translate, in practice, into principled support of the political leadership and service to the citizens as valued clients and customers.

Much has been made of responsiveness in contemporary literature. But such responsiveness must be qualified by professionalism, which is the quest for excellence in the responsible application of knowledge, competence, and skill. Competence and morality must be mutually reinforcing. And just as one of the tenets of the Hippocratic oath requires that physicians do not prescribe a medicine that might be harmful, or even that a patient can really do without, so government officials must learn to have the stamina to "speak the truth to power." Though servants of the citizens, they must also be stewards of their collective welfare. Service, in other words, both to political leaders and individual citizens must be offered without fear, self-interest, or favor. It must be rendered loyally, impartially, accountably, and objectively.

Efficiency and effectiveness are mentioned last. Of course, they are very important, but they are not ends in themselves. Their quest should serve a higher purpose. Efficiency, for instance, is a legitimate goal because all civil servants are guardians of the public purse and should have the taxpayers' interests always in mind. Effectiveness, moreover, should prompt all public servants to bring about improvements in the discharge of their functions and the delivery of services. But there are limitations to the pursuit of efficiency and effectiveness springing from considerations of legality, due process, and the principle of equality before the law. A compassionate and fair administration with a truly human face is the necessary antidote to pressures for efficiency, results-orientation, and managers who manage with less concern for the dignity and needs of the end-users than for the balance sheet in the year-end report. Ethics, in other words, are principles in action that people in democracies demand from the people who serve them. They are built on expectations, which constantly evolve; society's expectations of those appointed (or elected) to serve it; and the public servant's own response to the challenge that social expectations represent.

The impact of these principles on public service behavior is commensurate, in fact, to the role of the profession in the general scheme of governance and the nature of the tasks it is called upon to perform. It may indeed be argued that an essential weakness of ongoing anticorruption campaigns is that they are being conducted in an ideological climate still very heavily influenced by the antistate rhetoric that constitutes the legacy of Reaganism and

Thatcherism. They also seek to impose a set of standards, that have proved ineffective because they are at variance with prevalent conditions and corresponding attitudes in several countries, and tremendous inequalities of power and wealth, compounded by greed at the top and struggle for survival at the base of the social pyramid.

The urgency of restoring and reinforcing ethical values at the core of public service professionals is undeniable. But in the last analysis, this need has less to do with any apparent moral deficit among people in the public service than with prevailing standards in public life and the total scheme of national and international governance. Given the growing complexity of public life in an era of globalization, as well as great diversity and rapid change, the way to go about it should place less stress on sanctions and far greater emphasis on enhancing the role, image, performance, and professionalism of public servants.

Improving its capacity to attract the best and the brightest may be the number one problem of the public service in much of the world today. To be sure, the solution to this problem begins with the review of pay and career structures, especially in those countries where government is widely seen as the employer of last resort. However, all solutions begin with exploration. And exploration begins with debate. It begins with the recovery of principles and values, which from the beginnings of time, from ancient Greece and Rome, have made the public service a Great Profession.

References

Argyriades, Demetrios. 1996. Neutrality and Professionalism. In *Democratization and bureaucratic neutrality*, edited by H. K. Asmeron and P. Reis. London: Macmillan.

Giddens, Anthony. 1998. *The third way.* Cambridge: Polity Press.

Huberts, L. W. J. C. and J. H. J. van den Heuvel, eds. 1999. *Integrity at the public-private interface.* Maastricht: Shaker Publishing B.V.

Organization for Economic Cooperation and Development. 1999. *Public sector corruption.* Paris: OECD.

———. 2000. *No Longer Business as Usual.* Paris: OECD.

———. 2000. *Trust in government.* Paris: OECD.

United Nations. 1999. *Public service in transition: Enhancing its role, professionalism, ethical values and standards.* New York: Department of Economic and Social Affairs. ST/ESA/PAD/ SER.E/77.

United Nations Development Programme. 1997. *Corruption and good governance.* New York: UNDP.

———. 1998. *Corruption and integrity improvement initiatives in developing countries.* New York: UNDP.

————. 1999. *Human development report for Central and Eastern Europe and the CIS.* UNDP/ RBEC, New York.

World Bank. 1998. Fighting corruption worldwide. Special issue, *Finance and Development* 35 (1): 2–14.

17

Corruption and Democracy

Gerald E. Caiden

THIS PLANET STILL CONTAINS many unpleasant features—cannibalism, slavery, abject misery and poverty, persecution, violence, crime, and so on. It is the democratic spirit, the feeling of community, equity, regard for others, humaneness, and compassion that abhors such nasty features, that tries to work out ways and means of ridding humanity of them or at least minimizing their occurrence. So democracies devise moral principles, appropriate institutions, and workable processes and practices to ensure that at least their own societies, if not the world, reduce the incidence of these offensive features. Democratic regimes have now evolved many such devices, such as the promotion of the public interest and community service, the protection of individual civil liberties and human rights, representative and responsible government, the rule of law, independent agencies (judiciary, audit, ombudsman, electoral commissions, inspector generals, etc.) that ensure public accountability, openness and impartiality, division of power, fair competition among contenders, subordination of the military and police, promotion of civic culture, voluntarism and citizen participation, due process, and fair administrative practices.

Corruption is the exact opposite. Corruption in all its manifest forms gnaws at, undermines, and contradicts all the democratic elements. It embodies the antidemocratic ethos, for it embraces selfishness, self-centeredness, particularism, unfair privilege, exploitation of weaknesses and loopholes, unscrupulous advantage of the weak, the exploitable and the defenseless, and all manner of shady dealings. It is undeserved, unfair, unjust, and immoral benefit derived from positions of public trust and responsibility used for sleaze and unworthy actions. It is offensive to any notion of public guardianship on which the edifice of democracy is built.

These two contending forces are found in all societies. Sometimes one force is the clear winner. Corruption rules and it is a way of life, not merely a fact of life, and democratic devices are façades that fool only those who do not seem to know how things are really done in their society. Elsewhere, the democratic ethos rules and corruption is minimized and, when exposed, entails severe public condemnation and punishment. The narco-democracies stand at one end of the continuum and the small democracies of Iceland, Scandinavia, and New Zealand at the other. Between, there are various mixtures and combinations, with the line between democracy and corruption shifting all the time, first one way and then the other, as conditions, values, opportunities, and policing change.

Three major objectives are sought in this chapter. First, it attempts to concretize what may universally be agreed as constituting corruption in democracies, ruling out most of the abominations of autocracies although even democracies commit them. Second, it illustrates forms of corruption that afflict democracies. Do not be fooled by the countries quoted. They are merely examples that have been exposed quite recently and the evidence is irrefutable. But they could easily apply elsewhere, and evidence is building to suggest that other democracies are just more secretive or sophisticated. The systematic exploitation of public position is not just found in the rapacious elites of autocratic regimes; it is also found in kind in Japan, Western Europe, and North America and among the highest trusted positions elsewhere around the globe, even at one time in the reputable Scotland Yard in the United Kingdom, in the secret services of NATO countries, and in the banking industry in Switzerland, Luxemburg, Spain, and the Caribbean. Third, it emphasizes the internationalization of corruption and the failure of the world's democracies to protect themselves against foreign influences, such as the erosion of public service, the subordination of the public interest, and the infiltration of organized crime into virtually every aspect of respectable public life. Just as corrupt developing countries compete for aid, investment, and employment, so there are corrupt international and national agencies seeking new markets, new resources, and new channels of influence—and they are not fussy with whom they deal.

We look for new causes, reasons, and explanations, but there is little that is new under this particular sun. Human beings are imperfect and weak and they are manipulative, deceiving, and gullible. Scarcity is exploitable; competition can be fixed; and people tend to look after their own interests first. The unscrupulous are always creative about getting around any obstacles in their way. The righteous hate to demean themselves and deal with dirty business; they hope it will go away, or that it is not as bad as made out, or that it will not touch them— any excuse not to have to act boldly. In contrast, others see political life and public office as just another avenue of business for self-enrichment and reward to friends and relatives. They take advantage of the trust that democracies place in their public institutions and leaders to deceive the public and exploit their opportunities, and to entrench themselves in power through electoral manipulations and illegal campaign financing.

But corruption touches everybody. It corrodes the democratic ethos. If unopposed, it will spread its filth and eventually imperil democracy itself. One day, democratic states will become so soft that not much is needed to push them aside. It has happened in living memory to some of the strongest democratic states. Look how many so-called advanced democratic countries have failed at some time or other to prevent occupation and how many became willing tools of their tyrannical occupiers. Other countries that avoided this fate may just have been lucky. Although democrats may be tolerant, complacent, even lazy, there are limits to how much they can take. Anger them enough, and they will take to the streets, demonstrate, and fight within the system to halt corrupt excesses and to curb dirty hands. Recent years have witnessed public outcries against suspected (and too often proved) corruption in the democracies of Belgium, the United Kingdom, Sweden, Turkey, Argentina, Venezuela, Brazil, India, and the Philippines and public demonstrations against more sleazy self-styled democratic regimes around the world.

The Ubiquity of Corruption

That people lack confidence in their public institutions in nondemocratic societies is axiomatic. They have no alternative to putting up with whatever their autocratic leaders provide them, except to hope that one day they will be able to arrange things more to their liking. That people lack confidence in democratic societies is enigmatic. Why should people in open, liberal societies—in which they are encouraged to participate in public affairs and choose their own directly accountable government representatives, and whose public institutions uphold their fundamental human rights—lack confidence in the very public institutions they have fashioned for themselves and can redesign any time and in public leaders whom they can recall at their next available opportunity? How do they lose their confidence and why is not more done to restore it immediately? A simple explanation is that they lose confidence, for the following reasons: they no longer trust their leaders and institutions; they no longer believe they are getting good value; and they suspect that some are getting more favorable or favored treatment than they ought at others' expense. They feel they are no longer getting a fair shake because public leaders and institutions have been corrupted. There is too much of a gap between what is and what should be. Performance lags behind expectations either because the public have been deceived by leaders who promise too much or they have been let down by incompetent institutions that no one seems anxious to improve.

The very term corruption implies that things are not what they ought to be. They have been perverted, twisted, manipulated, distorted, bent, diverted, and otherwise made to depart from expected proper paths. In the process, the corrupt have unfairly gained or benefited in some way that should not have happened or otherwise would not have occurred, at the expense of everyone else. In a perfect world, this distortion would never happen. In this imperfect world, it inevitably does. As a result, some people reap unjust rewards at the expense of others, who, when they find out, feel cheated and victimized. In nondemocratic societies victims may feel this is their fate. But people in democratic societies do not expect to be treated this way; supposedly, they are to be treated decently and fairly, and any injustices are expected to be corrected or compensated. When democratic citizens feel that advantage is being taken of them, that they are not being treated decently or fairly, and that injustices are not being corrected or compensated, then their confidence in the public leaders and institutions blamed for perpetrating such discrimination diminishes. They know that if no corrective action is taken, the situation will persist and worsen. This feeling of not being able to make any difference, of being powerless to get corrective action, shakes their confidence in themselves and in democracy itself.

Every incident of corruption that comes to light, and the seeming inability or indifference of public leaders and institutions to correct it, disillusions people and serves to undermine their leaders' credibility. If the authorities do not seem to care, why should anyone else? At this point, some might argue that it is better if the existence of corruption or, rather, knowledge about its existence is suppressed because it will only breed suspicion and indulgence, thereby making matters worse. Unfortunately, suppression is doomed to failure. While corrupt acts may by their very nature be conspiratorial and furtive, they cannot in this day and age be committed by isolated individuals. Too much social activity these days is collective not individual, organized not random, public not private. Somebody is bound to know. Somebody is bound to be sucked into the conspiracy of silence. To silence them all requires too much repression, certainly too much for a truly democratic society. But even where intimidation may work, rumor and gossip about suspected corruption cannot be so contained, and the facts are likely to be exaggerated, embroidered, and distorted, further disillusioning people. For this reason, democracies pride themselves on openness not secrecy, on inquiry not suppression, and on exoneration as well as attribution. Sometimes, suspicions sour civil society more than the facts and unfounded rumors may be more damaging than the unpleasant truth. After all, corruption does not reflect well on any society, least of all democracies.

The worst aspect is the nature of corruption itself. It takes so many different forms and covers such a variety of public activities that often it is difficult for the common citizen to detect it for what it really is, for the corrupt are clever at disguising their corrupt acts and covering any traces. Moreover, it is very contagious. Corruption in one sphere of public activity quickly spreads like wildfire to another; few who come into contact with it can escape contamination, let alone stand up to it, especially when so many around them succumb to its temptations. Corruption is very beguiling. It promises undeserved rewards and so often delivers without detection, let alone retribution. If left alone, corruption will multiply, intensify, and eventually institutionalize itself, thereby becoming the norm, not the exception. When this happens, civil society is jeopardized and public authority crumbles. Rules are no longer rules. Standards are no longer standards. Uncertainty replaces order. Outcomes belie intentions. Public expectations are compromised at best and thwarted at worst, because the whole delivery system has been bent beyond all recognition, as self-interests replace the public interest, and private-regarding behavior is rewarded at the expense of public-regarding behavior. Indeed, corruption is so personally attractive and the opportunities for its occurrence are so widespread, the wonder is not that it infects so much public activity but that so little has been truly damaging and destructive to democratic society. Or have we all been living in a dream world for too long, preferring not to see the reality that is not hidden from the many victims of corruption, who are rightly growing more disillusioned with their corrupt leaders and institutions, democracy notwithstanding?

In recent decades, the mass media have become bolder in their criticism and less forgiving of officialdom. Gossip and hints of scandal are more newsworthy, and the private lives of public officials have become an open book. The public's appetite grows for the titillating and the sensational. The more public authorities try to protect their secrets, the more vulnerable they become. The more they try to retain their credibility, the more their indiscretions are glorified. The more suspicious and doubting the public becomes, the more willing they are to believe in wrongdoing in high places. Whistle-blowers increasingly take risks to reveal what they know. A veritable corruption information industry has sprung up. The world's serious newspapers regularly publish items and investigative stories on corruption. Television now considers corruption newsworthy whenever telecommunications can escape censorship, a factor that does not inhibit computer networks. Business associations, too, have not flinched from exposing corruption.

The internationalization of corruption has spurred public bodies to action. The United Nations hosted its first interregional seminar on corruption in December 1989, and the United Nations Criminal Justice Department (as it was called) in Vienna released its draft anticorruption manual the next year, following a draft resolution on international cooperation, which included the following Recommendation 8:

Because the corrupt activities of public officials can destroy the potential effectiveness of all types of government programmes, hinder development, and victimize individuals and groups, it is of crucial importance that all nations should: (a) review the adequacy of their criminal laws, including procedural legislation, in order to respond to all forms of corruption and related actions designed to assist or to facilitate corrupt activities, and should have recourse to sanctions that will ensure an adequate deterrence; (b) devise administrative and regulatory mechanisms for the prevention of corrupt practices or the abuse of power; (c) adopt procedures for the detection, investigation and conviction of corrupt officials; (d) create legal provisions for the forfeiture of funds and property from corrupt practices; and (e) adopt economic sanctions against enterprises involved in corruption. (United Nations 1990)

Since then, more countries have taken corruption seriously.

Current Major Concerns

In this imperfect world, corruption is bound to be happening somewhere; no country is exempt. It is impossible to eradicate completely and also impossible to measure with any degree of accuracy simply because much will be hidden and never known. The issue is: how serious a threat is it to society and whom does it harm? If unchecked, official corruption will eventually result in a "softness of state" comprising all manner of social indiscipline that prevents effective government and obstructs national development. "It will bring about a society in which little works [as it should], with increasing restiveness and resort to repression to prevent things falling apart altogether. Furthermore, it will lead to widespread cynicism, engendering hopelessness . . ." (United Nations 1996, 1).

What are the major current concerns about corruption? First, and on the top of Transparency International's list, is business bribery, which is rampant throughout the world and endemic in all transactions, public and private. Nothing gets done without some form of bribery, gift, favor, or other return. The bigger the stakes, the higher the propensity to exact economic rent as a condition of access. Despite United Nations and European Union resolutions adopted in the late 1990s, foreign paid bribes are still fully tax deductible as legal business expenses in many countries. Business bribery contaminates all contracting and seduces the highest public figures around the world into being rewarded for their contacts, influence, and intervention, if not directly then through their relatives and friends. The BCCI scandal caught many big fish, but BCCI was only one international bank in which bribe money was stashed; since then other banks around the world have been exposed as being involved in international money laundering.

Second, and related to business bribery, is the large amounts of money being laundered worldwide, with huge amounts of hot money sloshed around the globe daily. Illegal manipulation of the world's financial markets leaves national economies increasingly vulnerable. A significant portion of world financial assets are controlled by criminals who use their power and wealth to suborn governments, banking systems, and legitimate business; to steal and siphon monies from needed public investment and welfare; and to hinder public policy and management. Dirty money moves to weak political systems where controls are ineffective. "The corrosive effects of money-laundering on democratic and political institutions cannot be overstated . . . no financial institution and no country are immune" (United Nations 1996, 3).

Third, related to dirty money, is organized transnational crime, particularly the operation of crime syndicates and drug cartels, which cross borders at will to conduct "activities legally defined as crimes but against which law enforcement agencies [are] relatively powerless, either because of the involvement of high-placed individuals or because of circumstances reducing the likelihood of their being reported or prosecuted" (United Nations 1996, 3). These activities include terrorism, theft of cultural property, trafficking in women and children for sexual slavery, extortion, car theft, black-market trade in arms and nuclear materials, smuggling of migrants, drug trafficking, trade in human organs, environmental crimes, computer tampering, illegal lotteries, counterfeiting, violence against the judiciary and journalists, and trafficking in endangered species. "Entire populations are victimized as human vulnerability is targeted and various segments of society are entrapped in diverse illicit activities" (United Nations 1996, 3). The most serious of these organized criminal activities are those involving drug trafficking from Myanmar, Afghanistan, Laos and the Golden Triangle in Asia (heroin), Lebanon and West Asia (heroin and opium), and the South American Andes (cocaine), and engaging the crime syndicates of the Hong Kong Triads, Cali cartels in Colombia, the Italian Mafia, Japanese Yakuza, Russian Vory v. Zakanye, United States Cosa Nostra, and criminal gangs in Lebanon and Vietnam. The world is witnessing the emergence of narco-democracies, that is, countries "with a façade of democracy that are effectively controlled by drug kingpins who manipulate political systems with

[drug] money" (*Wall Street Journal* 4 April 1995, A14). Past presidents and other high officials in Colombia and Mexico have been fingered as being involved, and interdiction of drug smuggling from the Andes to the Caribbean and North America has been handicapped by corrupt governments and public agencies.

Fourth is the growing influence of money in political life. Countries are increasingly disturbed by (a) the direct buying power of money to secure the votes of electors and elected politicians to swing elections and legislation, influence party actions through legal and illegal campaign contributions, and obtain favored treatment through bribes and other personal rewards; (b) the purchase of commercial space and time in mass media to saturate the electorate; (c) the concentration of mass media ownership in the hands of fewer power brokers and public opinion makers; (d) the ability of well-placed insiders to manipulate mass media through public funding and other covert political activities and to smear political rivals through the use of privileged information, particularly where the mass media are largely government or party controlled; (e) asset-stripping, under the guise of privatization, to allow political backers to obtain public resources at bargain prices in return for party contributions, and other forms of the public financing of private political activities; and (f) tax avoidance and evasion, returning political favors through special legal loopholes or discretionary/discriminatory enforcement (or nonenforcement) of tax codes. Some of these are as old as politics, but what is new is the sophistication and ingenious devices employed to prevent common knowledge of political corruption, the spin placed on illegal political contributions when exposed, and the condescension in official circles toward the public—as if everybody does it and all the players should understand this is unavoidable in modern democratic politics.

Fifth is yet another traditional form of corruption, kleptocracy, where public resources are viewed as private spoils, state largesse is seen as a personal gravy train, and political activity is viewed as just another avenue for entrepreneurship. Public office is a means of self-enrichment with no holds barred. Public officials plunder the public treasury, steal, embezzle, run rackets, and conduct criminal activities and legitimate businesses out of their public offices. They are immune from prosecution, award relatives and friends government-protected monopolies and lucrative contracts, use public property as their private preserve, charge facilitation fees, and generally live well at public expense. In this scenario, citizens rightly consider all politicians as rogues and crooks not to be trusted. Foreigners dealing with kleptocracies find they, too, have to pay and must devise creative means of hiding the fact from their own organizations and governments.

Sixth is the embarrassing situation of the nongovernmental organizations, or NGOs, once seen as having the advantages of both public and private bodies but now viewed with increasing suspicion for having the disadvantages of both. Some NGOs are falling into disfavor, even disrespect, for being responsible or accountable only to themselves, beyond the reach of public accountability mechanisms. While some are indeed noble and heroic, others have become fronts for organized crime or merely self-aggrandizing, rewarding themselves handsomely for puny outcomes hardly worth the bother. Exposure of scandals among the worst offenders has disillusioned the public, resulting in loss of confidence and trust that has carried over into disrespect for even the trustworthy NGOs and suspicion of all bureaucratic organizations.

Now, if all this is well known, what is unknown? If this minister is caught, how many others up to the same tricks have yet to be caught? After all, "everyone" knows that politicians are rascals only out for themselves, and public employees get away with what they can. So why should scandals surprise? Such cynicism is particularly crippling to democracy as it breeds contempt for authority, apathy toward civic participation, and indifference to public maladministration.

Corruption in Democracies

All around the world, corruption is severely damaging the credibility of government in general and confidence in democracy in particular. Indeed, the inability or ineffectiveness to reduce corruption, to cleanse public institutions, and to secure honest governance has undermined popular support for the institution of democracy. While the situation is not as serious elsewhere, a dark cloud has appeared over all democratic regimes with every new revelation of sleaze in high places. People are expressing their unease by looking to nondemocratic extremes, forming new political parties divorced from discredited traditional parties, and refusing to participate in civil and political life. How serious a challenge to democracy is corruption?

The Newly Emerging Democracies

Clearly the most serious challenge to democracy is among the newly emerging democracies, the so-called transitional societies that have abandoned autocracy. Most have no experience of democracy at all. Setbacks attributable to democracy remind people of the "good old days" under autocracy—except things were so corrupt that few want to return. Given a choice between striving to make democracy work and returning to autocracy, most grit their teeth and hope that their sacrifices will eventually be worthwhile, if not for themselves, then for their children. On the other hand, they have grown up with corruption.

They have learned to live with it and turn it to their advantage when they can. Widespread corruption is nothing new. What is new is that, under democracy, the cast of villains has changed, law and order is collapsing as crime leaps, and newly created wealth is being exported, leaving many worse off than before. Unless the situation turns around soon, the contempt they had for their previous regimes will be redirected at their new public leaders and institutions.

Fortunately, history shows that long-established democracies also went through difficult transitions and suffered for generations from continued widespread corruption until new generations grew out of corrupt habits, new leaders and institutions managed to get a handle on corruption, and a new civic culture gradually brought a new moral basis to governance. Unless utterly poisoned, democratic shoots will eventually take hold and transform the way public business is conducted.

Russia   By all accounts, corruption in Russia has always been endemic. But it seems to have worsened with the collapse of Communism. Socialists, despite all the ideological chatter, did not turn out to be more moral given the hard realities of everyday life in the Soviet Union. The Communist regime kept a tight hold on disorder and crime and maintained strict discipline over wayward citizens. However, liberalization has loosened these controls and allowed the underworld to thrive. Organized crime and gangsters have taken advantage of new economic opportunities and, aided and abetted by corrupt officialdom, have become a serious menace to Russian society.

Less than three years after it began, the second greatest Russian revolution of this century is awash in corruption, opportunism, and crime. The Government not only has failed to pursue the evidence of its predecessors' venality; it has been unable to hold in check the greed of its own ministers. Scandal has become ordinary in the New Russia . . . In a murderous parody of free-market competition, mobsters fight open battles over territory in the streets . . . Criminal cartels, believed by police to control as much as 40 percent of Russia's wealth, infiltrate stock exchanges and the real estate market. Gangsters not only open bank accounts; they open banks. (Handelman 1995, 3)

Faced with so many other compelling problems, public authorities have yet to pose a serious challenge to corruption. There are few anticorruption laws and those enacted are weak and only selectively implemented. In the meantime, abuse of office appears to be soaring and citizens continue to bribe their way through Russian bureaucracy. Public employee remuneration is so low and uncertain that taking bribes is at least sure payment for services rendered, and extra payment is justified for expediting services which otherwise are expensive and time consuming. Administrative systems are so bad that people serve their own interests first. For example, army generals have embezzled large sums and kept serf battalions of conscript soldiers for building officers' dachas in Moscow suburbs, while ordinary soldiers lived on emergency rations and begged in the streets. Weary miners, unpaid for months, refused to work and unpaid power plant workers refused to operate electricity stations. Only a fraction of the money sent from Moscow to pay energy sector wages in Vladivostok arrived, as predators along the way took bites out to pay what was owed them (*Los Angeles Times* 3 August 1996, A1). This neglect of Russia's far east caused terrible misery in the winter of 2000–2001. Poorly paid Russian diplomats have shipped duty-free cars back to Russia as their own property then resold them at a mark-up while express customs services expedited the paperwork and collaborated with customs officers to extort car buyers. Russia's two biggest monopolies, the gas producer Gazprom (which holds one-third of the world's known gas reserves) and the power giant Unified Energy Systems (UES) are notorious for enriching top management at the expense of shareholders and the public through sweetheart deals and blocking reforms that endanger the oligarchy who run them and their corrupt deals.

Things may have always been done this way in Russia but money now replaces party connections (*protekzia*). More resented are the new black markets monopolized by gangsters and well-placed officials whose ill-gotten gains give them advantageous access to liberalized business opportunities and state divestiture of public property. In this scramble for wealth, the playing field is decidedly uneven, and the disadvantaged are left with a democratic façade that fails to stop the rot.

The newly liberated citizens of Communist societies form a dangerously unstable community in the post–Cold War world. One St. Petersburg engineer summed up the cynicism of his compatriots by cleverly turning around the old underground joke about Communism's secret pact in which the worker pretends to work and the Government pretends to pay him. "We pretend to vote and the Government pretends to govern . . . . It's the mafia which runs everything. (Handelman 1995, 340)

The danger in Russia as in other transitional societies moving from autocracy to democracy is that democracy may prove too fragile to withstand economic collapse, ethnic strife, and other possible catastrophes. They need strong, effective governance. They can do without the doubts cast by widespread corruption bequeathed by previous nondemocratic regimes. Ineffectiveness arising from corruption alone is unlikely to bring about collapse or replacement. But do things have to get worse before they get better?

Secure Democracies

At one period during the Second World War, it was estimated that only 12 genuine democracies still survived and several of those were under military or emergency wartime controls. Since then, their number has at least quadrupled. Occupied democracies were liberated and returned to their former democratic ways, notwithstanding wartime scars and occasional scares from nondemocratic movements within. Their colonies secured independence during the war or soon thereafter, along with the colonies of victorious Allies and defeated Axis powers. Unfortunately, many merely replaced imperialism with their own domestic forms of autocracy and, while they may describe themselves as democratic, they have yet to experience genuine democracy. In these countries, corruption is endemic. But so is corruption in secure democracies. Italy and Japan, now secure democracies, suffer from widespread corruption arising partly from one-party domination or the need for loyal coalition partners. However, corruption has tainted all their major political parties in efforts to keep political money flowing.

Mexico   One-party Mexican democracy has been so rife with corruption, the question is whether the country has ever experienced genuine democracy. Mexico is not a narco-democracy; drug traffickers do not dominate its economy. But recent revelations about kleptocracy by members of the Institutional Revolutionary Party (PRI) show how such corrupt patterns operate. Past presidents and their close relatives and friends have amassed fortunes not just from undisclosed secret funds and large self-awarded bonuses but also from payoffs, kickbacks, bribes, "loans," commissions, "fees," influence-peddling and money-laundering. Bribery runs throughout government and society. Taxi drivers and car owners have reported frequent shakedowns, and foreign tourists have complained of police beatings, robberies, and other abuses. Everyone suspects everyone else of being on the take and businesses take for granted that they have to pay off or cut in officials or face victimization—it is all part of the price for liberalizing the economy (*salinismo*) and privatizing public monopolies. Despite recent attempts to combat corruption, too many public leaders have too much to lose if corruption is tackled. Although the defeat in 2000 of the PRI presidential candidate promises a new era, anticorruption legislation remains weak, the courts impotent, and investigators subservient. Revelations and leaks continue to shake public opinion and confirm deep-rooted cynicism that gives the people little pride and confidence in public institutions while they wait for promised changes in the conduct of public business. On the other hand, President Vincente Fox raised eyebrows when on taking office he purged some notorious corrupt officials, cracked down on the police to diminish their petty corruption and generally demanded a higher moral tone in public life.

The Mexican situation is being repeated in other Latin American democracies. Most of their judicial systems are soft on corruption and white collar crime. Wealthy defendants can spin out cases for years and if it appears they might lose, they simply abscond. Even the judges are suspect. A former labor court judge in Brazil is accused of being the ringleader of a scam to embezzle some $92 million from the incomplete construction of a courthouse in Saõ Paulo, which also involved a federal senator and a presidential aide.

In Peru, after the fall of President Alberto Fujimori and the subsequent revelations of how corrupt his rule had been, the Vladi-videos continue to show the official elite making pilgrimages to the former chief of the National Intelligence Service (SIN) Vladimiro Montesinos to cut dirty deals. The daily soap opera at least galvanized the electorate into demanding cleaner government and more honest public leaders.

Things are a little better in India, where the rule of the once dominant Congress Party waned. Not only were government ministers forced to resign but so were leaders of opposition parties—for receiving *hawala*, or laundered money, illegal foreign exchange, and payoffs for help in landing contracts in the power, coal, steel, and railway sectors in the late 1980s, and for pocketing "illegal gratifications." Most claimed that the payments were donations that they faithfully passed on to party coffers. However, the police are still reputed to protect rather than prosecute crooked politicians.

The political class is seen as uninterested in justice for its own sake. Prosecutions are no longer seen as a means to convict the guilty, but as ploys to win elections. In any event, people with money rarely get convicted of anything. . . . (*Economist* 20 January 1996, 33)

This could also be said with equal force about other self-styled democracies around the globe. In them, democracy has failed to curb deep-seated patterns of corruption that persist for reasons that have little to do with democracy. The little that governments have done has soon been nullified. Consequently, the public has become hardened to political passivity and has a low opinion of politicians. Influential elites take advantage of their position to favor themselves and their causes, seemingly unmindful of the harm they do to civic society.

Entrenched Democracies

Finally, a group of well-entrenched democracies has long cleansed or attempted to cleanse governance in all walks of life. In them, scandal is rare and corruption the exception. Tolerance of corruption is low. Anyone even suspected of corruption has been bundled out of public life and disgraced. Public office is seen as an office of trust and its incumbent as a guardian of the public interest. Public officials are expected to serve as virtuous examples beyond reproach in their private as well as public life. Alas, few entrenched democracies have been spared scandal of late, rocked by corruption of a magnitude indicating all is far from well and, perhaps, has not been well for some time, just secreted. If the truth be known, there are more skeletons in the cupboard than ever suspected. The United States has never professed virtue. It has always admitted to corruption, justified to some extent as being the grease that enabled the complicated system of government to work more smoothly. And the United States has probably been more open than other countries in baring its corruption. Not so the Benelux countries or Switzerland or the United Kingdom, which have prided themselves on being relatively free of corruption. Not any more. Not only have people in high places been caught but they have tried to brazen themselves out of corruption charges, only to trap others and demonstrate their lack of morality. Such scandals may upset the public but they pose no real danger to democratic society because the democratic ethos is strong enough to stand such pinpricks, at least so far. But there is no telling whether and when some corrupt acts may cross the line into sedition and treason.

Germany   Since the Second World War, with relatively little experience of democracy, West Germany appeared to be doing well after the occupation by Allied powers determined to democratize the areas under their control. It appeared to become a model democracy with a professional bureaucracy almost free of corruption. This contrasted with East Germany where a Communist regime imposed one-party rule although corruption there also seemed to be contained. Reunification in the 1990s brought political strain but no open evidence of corruption. Then the roof fell in when, at the end of the decade, it emerged that the major political parties had financed themselves and their election campaigns through secret illegal funding from anonymous donors. The financial scandals fingered some of the most reputable public figures who were revealed as holding themselves above the law, taking illegal contributions, and enjoying a lifestyle beyond their means. Doubts have been raised about their trustworthiness and about just what kind of democracy exists, especially among former East Germans who still harbor doubts about capitalism. Certainly, the main opposition party has been weakened, even if temporarily. Germany's image as a law-abiding country has been compromised and its international reputation has suffered. On the other hand, some observers point out that this is exactly what should happen in a democracy. The democratic bedrock has not been disturbed. The democratic process has exposed wrongdoing and the wrongdoers have been punished for submitting falsified documents.

What is disturbing is that reputations so painfully built up have been destroyed and some of the most reputable continue their stubborn defiance of the law and fail to recognize their authoritarianism.

Other entrenched democracies have also not fared as well. Ireland has experienced economic success beyond expectations, with average incomes now exceeding other parts of Europe. But prosperity has also attracted immigrants whose presence has aroused latent xenophobia and who have been blamed for taking jobs away from the locals, keeping wages low, creating a refugee problem, and inhibiting the development of adequate public and social services. What has changed most are the revelations of corruption and massive wrongdoing by political and business elites whose lush lifestyle is maintained by business solicitations, misdirected party funds, unauthorized bank overdrafts, and secret offshore accounts. The country has become a land of "crooks and shirkers" with reluctance "to punish any of the culprits" (*Guardian* 19 August 2000, 14).

German pride, Irish pride, French pride, Dutch pride, British pride, even Icelandic and Fijian pride have been blemished by incidents of corruption in recent years. Corruption is indeed ubiquitous. But how serious is it becoming, for it does seem to be on the increase and taking increasingly serious forms on the global stage. As long as democratic societies take adequate steps to protect themselves, it is unlikely to harm them, if they bear in mind that corruption is cancerous. There is no way to prevent corruption altogether as long as there are rogues in public office who are tempted by their opportunities; as long as their corrupt acts are tolerated or even aided and abetted by their fellow citizens; as long as they can buy off prosecution because investigators are underfunded; and as long as society is indifferent, as people mistakenly believe that corruption is harmless and victimless. The truth is that all are its victims, everyone's quality of life is lessened, governance is compromised, and public confidence in leaders and institutions is undermined.

The Implications

Unless democratic regimes grasp the nettle of corruption, they intensify for themselves several challenges that assume far greater importance than they should. If allowed to get out of hand—and that is what is about to happen to the most complacent—these issues may well jeopardize, certainly compromise, democracy itself. First, by perpetuating popular discontent and resentment, they present opponents, particularly lunatic fringe groups, with golden opportunities to exploit public unease and to promise better prospects if the whole governance system were made to work more efficiently, more effectively, and more honestly—their way. Who knows what unexpected event will light the torch that sets discontent ablaze?

Second, the failure of democracy to deal promptly and deftly with crisis situations only intensifies the already prevailing lack of public confidence in public leaders and institutions. It weakens support for those who appear most blameworthy. It raises barriers between the governors and the governed. People become more passive. They prefer to stand on the sidelines rather than intervene in rescuing leaders and institutions in trouble.

Third, the shameless selling of politics in many democratic regimes distorts policy-making and makes the political playing field even more uneven. Money buys power, influence, access, and exceptional consideration. Elections cost too much. Raising public money becomes an obsession not just to finance mass media attention and election campaigns but also—from the first day in office—looking ahead to reelection, which becomes a continuous distraction and diversion of time and energy. Politics becomes trivialized and brought to the lowest common denominator, more for entertainment than education, more for self-promotion than public insight. The contributors disguise their self-interests behind a veneer of public beneficence. Meantime, the great majority of citizens who cannot possibly afford to participate grow increasingly alienated, resentful, and offended at this political mockery detrimental to their interests. They leave the political theater to insiders and political professionals with the right contacts, who start off with possibly an unbeatable lead and are adept at evading any legal restrictions imposed to ensure a more even playing field.

Fourth, the more people contract out, the worse the situation becomes as indifference succumbs to apathy, a disease that rapidly spreads and then infiltrates the public bureaucracy, which senses changes in public attitudes among friends, relatives, neighbors, clients, and colleagues who sympathize with their fellow citizens. In this situation, who looks out for the public interest and who is the public's guardian? More and more people turn inward and protect their own personal, selfish interests first. Community becomes a distant second.

Fifth, a crumbling civic culture diminishes the gap between democracy and its alternatives. What real difference do people feel? What do they have to lose? To win? If democracy cannot provide (not just promise) something better, someone else can. Unfortunately, that someone may be the one that provides mostly bread and circuses, diversions, and escapism from the daily dull routines, from the boredom of being civil all the time. So why shouldn't fringe groups be tempted to stir things up by shaking comfortable elites and complacent bureaucrats just to relieve their boredom?

Finally, if unconstrained, corruption only spreads. It contaminates everything it touches. It moves from one institution to another, from business to public administration, trade unions to voluntary associations, until all dealings come under suspicion and all performance is affected, all professions compromised, and everyone is pressured to go along and keep their mouths shut, until everything, in Gunnar Myrdal's words, "becomes soft." His description of soft states should be a dire warning to anyone who believes it could not happen here. It can; it does. Look around; not even the hardest democracies today are safe. Every society has to guard itself against the insidious effects of corruption or live to regret its complacency, democrats most of all.

References

Caiden, Gerald. 1997. Undermining good governance: Corruption and democracy. *Asian Journal of Political Science* 5 (2): 1–22.

Handelman, S. 1995. *Comrade criminal: Russia's new mafiya.* New Haven, Conn.: Yale University Press.

United Nations. 1990. Crime prevention and criminal justice in context of development: Realities and perspectives of international co-operation. Item 3, Document A/CONF., 144/8. Eighth United Nations Congress on the Prevention of Crime and the Treatment of Offenders. Havana, Cuba; New York.

———. 1996. CRIME. UN newsletter on crime prevention and criminal justice. Nos. 24/25.

18

Official Ethics and Corruption

Gerald E. Caiden and O. P. Dwivedi

ONE OF THE KEYS TO MODERN GOVERNANCE is the development of a trusted, trustworthy professional public service guided by honest public leaders. Nothing destroys public credibility in public institutions more than corruption in official circles or at least suspicion that the hands of the governors are dirty. Corruption undermines people's faith in their institutions. It casts deep shadows over official policies and actions. It destroys confidence in tax systems and in paying taxes for public projects that seem only to serve private interests and line other people's pockets. It diverts public resources from where they are most needed to questionable ventures that are probably overpriced and underperforming. It mocks the equal application of the laws and the reliability of public budgets and accounts. In short, corruption hollows out governance just like termites weaken wood.

What has been disturbing in the past quarter century has been the apparent spread of corrupt practices to infest places once believed immune and beyond question. It seems now as if no public institution anywhere has completely clean hands. As a result, reputations have been ruined by a few isolated indiscretions. The finger of blame has been pointed to the blurring between public organizations and private organizations, between the public and the private sectors, and between public behavior and private behavior. At one time, it was believed that they could be distinguished, that different ethical standards existed or should exist between them, and that public conduct was superior to private conduct. Perhaps in some countries this might have been the case, but that is not generally true today. Significantly, and within a short period, the international community, the major actors on the world stage, are gradually realizing that there cannot be two different codes of ethics or standards of conduct—one in the private realm and the other in the public realm. One cannot have a public sector free of corruption when the private sector actually tolerates if not rewards corrupt practices. Nor can there be a moral business sector when the public sector, the government, and the political system condone, not condemn, corruption.

Immoral business practices inevitably undermine public integrity. Corrupt behavior inevitably corrodes and corrupts everything that comes into contact with it. That has been the theme and findings of the International Anti-Corruption Conferences held around the world since 1987. Self-policing, the precious foundation of a moral society, works only insofar as people are willing to make it work. When they are unwilling, there is little anyone can do about it, certainly not weakened or ineffectual law enforcement which, by itself, cannot prevent the manufacture and trade of harmful products, gross swindles and frauds, or other shameful acts in a global society.

Moral organizations have found how difficult it is to deal with immoral governments, political bodies, public bureaucracies, and unscrupulous officials. Favoritism is based on personal considerations, not public interest rules. Competitive bidding or tendering is made a farce. Acceptable gift giving becomes unacceptable bribery. The great hopes that humanity once put into the international order have been dashed by the corruption and misbehavior of world leaders and international organizations with their sordid internal dealings and greed. Much public money is being stolen, secreted away, and misused by rich people in poor countries—often aided by rich people in rich countries who see their own poor people go without while squandering their ill-gotten gains on themselves. All are victims of the corrupt's unjust spoils, bias, incompetence, inefficiency, insensitivity, unaccountability, and secrecy. Their dirty hands dirty all.

Rethinking Official Ethics

In the past, public leaders the world over have watched terrible atrocities being committed by public officials elsewhere. Many of these crimes against humanity were too often instigated, planned, and executed by public servants. They still are. This contempt for human suffering arouses the moral indignation of the rest of the world, which all too often is not roused enough to intervene. The world since then has changed, sometimes for the better and sometimes for the worse. Because it has changed, regular meetings on official and public service ethics are necessary to enable public officials to step back from busy routines and urgent pressures, assess the trends, and use whatever initiatives and concerns they have to reduce the potential harm and increase the possible good they can do and enable others to do. But some new thinking is required, as traditional approaches are wearing thin. Fortunately, many areas are still amenable to traditional ethical guidance. They just require firmer political will to act, the enforcement of existing laws and regulations, the strengthening of deterrent strategies and tactics, the application of available technology, and the better training and discipline of public servants. But other areas can be very trying. Being new or novel—certainly without precedent—they require much innovation, creativity, and ingenuity.

For instance, among the novel ethical challenges not susceptible to easy solutions are the fast-changing relations between government and business. Business has been globalized way ahead of government, leaving many gaps in the provision of global public goods and services. Many of the international agencies that are supposed to fill some of these gaps cannot, because of the lack of international political pressure to enhance their performance, insufficient international public funds to help them improve their performance, and inadequate international public service professionalism. The business of international business is business. Although it is not lacking in social conscience, it rushes ahead not mindful of its social dysfunctions. International public agencies are unable to offset the adverse effects of international business on world problems of security, war and terrorism, environmental disasters and threats, transnational crime and harmful trade, and labor exploitation, de facto slavery, and unenforced human rights. Worse still, international business deserts just when it is most needed; it has a less acute moral sense when it feels that profits might be endangered. When most needed, it quickly flees and abruptly withdraws its investments—caring little about the social costs it leaves behind, the corruption and cronyism it fostered, the damage to civil society caused by such irresponsibility, and the poverty, misery, unrest, and violence left in its wake.

Governments cannot bully private parties to end such harmful activities, in fact, government agencies are not much better. What is required are new forms of voluntary cooperation and partnership in place of coercion. Just as public authorities have to be trusted to police themselves, so private bodies also have to be trusted to police themselves, encouraged to find their own solutions, and at least at the outset, given or offered public incentives to do the right thing. In some areas, even this risk cannot be taken because the consequences of trading in atomic, biological, and chemical weapons or trading in narcotics and other harmful products are just too disastrous: so coercion is still unavoidable.

Thus a key issue in the contemporary global society is whether the newer occupiers of positions of responsibility in any organization, public and private, really know right from wrong, whether they seek help for their daily moral dilemmas at work, whether they choose the path of self-respect, honesty, and integrity, and whether they resist the many temptations to pull them off course.

Given the changes in today's ethical environment, there is no longer any guarantee that they will know right from wrong, correct from incorrect behavior—
especially not when the whole apparatus of governance itself may be out of sync
with society and acts immorally or indecently, when political and bureaucratic
elites misbehave with apparent impunity, when colleagues continue to deceive
and abet wrongdoing, when fellow citizens seemingly go along with anything
and raise no protest, and when one's own judgment has been befuddled by
contradictions, mixed messages and ambiguities. To repeat, all have to recognize that they want the same morals to dominate all organizations, public and
private, governmental and nongovernmental. The same set of morals, the same
expectation of personal integrity, has to be universal. There cannot be different
ethical standards for one set of people and another for another set, not when
they do business daily together.

People have come to realize that the danger to them as individuals does
not come so much from the wickedness of others as from the wickedness of
organizations. More than ever before, people depend on organizations doing
the right things, behaving responsibly, being moral. People can still avoid dangerous individuals but they cannot avoid evil organizations intent on doing harm:
organizations that deliver weapons of mass destruction; poison air, water, and
food; carry out ethnic cleansing and other terrible crimes against humanity—
organizations that do not improve the lot of humankind but worsen it. People
in groups do things that they would never do by themselves. Organizations
blindside people into committing evil acts and worse still, the most evil of them
keep detailed records of their misdeeds as a historical boast.

Some Major Trends in Official Ethics Reform

The above information does not mean that people are standing idly by and
ignoring these issues. On the contrary, complacency has given way to concern.
Around the world, all kinds of groups have been getting together, devising reforms to update and modernize official ethics and restore the former respect
for public service ethics, and looking ahead to face the challenges likely to arise
in the next two decades. These ambitious groups have tried to avoid stooping to
the levels of public discourse all too often employed to denigrate the institution
of governance, the concept of public service, and the image of professional
public servants. They have endeavored to be civil, positive, creative, and influential (Cooper 2000).

Three major transformations that these groups have been instrumental in
bringing about in less than twenty-five years encompass most current trends in
official and public service ethics reform: publicity and transparency, institutional

capacity, and confronting corruption. To begin with, the reformers have become victims of their own successes, particularly in ridding the world of whatever taboos may have surrounded the subject of official ethics. Where once people may have been silenced, they cannot be any more. Even in the most repressive regimes, modern computer technology can overcome suppression. Countries that once allowed no public discussion openly admit their problems with official ethics and seek international help. International organizations that once avoided the subject advocate reforms in official and governance ethics and boast of their schemes to provide technical assistance to members who seek help. Public administration textbooks have almost compulsory inclusions, which are used to educate and train public servants. A flood of new books, journals, and articles specializing in public ethics threatens to drown readers. This is an amazingly successful transformation in only two decades. Credit must be given to worldwide mass media in fearlessly exposing wrongdoing in public office, often at great cost and sacrifice and to Transparency International (TI), founded in 1993, which has become the forefront in demolishing taboos, confronting both public and private corruption, and keeping an ongoing record of most reform campaigns.

The downside has been the excesses of mass media in exposing official misconduct so that little is sacred. Exaggerations distort reality and public figures have been intimidated, hounded, and falsely accused enough to scare off good candidates or at least give them cause to think twice about running for office. Perhaps transparency in the private affairs of public officeholders has gone too far in the sensational media, but the pendulum will no doubt swing back. In the meantime, officeholders are warned that there can be few secrets, little accepted deviation from the straight and narrow, and no bending the truth without adverse consequences when public indignation is aroused.

The debate over whether to codify official ethics has ended with the sweeping victory of the codifiers, who argued convincingly that there would be little harm but possibly much good in codification. Their efforts reveal how difficult it is to put to paper the unarticulated mores that supposedly govern or should govern official and public service ethics. Finding the right words is just one difficulty. There are also the embarrassing gaps, along with the ambiguities, contradictions, double standards, and sophistry. Once satisfactory solutions have been found, the next task is to convince public service organizations to adopt the codes, verify that everyone understands their provisions, and ensure compliance with them. Then come the even harder tasks of framing and amending legal codes to echo their moral precepts and institutionalizing arrangements to see that the law is obeyed without discrimination, fear, or favor. Of course, devious officeholders still find ways to avoid or evade them; so new counter measures have to be formulated. This unforeseen consequence of codification has become a vicious circle seemingly without end, as authorities try to outwit the cheats and the cheats try to keep one step ahead.

The simple idea of codification has ballooned into major institutional rearrangements as it pointed to the need for significant overhaul and reform of legal and judicial systems, professional education and training, extralegal arrangements (such as special prosecutors), new legal and investigatory tools (such as inspector generals, and complaint mechanisms), novel methods of information gathering (hotlines, witness and whistle-blower protection, undercover agents) and concerted attacks on a wide variety of organized crime. In short, codification has snowballed into elaborate and expensive reform campaigns covering virtually every aspect of conducting public business. The term governance is now preferred to denote how inadequate the term government has become for reforms that extend beyond government itself to include every group touched by the modern machinery of government, which means practically every resident, taxpayer, welfare recipient, contractor, beneficiary of the law, and receiver of public money. It is no longer confined to career public servants or noncareer public employees and their bosses. Of course, many other factors have been responsible for this explosion of administrative reform and codification may well have been incidental. But the total impact of official and public service ethics reform has been profound, with the reexamination of internal arrangements ranging from the highest level of global organizations to the lowest level of local community organization, especially the push for democratization and improving civic culture. This process, once begun, has no end. It is a process that links the past to the future, what has been to what should be. The here and now presents enormous opportunities and challenges to reshape public service ethics as never before. It is an exciting time to be so involved and to contribute.

No better illustration comes to mind than the current worldwide confrontation with corruption, the very antithesis of public service ethics. The turnaround in recognizing that corruption has become so dysfunctional to human progress and world development has been truly amazing. And it has taken less than 25 years. Indeed before 1991, reformers were upset that their efforts had not borne much fruit. Now they rejoice for they have won over international opinion, as evidenced by pronouncements, restatements of organizational missions, and other formalities issued in the past eight or so years. While not underestimating this profound transformation in climate, warning must be given that such rejoicing may be premature until intention is realized fully in practice. The world has witnessed several attempts to confront corruption. Some have been disastrous; others have been successful but only for a limited period.

Somehow corruption revives and spreads again, and, learning from previous errors, the corrupt become smarter and harder to remove from public office. The information age has presented powerful tools to tackle corruption. But it has also presented novel forms of corruption. Computer fraud is a growing concern: it is a rapidly growing business in which evidence can be destroyed instantaneously. Imaging can falsify reality; history can be recreated. Seeing is no longer believing. The related fields of medicine, pharmacology, and biology have new technologies that compel the rethinking of life and death, illness and wellness, expendable and nonexpendable, harmful and harmless, toxic and nontoxic. In the same way, corruption must be redefined, laws rewritten, and the debate over what should be permitted or not has to be reopened. Indeed, the debate over public ethics is continuous and nothing should be considered written in stone.

Toward Good Governance

Recognition of the moral dimension of governance points to a concern for improvement of the quality of public service and governmental conduct. The broad principles that should govern official conduct are not obscure; rather, they mark the direction toward which those who govern must channel their acts if they are to serve the society. These principles include the call for individual responsibility and obligations, sacrifice, compassion, justice, striving for the highest good, and acting morally. Morality provides the main foundation for the governing process because public confidence and trust in liberal-democracy can be safeguarded only when the governing process exhibits a higher moral tone. However, that moral tone is but one of the several prerequisites of good governance. A broader list includes the following values:

1. *democratic pluralism*, a cornerstone of liberal democracy, is based on the three implicit values (equality, empathy, and tolerance) and draws from three basic ideals: fundamental freedoms for all, equality of all, and universal participation in the governing process

2. *legitimacy* of the governing process so that those who govern derive authority and power from legitimate constitutional instruments of governance

3. *consensus* among different and differing interests in the society, and *equity* assured to all individuals so that they may improve their well-being

4. *public participation* in decision making

5. *rule of law* that is enforced impartially

6. *responsiveness* of institutions to the needs of all stakeholders

7. *effective and efficient responsibility and accountability* of institutions and the statecraft that meets basic needs of all by using state-controlled resources to their optimum accountability

8. *strategic vision* of the leaders toward broad-range, long-term perspectives on sustainable human development

9. *transparency* for access to governing process (including institutions and information sources)

10. *moral governance* that reflects such values as the common good, democratic pluralism, public service ethics, controlling corruption, and seeking spiritual guidance for secular work, and where governing elites dedicate their lives for service to the public. Good governance and sustainable human development, especially for developing nations, also require conscientious attempts at eliminating poverty, sustaining livelihoods, fulfilling basic needs, and offering an administrative system that is clean and open.

The profession of an equitable administrator includes not only those values which are considered an essential part of an objective accountability (such as objectivity, effectiveness, impartiality, integrity, and probity in the conduct of public affairs) but also those ideals (such as the spirit of self-sacrifice for public duty, serving the public and community as a higher ideal, maintaining the highest standards of personal honesty and integrity, and protecting the common good) that are an integral part of moral accountability. These expected and perceived ideals mean that public officials are expected to act within legal bounds and within a moral context. Of course, public officials are a mirror of societal mores and conscience including prevailing morals and ethical standards. If the leaders do not exhibit the highest standards of ethical behavior in the conduct of public business, then it is difficult to expect their underlings to behave in an exemplary manner. At present, there appears to be an emphasis on objective accountability without paying much attention to the subjective or moral side of the coin.

Thus, no amount of laws, codes of conduct, and threats of punishment can force public officials to behave ethically, and to promote just government. Unless they are guided by a sense of vocation, serving others, and accountability, it is impossible to expect a moral government.

This belief holds that government is a public trust and public service is a vocation for persons who should know how to behave morally. Behavior emanating from ideals associated with service as the highest calling includes possessing and exhibiting such virtues as honesty, impartiality, sincerity, and justice. Further, it is equally desirable that the conduct of public administrators should be beyond reproach; and that they should perform their duties loyally, efficiently, and economically. (Dwivedi 1995, 297)

Moral lassitude is as undesirable in the public life as it is in the family life, thus the constant need for spiritual guidance in secular affairs so that basic ethical ideals are sustained. Morality can lead to mastery over such base characteristics as greed, exploitation, abuse of power, and possibly mistreatment of people. Morality requires self-discipline, humility, and resists the arrogance that can come with holding a public office. It enables people to center their values upon the notion of a cosmic ordinance and a divine law that must be maintained. Spirituality serves both as a model and operative strategy for the transformation of human character by strengthening the genuine and substantive will to serve the common people. And, if the goal of such formation is to serve and protect the common good, then it can provide the incentive for public officials to serve the public with dignity and respect.

In addition, there is a need to consider other strategies toward good governance. Some of these include the need to emphasize on righteous action by public officials so that they are able to serve and protect the common good, and how to inculcate the feeling of care among them.

Righteous action in the public domain relates to a system of ethics and moral duty. Persons performing a public duty may be capable of both good and evil actions; if they remember that it is their duty to sustain the general welfare of all people, they should act righteously. For public officials to act righteously they must act in the service of others and avoid exploiting other human beings, because public officials who are morally committed to upholding the common good also know that it is their duty to serve others. By undertaking such righteous actions they will be fulfilling two-fold duties: one to the self, whereby one seeks inner strength through spiritual action, and the other to the community at large, whereby one works for the common good. As such, spirituality or morality regulates human conduct and molds individuals into the right character by inculcating in them spiritual, social, and moral values strengthening the ethos that holds the social and moral fabric of a society and nation together. That morality also becomes a foundation for good governance by maintaining order in society, building individual and group character, and giving rise to harmony and understanding.

The moral foundation of any public sector organization in a democracy requires that public officials show genuine caring for their fellow citizens. Devoid of such a moral foundation, a situation could emerge akin to the Nazi bureaucracy when state administration was enlisted in the cause of evil led by self-righteous people in government who sacrificed moral obligation to protect the common good. Hannah Arendt has very aptly demonstrated the absence of any moral qualm among those public servants of the Third Reich who knew about the transportation and mass murder of Jews and others (Arendt 1969). What happened in Nazi Germany must not be repeated elsewhere. There is a great need to sensitize public administrators worldwide so that they show unwavering commitment to such democratic values as equality, rule of law, justice, fundamental freedoms, and respect for cultural diversity. As public servants they are obligated to uphold these values.

Caring public officials should concern themselves about the country and society and care equally about the impact of their actions on those within and outside the borders of a country. Such caring actions taken and expressed in accord among those public officials become collective sentiments that in turn relate to the common good. In any case, the most important function of public officials is how they can serve the common good and good governance. In a liberal democratic system of governance, there is no higher public service value than its mission of caring for and serving the public.

The human governance system in a liberal-democratic state can be assumed to exist for the sustenance of the common good. This is achieved through certain institutions of the state whose actions and decisions the public accepts. The purpose of such institutions, and of the state itself, is to perform certain duties and fulfill acquired obligations. The justification for the state to pursue the common good is actually the justification of its own existence. The basic thrust of the concept is to motivate people in government so that they can make a full contribution of their capabilities in serving their nation and the community.

The objective of good governance is to create an environment in which public servants as well as politicians are able to respond to the challenge of good governance. That challenge for public officials involves a notion of duty, as well as acting morally and accountably. If these two dimensions can be brought together in public sector management, it may become possible for a public servant to rise above self-interest by placing collective good above private interest and greed. Strengthening of such a notion also creates a shared feeling or a spirit of public duty among those who govern. Of course, such a classical notion includes other values such as probity, applying objective standards universally, willingness to speak truth to leaders, an appreciation of the wider common good over and above the narrower political interest, equity, and a sustainable concern for democratic ideals. Such is the duty of those who wish to be involved in the difficult and complex world of governance. This is the essence and basis of a moral state. Confidence and trust in democracy can be safeguarded only when the governing process exhibits a higher, credible, and real ethical stand, deriving from justice, equity, and morality. Bringing moral and procedural domains together provides a strong fight against corruption, mismanagement, and bad governance. No society, no matter its political and religious orientation, can live in a spiritual or moral vacuum. Furthermore, there ought to be some articles of faith (drawn from the societal values, cultural traditions, and moral ideals) governing people's lives that must be encouraged and reinforced. In the final analysis, good governance is essentially a moral enterprise.

References

Arendt, Hannah. 1969. *On violence.* New York: Harcourt, Brace and Wood.

Barnard, Chester I. 1948. *The functions of the executive.* Cambridge, Mass.: Harvard University Press.

Canada, Royal Commission on Financial Management and Accountability. 1979. *Final report.* Ottawa: Supply and Services, Government of Canada.

Cooper, Terence, ed. 2000. *Handbook on administrative ethics.* New York: Marcel Dekker.

Corry, J. A., and J. E. Hodgetts. 1957. *Democratic government and politics.* Toronto, Canada: University of Toronto Press.

Dwivedi, O. P. 1995. Reflections on moral government and public service as a vocation. *Indian Journal of Public Administration* 41 (3).

Frederickson, H. George. 1997. *The spirit of public administration.* San Francisco, Calif.: Jossey-Bass Publishers.

Gawthrop, Louis C. 1984. *Public sector management, systems and ethics.* Bloomington, Ind.: Indiana University Press.

Kooiman, J. 1993. Governance and governability: Using complexity, dynamics and diversity. In *Modern Governance: New Government–Society Interaction,* edited by J. Kooiman. London: Sage Publishers.

Mosher, Frederick C. 1968. *Democracy and the public service.* New York: Oxford University Press.

Index

Also from Kumarian Press...

International Development

New Roles and Relevance: Development NGOs and the Challenge of Change
Edited by David Lewis and Tina Wallace

Patronage or Partnership: Local Capacity Building in Humanitarian Crises
Edited by Ian Smillie for the Humanitarianism and War Project

Street Level Democracy: Political Settings at the Margins of Global Power
Jonathan Barker

Transcending Neoliberalism: Community-Based Development in Latin America
Edited by Henry Veltmeyer and Anthony O'Malley

Environment, Conflict Resolution, Gender Studies, Global Issues, Globalization, Microfinance

Bound: Living in the Globalized World
Scott Sernau

Exploring the Gaps: Vital Links Between Trade, Environment and Culture
James R. Lee

Inequity in the Global Village: Recycled Rhetoric and Disposable People
Jan Knippers Black

Mainstreaming Microfinance:
How Lending to the Poor Began, Grew and Came of Age in Bolivia
Elisabeth Rhyne

Promises Not Kept: The Betrayal of Social Change in the Third World
FIFTH EDITION John Isbister

Reconcilable Differences: Turning Points in Ethnopolitical Conflict
Edited by Sean Byrne and Cynthia L. Irvin

War's Offensive on Women:
The Humanitarian Challenge in Bosnia, Kosovo and Afghanistan
Julie A. Mertus for the Humanitarianism and War Project

When Corporations Rule the World
SECOND EDITION David C. Korten

Visit Kumarian Press at **www.kpbooks.com** or call **toll-free 800.289.2664** for a complete catalog.

Kumarian Press, located in Bloomfield, Connecticut, is dedicated to publishing and distributing books and other media that will have a positive social and economic impact on the lives of peoples living in "Third World" conditions no matter where they live.